TORN APART

TORN APART

The True Story of Two Sisters
Who Found Each Other After Sixty-
Five Years

Sybil and Blanche Le Fleur
with Derek Flory

CHIVERS

British Library Cataloguing in Publication Data available

This Large Print edition published by BBC Audiobooks Ltd, Bath, 2009.
Published by arrangement with Mainstream Publishing Company
(Edinburgh).

U.K. Hardcover ISBN 978 1 408 42157 4
U.K. Softcover ISBN 978 1 408 42158 1

Printed and bound in Great Britain by CPI Antony Rowe, Chippenham
and Eastbourne

CONTENTS

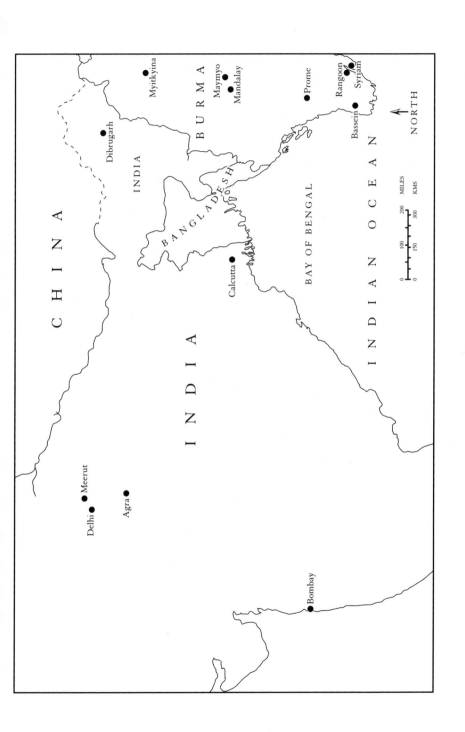

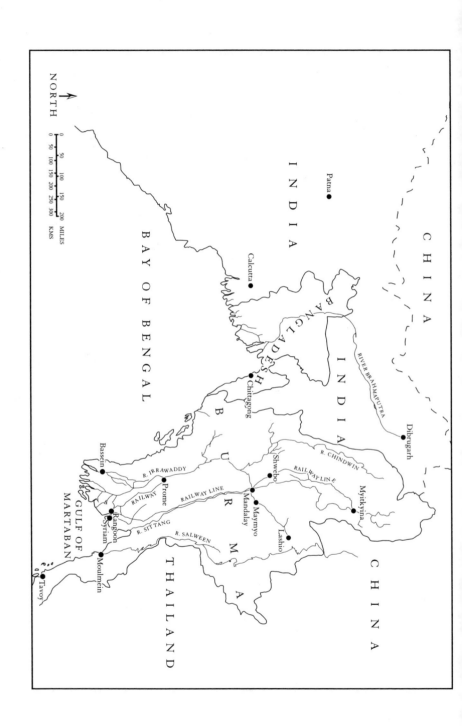

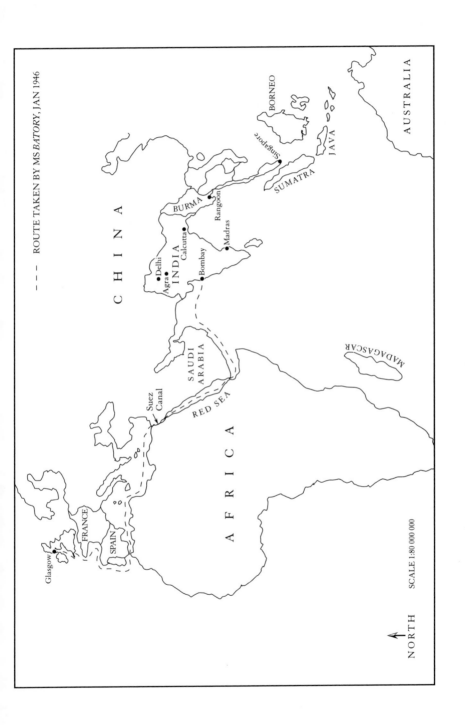

- - - ROUTE TAKEN BY MS *BATORY*, JAN 1946

PREFACE

At the beginning of June 2007, my sisters and I knew little of our mother's early years and her life growing up in Burma. We knew even less about her family. On 11 June, that began to change. Through a chance set of circumstances, we were to discover not only the details of her childhood and her large family but also stories of her escape from the Japanese occupation of her country. We learned about her subsequent journey to safety, her marriage to our father, a Scottish soldier stationed in India, and of her making a new home in Scotland, halfway around the world from her birthplace. What had the greatest impact on all of us, including my mother, was the revelation that not only did Mum have a sister living in Calcutta but we had a whole family in India, Burma, Hong Kong and Australia that we had known nothing about.

This book tells the story of the two sisters: my mum, Sybil, and my aunt Blanche. I pass on their tales here as they related them to me. I quote Aunt Blanche directly more often than my mother, and this is a reflection of their personalities. Mum is more quiet and reflective and is less inclined to talk in an emotive way, as she has had to suppress many of her fears and anxieties over the years. Aunt Blanche, on the other hand, is very emotional and expressive and is certainly not afraid to talk of the traumas she experienced.

I hope you enjoy the journey as much as we have.

Derek R. Flory
Milnathort, Scotland
May 2008

PROLOGUE

13 June 2007

HUNTLY, SCOTLAND

It was the phone call she thought would never happen.

At the prearranged time, I dialled the number in Calcutta and waited for an answer. I spoke briefly to the person on the other end and handed the phone to my mother.

'Hello, Blanche,' she said in a quivering voice that betrayed her anxiety and uncertainty.

'Is that really you, Sybil?'

And then came the question Blanche had been waiting 66 years to ask: 'What happened to you, Sybil? Why didn't you come home from your Christmas shopping?'

It was the first time since December 1941 that my mother had talked to the sister whom she had been forcibly parted from on the other side of the world. In all that time, neither knew that the other was still alive or what had happened all those years ago. This was the call they thought would never happen.

The effect of the conversation on my mother was instant. It was as if a huge load had been lifted from her shoulders, and she went around the house singing to herself with an energy that belied her 86 years.

'Well?' we asked, hardly able to contain ourselves. 'What did she say? What did you talk about?'

'Oh, we just talked about everything—about the food we used to eat and the people and places we remembered. We talked about Irene and Uncle Bertie, and of course when I laughed so loud, it was because Blanche told me that Daisy Boyce had died.'

We looked at her in wonder. Who were these people whom she spoke about with such familiarity, people whom we had never heard of before? And what about Daisy Boyce? What was it about her death that made my mum laugh? This was totally out of character, as she never has a bad word to say about anyone.

Over lunch in the local café, we could talk about nothing other than the discovery of Blanche and our whole new family. Mum laughed as we had never seen her laugh before, and I don't think I have ever enjoyed a simple meal so much.

When we returned to the house, Mum decided to call Blanche again. This time, the 'Hello, Blanche' was said with joy and confidence, and there was no stopping the sisters as they began to share their memories and talk about their happy girlhood together. This time the call lasted two hours, as Mum also talked to Blanche's daughter Anita and grandson Peter. By now, everyone was laughing, and the stories were coming thick and fast.

As we drove home from Huntly in the early evening, my wife, Caroline, and I reflected that our decision to tell Mum about the discovery of her sister and family had been absolutely the right one to have made. This news had brought us immense joy and filled us with emotion.

*   *   *

Sybil Maud Flory. This was our mother, a person who had lovingly brought up her four children in a country far from where she was born, who had nursed us when we were sick, who had stood by us in difficult times, who had fed us our favourite foods and who had looked after her husband as if she had been born to do so. We were taught by her to be proud of our Scots heritage and of her husband's family, part of the Robertson clan. She instilled in us Christian values and beliefs, and she took pride in our achievements, giving us the support, encouragement and strength to excel at what we did. Never once did she think of herself or hanker after her past life—or if she did, she successfully concealed from us all her hopes, dreams and remembrances.

Over the years, we had come to learn a great deal about my father's side of the family—his mother, Flora; his aunt who had nursed a prince back to health; his uncles, William the butcher and Patrick the farmer, and Arthur and Alfie who had emigrated to America and had succeeded in banking and commerce—but we knew next to nothing about the life of our mother, Sybil, before she lived in Scotland.

Now, after six decades of silence, the floodgates were open. Over the next weeks and months, we were to find out so much more about our loving, quiet (and, we had thought, unremarkable) mum, her family and her life in Burma. We were to learn about her childhood in the port of Syriam, her school days, her first jobs and what happened to her on that fateful day, 23 December 1941. We were to discover the events that had shaped our mother and determined what she did and how she reacted in everyday situations. We were to hear stories of joy, excitement and love, stories of disaster and desperation, and of courage in the face of adversity, during a war that ended the lives of tens of thousands of people—stories that brought us nearer to understanding our mother's strength and ability to cope with the tragedies she faced. We heard of fear and hunger, disease and death, and of how a will to survive and dogged determination saw her through.

Above all, we were to hear of a belief and faith in God that kept a hope, a dream, alive for many long years, and which underpinned everything she and her sister had done over a lifetime.

This story of her life made us laugh, cry and reflect on how easy our own lives had been, but above all it made us realise just what a special person our mother is and that we should never forget the enormous debt we owe to her.

And, yes, we were to learn all we needed to know about Daisy Boyce.

CHAPTER ONE

December 1941

RANGOON, BURMA

Rangoon was preparing for Christmas. As for so many Christmases before, the shops, bars, gentlemen's clubs and hotels along Dalhousie Street were making an enormous effort with their window displays. Inside Rowe & Co., the big department store, the tall Christmas tree stretched high above the sales counters. Brought specially from north of Maymyo, it was a magnificent specimen. Huge loops of tinsel and decorations hung from its branches, and glass baubles sparkled under the lights. At Whiteway, Laidlaw & Co., the furniture store, the scene was the same, except that, in a spirit of one-upmanship, they had selected an even taller tree and imported a new set of decorations from London. The only thing visibly different about this Christmas was that the grand street decorations and lights, which in the evening usually drew crowds from all around Rangoon to gaze in awe at their splendour, were no longer lit, under orders from the Governor. It was one of the few signs in Burma, otherwise apparently peaceful, that things were about to change. In

Britain and Europe, the war was being prosecuted with a vengeance, while in idyllic Burma life carried on as normal, and there was a determination to make this an even more memorable Christmas than usual. That peaceful life would soon be over.

From Judson Baptist Church on the university campus came the sounds of massed choirs rehearsing Handel's *Messiah*, along with traditional carols. Sybil loved this time of year and had already taken in the sights and sounds, having made regular trips into town to window-shop, visit the stores and choose carefully from the many delights that appeared each December. Sybil was working as a seamstress and was temporarily making her home with her sister Blanche, Blanche's husband and their son on 53rd Street, Rangoon. Blanche had married her husband, Manu Desai, a radio broadcaster and businessman, when she was in her late teens. He was a tall, handsome, elegant man with jet-black, wavy hair and a ready smile, and he exuded confidence and charm. An electrical engineering graduate, he had moved into broadcasting and also owned and managed an electrical supply and repair shop in the city centre.

On 23 December, Sybil had some last-minute shopping to do, and she had arranged to meet her friend Bertha in town. After a traditional breakfast of *mohinga* (a fish soup with noodles, boiled eggs and gourd fritters) to set her up for the day, she said goodbye to Blanche and her baby son, Leslie. Blanche was expecting a second child and had much to do to prepare for Christmas.

'I'll just get a few things with Bertha, and I'll be home in time for dinner. Is there anything you need me to get?'

Blanche gave Sybil a short list of items to be purchased in town and added, 'I'll take Leslie to the park later. He loves the swings and the slide, and he's made some friends there. Besides, it gives me a chance to chat to the other mums.'

'See you later,' Sybil said, and with that she was off to town.

Sybil and her sister were the children of a Burmese mother and a French-Portuguese father. The girls stood 4 ft 11¾ in. tall in their stocking soles and were fashionably slim, with features like those of fine porcelain dolls. There was no denying their beauty, and they drew attention wherever they went. Sybil made her own clothes, the designs copied from the latest magazines from the West, and she knew what suited her. Her perfectly oval face was the setting for dark, laughing eyes and a delicate nose. She possessed a smile that lit up a room, showing off brilliant white teeth. Her thick, wavy hair was kept in a short style for simplicity, but it only added to the picture of style and elegance. Her skin was as smooth as silk and the colour of milky coffee. She was a free spirit, an adventurer, a traveller with a love

3

of new experiences; although temporarily back in Rangoon, she fully intended the stay to be a short one and had plans to see more of her country.

That morning, she had chosen her favourite blue dress—a recent creation—a matching silk scarf to add some flair and a pair of sensible shoes. She loved high heels, but they were hardly practical for the walk into town.

Sybil hoped to pick up a few presents at Rowe & Co. before heading for home. She carried out alterations for the department store, among other clients, and had come to know the salesgirls well. She played hockey for the Rowe & Co. team, the Watsonians, and was a popular member of the side, scoring many goals from her position as a forward. She was small and fleet of foot and could deftly get round the larger players on the pitch. When it came to shooting for goal, she had a strength and a will that far exceeded her physical size. The name of the team had initially mystified her: Watsonians would have been a more appropriate name for a team playing for Watson and Co., the big motor engineers in the centre of Rangoon. She found out that the team had been named by one of the senior managers of the firm, remembering his schooldays in a city called Edinburgh many thousands of miles away and in a country they had only read of, a cold, bleak and dark place called Scotland.

Walking along the busy streets, Sybil drank

in the sights and sounds of the city she loved: the smells of the fresh fruit and vegetables; the spices of all colours piled high; the calls of the street vendors advertising their wares to the populace in time-honoured tradition, while simultaneously negotiating with the current crop of customers. Meat and poultry stalls stood side by side with barrows covered with bales of silk material of all colours: scarlet reds, deep blues, shocking pinks and bright lime greens. There were carts bearing baskets of freshly picked flowers and crates of vegetables and fruit of all shapes and sizes. Spices in all the colours of the rainbow, sending out aromas that made your mouth water, were piled in pyramids atop wicker baskets. The vendors deftly measured out precise quantities, wrapped them in paper and, in exchange for the right amount of cash, handed them over. Sybil stopped to examine the silks, feeling their quality and weight, enjoying the smooth silk textures and the intricate patterns. Women, laughing and vociferous, jostled to get closer to the stalls. Several times, Sybil felt a sharp elbow in her side or arm as she was nudged out of the way by someone even more determined than she. Sybil decided to return to the stall on her way home when it would be quieter, to buy several yards of scarlet silk and also some light-blue material. She already had in mind a pattern she had seen in one of her magazines. She would make one dress for herself and one for Blanche.

Sybil loved the clothes of the women in the crowd most of all. The brightly coloured silk *longyis*, or skirts, and the equally vibrant *eingyis*, or blouses, of the Burman women, the small tops and saris worn by the Indian women and the linen suits and dresses of the Westerners caught her attention, and she inspected them with the eye of a trained seamstress. Watching this rainbow of colours pass her by, she wished the Watsonians hockey strip could have been more colourful, perhaps a deep purple or vibrant blue. Instead, the skirt was patterned with black and white diagonal stripes and the blouse was plain white. No wonder some of their opponents called them 'the Zebras'. Maybe next season she would suggest a change.

Rangoon was an enigma. It was a place of beauty dominated by the gold-covered Shwedagon Pagoda, a commercial centre where wealth was considerable and ostentatious, a seat of learning where the education system rivalled any in the world. It was also a place of heartbreaking poverty where adults and naked children begged in the streets. The poor scavenged among the waste at the side of the road, picking up rotting vegetables and overripe fruit. They were often in competition with the much larger scavengers that were to be found lumbering slowly and sedately along the streets: the oxen.

It was a city where the latest cars from Europe raced past rickshaws pulled by barefoot, stick-thin men, and they in turn jostled with the slow-moving bullock carts of the poorer merchants; a place where finely dressed Westerners moved among ragged urchins, not even giving them a glance to acknowledge their presence. For many members of the wealthy ruling classes, the poor and needy simply did not exist.

Sybil found the contrast between the affluent Westerners and the hungry children upsetting. Why was there this huge divide between those with access to good food and the best medical treatments available and those who starved, suffered and died from the most debilitating diseases imaginable? How could these people survive on rotting fruit and stale discarded bread? If rice was inadvertently spilt by a harassed stall owner, it was scraped almost instantly off the street by an observant pauper. The thought made Sybil shiver, and she considered herself very fortunate indeed.

It was early morning and there were only two shopping days before Christmas. Sybil had so much to do and so little time. It was a beautiful, clear, warm day. The energy-sapping, humid, wet, windy and unhealthy monsoon season was a distant memory; the cooler and drier months of October and November, with their chilly nights, had given way to a time of blue, cloudless skies, warm, dry days and cooling breezes coming off the Gulf of Martaban. Sybil had a plan. She would make her way from her sister's house on the outskirts of Rangoon to the home of her friend Bertha De Alvis, who lived in Fraser Street. This was the perfect base for Christmas shopping, right in the centre of town. Bertha was her best friend. They had shared many fun times together, and this was going to be another great Christmas. An additional attraction of Fraser Street was Theo De Alvis, Bertha's elder brother and Sybil's boyfriend, and she hoped to meet up with him that morning.

The airy, modern streets of Rangoon had been laid out on a grid system planned by a Scottish military engineering officer by the name of Lieutenant Fraser and a surgeon turned town planner, Dr William Montgomery. They started with the imposing Sule Pagoda in the centre of Rangoon as the focal point. The layout was developed so that roads running west to east were very broad and lined with trees, while roads running north to south varied in width and were arranged symmetrically. The smaller roads were numbered, while the boulevards were named after eminent persons of the time. Fraser Street and Montgomery Street bore the names of their planners, while Dalhousie Street, for example, was named after a governor general of India. Strand Road, with its famous Strand Hotel, was an imposing street running from west to east along the sea front; the views of the Gulf of Martaban were spectacular on a clear day.

The impending Christmas celebrations had brought more people than usual to central Rangoon, and the streets of the city were thronged with life. Traders were doing brisk business at the stalls that lined the wide thoroughfares; shops were crowded as people stocked up on last-minute purchases. Coolies—unskilled labourers from India and China—carried their heavy burdens with haste and dexterity through the traffic, messengers ran hither and thither delivering parcels and documents, rickshaws trundled along the streets and cows meandered through the crowds. The cattle and water buffalo were part of everyday life, jostling with shoppers, chewing lazily on discarded fruit and vegetables and lowing contentedly. Rangoon was a great bustling melting pot of cultures, and this time of year was very special. Sybil loved it dearly. To her, the familiar sounds, the sights and the smells were comforting, and the buzz was exhilarating.

Often, she would walk along Dalhousie Street towards the Sule Pagoda with Blanche, and, if they felt like it, they would go to one of the many cinemas. Past the Sule Pagoda, they would turn right into Mogul Street and buy ice creams—cones piled high from a choice of every flavour imaginable and sprinkled with hundreds and thousands, or knickerbocker glories with fresh fruit and whipped cream topped with a bright red cherry. It was all they could do to finish them before the heat of the day made them drip onto

9

their hands and clothes. Today, Sybil planned to take Bertha to Scott Market to buy the delicious chocolate-covered Yule logs on sale there. Chocolate was a treat very much associated with Christmas.

Sybil entered the grocer's at the top of Fraser Street and bought the items that Blanche had requested. They were wrapped in brown paper tied neatly with string, and the parcels were finished with a flourish and a fine bow on top. The Indian shopkeeper, Mr Singh, wished her good day and a happy Christmas. It didn't seem to matter what religion they were, the people of Rangoon celebrated every religious festival with joy and with a tolerance that was the hallmark of their open, liberated society. It was often said that there were twelve months in the year and at least twice that many religious festivals.

It was still early when Sybil reached Bertha's house, and, as always, they chatted animatedly about their news, discussed the latest fashions, films and gossip, and, of course, Sybil took delight in showing Bertha the few purchases she had already made en route to Fraser Street. They were tempted by the large chocolate bars, but Sybil was supposed to take them home for Blanche. Time flashed past, and soon they had been chatting for over an hour. Sybil checked her watch: 10.40. It was time they made a move, or the best bargains would be gone. Saying their goodbyes to Bertha's family, they

10

opened the door to leave.

At 10.42, the air-raid sirens began to wail. This was not the first time they had sounded in Rangoon. There had been a few false alarms over the past few weeks; they had always ended with the sirens emitting a steady note to signal the all-clear. Surely this was just another such event? But this was no false alarm. War had arrived in Burma, and the IJAAF (Imperial Japanese Army Air Force) was hell-bent on the destruction of its capital.

As a formation of Japanese fighters from the 10th Hikodan, or brigade, bombed Rangoon's airstrip, another made up of heavy bombers reached the city. The 98th Sentai of the 7th Hikodan, under the command of Colonel Usui Shigeki, circled at 20,000 ft before beginning its bombing run against the dock area and centre of Rangoon. A formation of 18 Allied fighter planes with altitude advantage attacked from behind and caused the group to fly off course. One bomber was shot down and crashed near the docks. The 98th Sentai regrouped but could not line up on its intended targets, the port buildings and warehouses and the considerable number of freighters at anchor in the docks and river. Instead, it bombed central Rangoon, hitting, amongst other buildings, the government headquarters, the post office and the telephone exchange. A second bomber was shot down, and Allied fighters pursued the formation as it left the scene of destruction.

11

While this was going on, a third formation approached Rangoon from the ocean and flew over the east side of the city, dropping its bomb load on central Rangoon, the dock area and the cargo ships anchored there, scoring direct hits on key buildings, disabling the harbour facilities and sinking a medium-sized ship. Stray bombs also exploded to the north and east of the centre.

In and around Fraser Street, the sirens caused mixed reactions. Curiosity and naivety overcame fear in many. Coolies laid down their burdens, market traders left their stalls, shopkeepers and their customers ran into the streets, office workers opened windows and leaned out, worshippers left churches and pagodas, and women and children ran from their houses, all peering intently upwards to watch the spectacle unfolding before their eyes. They watched the developing dogfights as the few fighters of the RAF and AVG (American Volunteer Group) tried to defend the population below. It was only when they heard the bombers overhead and saw for themselves the swarm of silver cigar-shaped aircraft with the Rising Sun emblem on the wings that they realised that this was no drill. They watched in awe and amazement as the bomb doors opened and silver missiles rained down from the sky like the teardrops of a glass-beaded curtain. Up until now, the inhabitants of Rangoon had been untouched by the horrors of the war in Europe or the terrible destruction rained down upon the Pacific Rim islands and Pearl Harbor. They were totally unprepared for this or any other kind of war.

The people in the streets and offices could see and hear the aeroplanes and sense the vibrations in the air as the bombers flew low. They could feel the pain of flying shrapnel from the fragmentation bombs, the agony of loss of limbs, the destruction of vital organs and the pumping of blood from severed arteries. But they had no concept of the nature of the weapons used against them or their destructive power.

Within minutes, the centre of Rangoon was destroyed. Buildings collapsed, large fires blazed and the streets were littered with the dead and dying. Burst mains spewed out torrents of water; power cables lay sparking on the ground or swung precariously overhead. Some of those who survived the bomb blasts and shrapnel were electrocuted in horrifying dances of death, as if a greater power had decreed that they should not survive a moment longer. The once bright Christmas lights were reduced to so many pieces of glass piercing the flesh, causing pain where moments before they had given pleasure. A few miles away at the end of Blanche's street, bombs flattened several buildings and totally obliterated the small play park, which was crowded with mothers and small children. More people died in the 20-

minute period during which these bombings took place than were killed during the heaviest all-night raid on London. Some 1,500 people—busy, happy and festive just minutes ago—lay dead in the streets, and an even larger number were gravely wounded.

In Fraser Street, in the initial excitement caused by the siren, Sybil, Bertha and the family ran out onto the balcony to watch the planes flying overhead. Down below, directly across the street, Mr Singh was working outside his premises when bullets struck him down, killing him instantly. One hour earlier, Sybil had been talking to him, promising to return with Bertha to purchase some small items. Sybil and the De Alvis family saw Mr Singh fall to the ground and were horrified. They fled to the relative safety of the interior of the building, suddenly aware of the danger they were in. They would shelter in the stairwell until the all-clear was sounded—this was no false alarm. All the inhabitants of the building joined them. The family held one another close for comfort, and Sybil and Bertha hugged each other tightly and prayed. They heard the low drones of the heavy bombers and the much higher-pitched sound of the fighters, and they felt the tremors as wave after wave of incendiary devices and fragmentation bombs found their targets. From the stairwell, they heard the screams of the injured and dying. Although it lasted little more than 20 minutes, the raid seemed to go on for an eternity.

When the all-clear sounded, Sybil and the De Alvis family made their way out of their shelter. They were met by scenes of total carnage. The once bustling shopping area was unrecognisable; market stalls, shops, offices, whole streets lay in ruins. Bodies were everywhere, and the cries of the injured and dying broke the eerie silence that pervaded the city, shrouded in smoke and dust from the attack. Wandering slowly, in a daze, through the scene of desolation, Sybil wondered what monstrous hand had delivered such a crushing blow to her Rangoon.

People rushed past in all directions. The multicoloured clothes were now predominantly bright red, as if some demented artist had thrown paint over everyone. All around lay bodies with limbs missing or heads blown off, body parts arranged haphazardly and entrails spilt on the dusty ground. It was like a grotesque and macabre dolls' hospital. Beggars were helping themselves to whatever they could lay their hands on—bread, meat, fruit and vegetables. A wailing man cradled a watermelon with its skin blown away and its innards looking like a head with half its brain missing in his arms. Sybil looked again. The melon had a tiny body and grubby arms and legs. She retched.

Looters entered shops through the holes blown in the walls and emerged with whatever they could carry. The normal street smells of foods and spices, bougainvillea and delphiniums had been replaced by a sweet, sickly stench that caught in Sybil's throat and made her gag. In time, some semblance of order returned and municipal wagons made their way tentatively through the streets. Sybil and her friends watched as bodies and parts of bodies were loaded onto the trucks and driven away. So much had been learned in so short a space of time. For Sybil, a girl of 21, the lesson of how cruel life can be was imprinted on her mind forever.

By a stroke of luck, Bertha's stepfather, a wealthy silk merchant called Mr Younis, found them wandering near Fraser Street. He had managed to escape from his office to an air-raid shelter just before the first bombs struck. He had crouched in the small slit trench, not caring about ruining his smart suit, his mind focused on his family, who were caught in the midst of the bombing with nowhere to take refuge. His joy on finding them all alive was tempered by his continued concern for their safety, and he decided that they should leave Rangoon immediately.

The information Mr Younis had was that the Japanese had invaded the south of Burma. Many officials still believed that the Japanese would advance no further, leaving Burma as a buffer between Allied and Axis areas of control. Others had an even less realistic view: that in the event of further invasion by the Japanese, British and Commonwealth soldiers, with locally conscripted troops, would be able to

16

repulse the enemy. It was the opinion of the General Officer Commanding (GOC) Burma, Major General D.K. McLeod, and a view widely held within the colonial government, that the Japanese lacked skills as fighting men, and there was a gross underestimation of the abilities, tactical expertise and courage of the Japanese army, as well as of the sophistication of their weaponry.

Mr Younis was not convinced by the bravado of the British. He had been taking a keen interest in the war in the Pacific, and in Malaya and Siam. Through his business contacts, he knew that the Japanese were a formidable fighting force, experienced in jungle warfare, survival in extreme conditions and advancing quickly over difficult terrain. Nor did they have obsolete equipment or outdated aircraft, tanks and artillery. Four years of war against the Chinese had given them all the training they needed. Mr Younis had also heard that the Japanese were treating their prisoners, both military and civilian, with a total lack of humanity, while determinedly pursuing their expansion plans. He saw the immediate threat and was not prepared to risk his family for the foolish and naive beliefs of others.

He had to consider the options open to them. Staying in Rangoon did not seem like a sensible thing to do given the level of destruction caused by only one bombing raid. Leaving by sea meant taking the risk of being bombed, and there would undoubtedly be submarines waiting to pick off any unsuspecting ship. Besides, Mr Younis had a fear of drowning and considered that option only very briefly. The decision was taken to travel north, and in making that decision they were not alone. That first bombing raid on Rangoon heralded the departure of tens of thousands of others who feared the worst.

Bertha, a British Army nurse at the military hospital, knew she would be needed and decided to return to her base early to help attend to the wounded. It was with a heavy heart that she said goodbye to her family. With tears in her eyes, she gave Sybil one last hug before heading back into the mayhem. She looked back only once, waved, turned round and strode purposefully into the crowds.

Shocked and very frightened, Sybil and her companions were caught up in the stampede to run away from the bombs, to flee the city. There was no time for Sybil to retrace her steps across town to Blanche, no way to find out if she and her baby were safe. She had to trust in her own instincts and in the decisions taken by Mr Younis. She had to put her own survival first.

*　　*　　*

In her house on 53rd Street, Blanche was getting ready to take Leslie to the park when she heard the drone of aircraft. Then the noise began as bombs exploded nearby. The Japanese

18

had showered the city with leaflets telling the inhabitants that they would be dropping pumpkins for Christmas, but the gifts turned out to be rather more deadly.

Blanche heard the explosions and the sound of gunfire; she saw swarms of birds take to the sky and their shrieks filled the air. Taking shelter in the front room under a sturdy table, Blanche prayed for the safety of her family. With a tremendous bang, a bomb dropped close to the house, and the back door was blown right off. Blanche took Leslie in her arms and was about to run out into the street when she was stopped by an air-raid warden, who abruptly told her to go back inside until the all-clear sounded. The bombs kept dropping, and with each impact Blanche shuddered and prayed even more. After what seemed to be an eternity, the noise stopped and all became deathly quiet. Blanche, cradling a crying Leslie in her arms, walked out of her house and was greeted by a scene of devastation. Houses had been destroyed, bodies lay in the street and a thick cloud of dust hung in the air.

'We didn't know what was happening at first,' she remembers. 'We didn't bother, we didn't know what war was. Suddenly, when people started shouting, we realised that something was happening. The planes were overhead. People were caught unawares, and most of them were killed. The big banks, shops and companies were bombed and destroyed.

The bombs fell at the end of our street, and many women and children were killed. They said they would drop pumpkins but these weren't pumpkins. How could they do such an evil thing?'

After the bombing came a large number of municipal lorries, and the bodies were loaded onto them like slaughtered cattle.

That afternoon, Blanche's husband returned to their house. As a broadcaster and radio announcer, he was more aware than most Burmese of the circumstances affecting the country and knew that it was no longer safe to stay in Rangoon, the principal target for the Japanese bombers and a port vital to the enemy. Gathering the family together—Blanche, Leslie and Manu's brother and sister-in-law—he explained to them the need to flee and outlined his plan to take them to safety. First of all, he organised the packing of essential supplies and the distribution of all their money and valuables, ensuring that each adult had sufficient funds to help with their survival. Only staple foods were packed and basic clothing selected. Blanche had to leave behind all her fine clothes but took with her a silk dress that Sybil had made for her.

Blanche and her family set off for the shops to get more food and were confronted by looters taking whatever they could get their hands on. Her friends who owned the local grocery were nowhere to be seen. It was with a heavy heart that she too began taking what foodstuffs she could get her hands on. Bags of rice, tinned foods, fresh vegetables and fruit were all acquired, and finally Blanche went into the confectioner's next door and took as many cakes and sweets as she could carry. They were for Leslie, so he would be quiet and happy. Blanche vowed that after the nightmare had ended she would return to pay for the food they had taken and hoped that God would forgive and understand her actions.

For now, their survival was all that mattered. How different this all was from their former life. How Blanche prayed for a return to normality.

The war had begun in earnest and the family's idyllic life was over.

CHAPTER TWO

1920–26

SYRIAM, BURMA

For many in the port of Syriam, lying just east of the capital across the mouth of the Rangoon River, 8 April 1920 was just another day. But it was on that day, at 7.15 a.m., that Sybil Maud Le Fleur made her first public appearance. The midwife who attended the birth was the same woman who had assisted at the birth of Sybil's brother Austin some three years before and her sister Eunice Olga three years before that.

Their mother, Lucy, was an organised and punctual woman, and it seemed that Sybil would take after her, for she arrived exactly on her due date. It must have been a relief to Lucy that her baby had been born so early in the morning. At this time of year, as the day progressed the temperature outside steadily rose to a level that made any form of exercise or effort quite unbearable, and despite the substantial thickness of the walls, it was necessary to sit quietly in the shade. Childbirth was certainly not something one would wish to go through in the heat of the day.

By all accounts, Sybil was a live wire from

the very start. Not for her the undignified ritual of being held upside down and slapped on the bottom to let her know it was time to wake up and take her first breath. She was already exercising her lungs in annoyance at the rude interruption to her quiet life before the midwife had had a chance to sever the umbilical cord.

'She's a stubborn one, and noisy as well,' the woman commented as she handed the baby to her mother. Sybil was wrinkled and prune-like, as most babies are, and at 8 lb she was no delicate or fragile creature. Sitting atop her head was a shock of straight jet-black hair. As Sybil nestled in her mother's arms, Lucy looked down at her and felt an overwhelming joy. She held the new baby tightly in her arms and sang softly in her soothing voice.

That year, 1920, was one of some significance in the history of Burma: the first obvious signs of the unrest that would eventually lead to Burmese independence appeared. The British had governed Burma as a province of British India since their victory in the Third Anglo-Burmese War of 1885, following which the Burmese royal family had been exiled. In 1920, students at Rangoon University staged a strike. It was to be the first of many. These well-educated young Burmans had grown to resent British rule. They wanted more freedom for their country, constitutional reform and a return to Buddhism in place of the Christianity that had been forced on Burma by missionaries from the West. The nationalist struggle was to lead to much unrest during Sybil's childhood, some of which would have an impact on her future. But for the time being, the family were content in their haven in Syriam, largely unaffected by politics or civil unrest.

Sybil's father, William Thomas Le Fleur, whom they called 'Dada', was an engineer employed at the Burmah Oil Company. It was but a short walk from his doorstep to the company's massive Syriam refinery, situated on an outcrop leading directly to a huge oil terminal, the great Indian Ocean and thence the world. William was a tall, fine-featured man of slight build. He had a long, thin face, piercing brown eyes, a small mouth and prominent ears, but it was his hands that drew most attention: he had long, slender fingers—perfect for his work as a precision engineer. Lucy was a complete contrast. Barely 5 ft tall, she had a round, smiling face, a slightly flattened button nose, dark almond-shaped eyes and a smile that spread from ear to ear. Her smooth skin was like milk chocolate, and her hair was jet black and tightly curled.

Some weeks after the birth of their new baby, she was christened at the local Roman Catholic church, where her parents were regular and devout parishioners. Sybil's parents and grandparents, her sister Eunice and brother Austin and a large congregation gathered to watch the happy event.

'I now baptise you Sybil Maud Le Fleur, in the name of the Father, the Son and the Holy Ghost. *In nomine Patris et Filii et Spiritus Sancti.*'

'Amen,' said the congregation, as the priest threw water over her face. She screeched out loud, and Lucy had to take her from him before she squirmed out of his grasp.

Although she had been christened with the grand and very English name Sybil Maud, she was soon nicknamed 'Baby'. Eunice's nickname was 'Buddie' and Austin was called 'Buddha'.

And so it was that Sybil started on her long journey through life: it would take her to the other side of the world, bring incredible happiness and unspeakable sadness. It was a journey that would require her to face great challenges and would many times test the faith into which she had been born.

*   *   *

Sybil's father was the son of a wealthy French merchant, Albert Le Fleur, who was born and brought up in Rangoon. There was some talk of Albert's father having been a French nobleman forced to leave his homeland in something of a hurry, but, other than rumour, the Le Fleur girls knew little of their great-grandparents, although their father's side of the family had clearly been well-to-do. Albert met and married a beautiful young woman of French-Portuguese descent. (A significant number of Portuguese, Armenian and French families had been resident in Burma since the early eighteenth century.) He was some 15 years her senior, but their relationship was strong. They were devoted to each other, constant and inseparable companions. Their marriage had been blessed with five children. William had three brothers and a sister: Clifford ran a large diamond and ruby mine (the 'pigeon's blood' rubies to be found in the mountainous north-east of the country were famous around the world); Mervyn managed the local corporation sewage treatment works; Arnie did odd jobs and maintenance in houses around Syriam; and Mary was very artistic and an accomplished musician.

Sybil never met Albert because some years before she was born he contracted a fever during the monsoon—a not uncommon occurrence—and despite receiving the best medical care available, he died. Some time afterwards, William's mother married for the second time. Her new husband, Sonna Fonseca, was a friend of the family, of Spanish-Portuguese descent, and had been very close to Albert, as he was to William and his siblings, whom he looked upon almost as his own children. It was therefore quite natural that he should assume such a position on a more formal basis. Mr Fonseca had been employed for a number of years as a senior draughtsman at the Syriam refinery, where Sybil's father would go to work on completing his engineering degree. Sybil's step-grandfather was to be a strong influence on her, and his love for all the children was unbounded. William's parents lived in a quiet corner of town, not far away from the young Le Fleur family, and the children visited them frequently when they were old enough to be allowed out on their own.

Lucy, christened Lucia, was the daughter of a successful Karen businessman and his Burman wife. The Karen were a fiercely independent people, descended from Tibetan refugees. Under the British, they became an integral part of the colonial police force and many were recruited into the British Army. Lucy's father, like many Karen, was a Roman Catholic and had made his fortune trading with Siam (modern Thailand) and China. Lucy had inherited her father's wit and intelligence and her mother's artistic nature, sensitivity, striking features and large brown eyes. William used to say that when she looked at him, he simply melted inside. 'I knew the first day I met her, there and then, that I would never have peace in my heart until I had married this beautiful girl with the sparkling eyes and the gentle nature. She was all I dreamed about. She was my princess,' he would say to his children.

And so, after a suitable period of courtship, they married, and their union was a happy one.

Burma was a multicultural country with a high proportion of Anglo-Burmese and Anglo-Indians, so the Le Fleurs' marriage was not at all unusual. The couple grew prosperous, and they settled among the Eurasian community in Syriam.

The Le Fleur family had found a niche in colonial Burma's lively society, centred on Rangoon and Syriam. Foreigners dominated the thriving modern export market, as well as the equally healthy local economy. British—in fact, Scottish—entrepreneurs owned the Burmah Oil Company, as well as the Irrawaddy Flotilla Company, which was founded in 1865 and had grown by the 1920s into the largest fleet of merchant ships in the world.

Many successful import and export businesses were run by Indian businessmen, and indeed there was a perception among the Burmese that their wealth was gained at the expense of native Burmans. Tamil Indians tended to work as labourers and generally remained poor, but other Indian ethnic groups made up the lower and middle ranks of the civil service, provided many of the country's physicians and also served in the police and army. Indians also provided Burma with merchants, shopkeepers and craftsmen. There was a much smaller Chinese community, created over hundreds of years of trade between the neighbouring countries, whose members were well assimilated into Burmese society and suffered less resentment than did their Indian counterparts.

Many British citizens also made their way to Burma, often via India, to work in civil service and government posts. Eric Blair, better known as George Orwell, worked in Burma from 1922 to 1927 as a member of the Indian Imperial Police. From January to October 1925, he was posted to Syriam as head of security at the Burmah Oil Company refinery, and he was well known to William and to his stepfather. Orwell's famous essays 'A Hanging' and 'Shooting an Elephant' describe incidents that took place during his time in the colony, and his first novel, *Burmese Days*, was loosely based on the people he met and his experiences there.

The Le Fleurs' house, like many others in the street, was a bungalow in a colonial style with a red tile roof. It had big arched windows with shutters and a wide veranda running all round the house. For most of the year, the windows were left open and a fine net curtain hung down to prevent the many airborne bugs from entering while allowing a pleasant breeze to flow round the house—aided by the three fans.

The family measured their wealth and status not only by the size of their house, the land surrounding the property and the servants in their employ but also by the number of ceiling fans in their home. William had used his skill and knowledge to construct three large fans, one in the living room, one in the dining room and one in his and Lucy's bedroom. These contraptions would whirr loudly and swing to and fro as they spun around on fragile spindles connected to small electric motors. From the children's viewpoint, close to the ground, they looked as if at any moment they might detach themselves from the ceiling and fly off, beheading anyone in their path. Despite the frequent power cuts that rendered the fans inoperative, the Le Fleur family were the envy of their friends, many of whom had only one ceiling fan, in the living area, and there was no doubt that Dada's arrangement made the house a more pleasant place to live.

The bungalow was situated in the middle of a walled and gated compound. They were relatively safe and secure, although William always kept spears at the door in case they should be threatened by local dacoits, or bandits. During the dry seasons of the year, the land inside the compound was dusty packed earth dotted with a few of the more hardy local plants, shrubs and mango and papaya trees. During the monsoon, it became a sea of mud, with strange and unidentified plants shooting up where previously there had been nothing.

The family had four servants. William's manservant looked after all his clothes and belongings with such dedication and attention to detail that he would not allow even Lucy to touch them. She used to tease William and say that his manservant was jealous of her, but he only laughed and kissed her. A cook made all the

30

meals, and she and Lucy would go to the market together to buy the fresh ingredients. The children were looked after by an ayah, or nanny, who played games like hopscotch, skipping, and hide and seek to keep them amused. The final member of the little retinue was a gardener, who also looked after many of the neighbouring compounds, as he was only required at any one of them on a part-time basis.

When Sybil was two years old, Blanche Miranda was born. This new arrival presented her parents with something of a dilemma. Sybil was nicknamed 'Baby' but she was no longer the baby of the family. They settled on calling Blanche 'Boo Boo'.

Blanche was a happy child. When she was a baby, Sybil would sit with her cradled in her arms, paying particular attention to holding her head up. Blanche would look up, and her face would break into a broad grin and she would chuckle and gurgle loudly. Lucy used to say that it was probably down to wind, but Sybil knew they had a bond. As Blanche grew up, she would follow Sybil around, first of all on her bottom, having developed a shuffling technique that saw her move at quite alarming speeds across the highly polished teak floors. The girls played well together, although sometimes Sybil, as the elder sister, felt the need to exercise a little authority and make it clear to Blanche that certain toys were hers and hers alone.

The Le Fleur girls' first language was

English, and they would also learn Burmese and a smattering of Tamil. However, it was some time before Blanche spoke at all. She had no reason to try. What need had she to talk when Sybil was there to do it for her? When Sybil asked for a drink, Blanche was given one too; when Sybil ate some fruit, she too had a piece. When Sybil lay down because she was tired, her little sister would lie down beside her, and Sybil would put her arms around her for comfort. Blanche's first objective was to learn to walk so she could chase her sister around and get involved in all the games they played. They would sing and dance together, and at the end of their games, when they were finally tired, they would rub their noses together in a show of tender affection. Sybil looked after her with such love and affection that Lucy would say, 'Here comes our little ayah,' and she would clap her hands with delight.

One day, when Blanche was still just a toddler, they all journeyed to Rangoon. Eunice and Austin were at home for the holidays. (Austin was a boarder at a monastery run by the De La Salle Brothers, while Eunice attended St Philomena's Convent, where she was taught by the Good Shepherd order of nuns.) William dressed in his best black suit, a white shirt with starched collar, gold studs and cufflinks, and a smart striped tie. Lucy spent a long time getting ready, putting on her best dress, her double strand of pearls, carefully applied make-up and her shiniest shoes. The children wore their Sunday clothes, and, with hair carefully combed and skin scrubbed clean, they set off for Rangoon. They travelled to the ferry landing in a one-horse gharry, a light carriage. It moved with a rocking motion that seemed designed to induce sickness over a journey of any length. Luckily, the trip to the ferry was a short one. The family crossed the Rangoon River and, after a short walk, entered a shop just off Dalhousie Street. The sign above the door said 'J. Thomson—Photographer'.

Inside was a treasure trove of cameras, from simple box Brownies to large wooden models with gleaming brass fittings and accordion-like bellows. Metal signs hung on the wall advertising Eastman Kodak, Houghton Ensign, Graflex, Gundlach and myriad other exotic names. A small Indian man ushered them through a doorway and into the back of the shop. Standing in the middle of the room was a tall man. Sybil looked him up and down. He was taller even than Dada, but that wasn't what frightened her. He looked like a ghost; his face was as white as the cotton towels they dried themselves on. His hair was a shock of red, and he had a thick red growth of hair above his mouth. Sybil hid in the folds of her mother's dress until she was gently persuaded to come out. Maybe the giant wouldn't eat her after all. She listened to what he was saying and thought she recognised some words, but he spoke so strangely that she thought she might have been imagining it. After some arranging of the subjects, the giant took his place behind one of the bigger brass-and-wood boxes. He came back round to the group, made some further adjustments and returned to the camera. 'Hold still,' he said, and with that he took the first family portrait to feature little Blanche.

They left the shop and walked the short distance to Mogul Street, where they were each given an ice-cream cone. The ice cream was deliciously cold, but it gave Sybil a headache as she ate it too quickly; she felt as if her brain was freezing. They bought a few provisions in Rowe & Co. and made their way slowly back to the docks. By the time the gharry arrived at their compound, Sybil and Blanche were asleep in each other's arms.

When Eunice and Austin were away at school, life settled into a routine. William would leave for work at seven, having had a substantial breakfast. The family would then have their meal: vermicelli with coconut sprinkled with sugar and doused with milk, cereal or, on cold mornings, mohinga. At midday, William would come home and the family would have tiffin, or lunch, which was a fairly substantial meal of chicken casserole or chicken dahl, or perhaps duck, beef or lamb in a rich curry sauce with potatoes and boiled or fried rice. Sometimes they had Sybil's favourite, *ohn-no khaukswe*, a chicken curry prepared with coconut milk, served with noodles and dressed with a sprinkling of coriander, finely chopped red onion and some freshly squeezed lime juice. On Fridays, they always had fish. When William returned from work, they had a simple, light meal, tea leaf salad or *jia san hinga*, a soup of fish, glass noodles and vegetables.

When the cook had her day off, the ayah, who was a Tamil girl, would cook rich Indian curries, and the children would help her by crushing fresh herbs and spices with a big marble rolling pin. They became very familiar with these: turmeric, with its pungent earthy smell; cumin, aromatic and smoky; coriander, with its fresh taste and aroma; and lime leaf, which produced a mild and delicate citrus flavour, perfect for adding the finishing touches to soups and mild curries. They would watch as their ayah fried red chillies and added fresh, finely chopped onion, which stung their eyes. The smell of the meat or fish cooking would make their mouths water. Coriander, ginger, cumin, garlic and fresh vegetables would join the meat, and all would be cooked until the flavours were mingled. Turmeric was added to the rice to give a rich colour and delicate flavour. They all loved the different flavours of Indian curries, which were stronger and spicier than the delicately flavoured Burmese meals they ate most of the time.

Their ayah could not read, but she would tell

them the stories that she had been told as a child. Tales of great adventure and maharajas, of tiger hunts and elephants, of heroic deeds, of monsoons and earthquakes, all set in a country quite different from Burma. She told of the great god Shiva and his bull Nandi and of Rajaraja, the ancient king of kings. Sybil and Blanche would dream of the land their ayah told them about. For now, they travelled to India only in their imaginations, not knowing that the country was to play a significant role in both their futures.

Every morning, after William had gone to work and the sweeper employed by the municipality had emptied the night-soil from the commode in the bathroom, the children would take a bath in the big enamel tub. Water had to be bought every day from the coolies, and it was quite a science knowing how much the household would need. Once purchased, the water was kept in huge earthenware containers in a room beside the kitchen. Depending on the time of year, the bath water was either freezing cold or tepid. It was all right once you were immersed, but teeth had to be gritted at the point of entry. Hot water was found only in the kitchen, in the blackened kettle hanging from a steel hook over the open range or in the large metal saucepans used for cooking. The soap the family used was lightly scented and produced a rich lather that frothed easily. The children would scoop up handfuls of soapsuds and blow them in the air to watch the light play on the bubbles, reflecting all the colours of the rainbow. Covered in goosebumps, they would emerge after a good long soaking and shiver as they dried themselves with thick white cotton towels.

In the evenings, when William wasn't working, he and Lucy would read to their children and do jigsaw puzzles. Sometimes their parents entertained friends or William's colleagues, and the girls would be allowed to stay up for a little while as long as they were well behaved. It was a very happy and joyful home, full of laughter and merriment, and Sybil and Blanche felt they were the luckiest children in the world.

When William's work took him to Rangoon, he would come home with small toys for his children and gold bangles for his wife. He also brought jars of durian preserve, which Lucy loved and kept in a cupboard out of reach of her inquisitive children. The durian fruit was an interesting specimen. Growing up to a foot long and with a husk of prickly thorns, it had a distinctive strong and unpleasant odour. William would never allow one within the compound, let alone the house. If the smell could be tolerated and the husk removed, the soft inner flesh waited, and it was unsurpassed for flavour. Creamy custard flavoured with almonds and sherry, along with a multitude of other sensations, assaulted the taste buds, and it seemed the more you ate the more you wanted.

When she was about four years old, Sybil began to notice and take interest in more grown-up things. When her parents went out to dances or parties, they would dress up in their best clothes, and she would sit and watch as Lucy carefully went through her wardrobe and tried first one outfit then another before saying to William, 'I have nothing to wear.' Sybil looked on as her mother carefully put on her make-up, emphasising her big eyes and fine features. A fine dusting of powder here, a bit of rouge there, a flattering shade of lipstick and a puff of perfume from the glass container with the fancy bulb spray, and she was every inch the princess of Dada's dreams. There was no need for much make-up, as even without any Lucy was a strikingly beautiful woman. Sybil was fascinated by the bright lipsticks of all shades, the eyeliner, the powder and the jewellery that her mother would try on, matching it to her choice of outfit. Sybil longed for the day when she too might have occasion to use make-up and lipstick like Mummy.

That day was to come sooner than anyone thought. One afternoon, Blanche and Sybil managed to give their ayah the slip while she was in the kitchen preparing tiffin. She had her hands full that day and didn't notice when they sneaked away. Hand in hand, they went into Lucy's bedroom, and with the confidence that only a four year old possesses, Sybil began to apply make-up to Blanche. She managed to give her a pale face and rosy red cheeks, with only the faintest amount of powder and rouge missing their target and landing on the bed. All was going well until it was time for the lipstick. Although her coordination was quite good, Sybil hadn't reckoned on Blanche laughing as she carefully applied the red substance to her face. The result was dramatic and a little terrifying. It reminded Sybil of the little dragons that their ayah used to tell them about. Sybil made a much more successful job of applying her own make-up, and the two of them were tottering around in Lucy's shoes when she and their panic-stricken ayah walked in.

Sybil could see they were cross, but she detected the hint of a smile on Mummy's face. She made the sisters promise never to do it again—although poor Blanche was more the innocent victim than the perpetrator of the deed.

Lucy wasn't so forgiving one day when Blanche and Sybil were supposed to be visiting their grandparents. Sybil had taken it into her head that she needed to trim her hair, but she decided to try it out on Blanche first. The results were certainly impressive, and seemed rather stylish to her, so she set about her own hair with the small pair of scissors she had found. When their mother saw them, she took them by the hand and marched them straight to her husband.

'What on earth am I going to do with these children? How can we go to see your parents with them looking like this? They're bound to wonder what kind of a mother would allow this to happen to our beautiful little girls.'

William looked surprised and upset. Sybil hadn't realised how much he loved their long black curls, and it was obvious that the results of her attempt at hairdressing had shocked him. Of course, their hair would grow back in time and all would be forgiven, but standing there, being inspected so closely, Sybil began to realise that maybe, just maybe, on this occasion she had pushed them a bit too far. Lucy did her best to tidy them up and make them look as presentable as possible, and eventually they went round to Grandfather's house. When the family went in, not a word was said by either parents or grandparents about how Blanche and Sybil looked.

When Sybil was five, she followed Eunice to boarding school at St Philomena's Convent in Rangoon. Although she made many good friends, she would sometimes cry herself to sleep. She missed Dada and Mummy, their cook and their ayah; but above all she missed her sister Blanche.

St Philomena's was an imposing red-brick school situated in 15 acres of grounds on the Prome Road. The two-storey buildings formed an open courtyard. One wing was for senior pupils, with dormitories upstairs and classrooms downstairs. The other wing, a mirror image, was for juniors. From the end of each wing, a teak staircase led down to the classrooms, and it was therefore rare for the older pupils to come into contact with the younger ones. Because of the age gap between them, Eunice and Sybil were not often together and saw each other only at mealtimes. They each had their own group of friends, although when they were at home they got on like a house on fire. The upper floor of the central section was home to the nuns and resident teachers, while the offices, library, kitchens and refectory were on the ground floor. The grand main entrance led to a central hall, which had a floor constructed of alternate squares of black and white marble, like a giant chessboard. A very grand, ornately carved staircase, used only by the nuns and teachers, led up from the hall to the first floor.

The children of St Philomena's would have felt at home in any school in Britain, as it was run on Western lines, basing its curriculum on the English school system. The timetable would be familiar to British pupils even today. There were classes in English literature and language, mathematics, history, geography and science. The uniform consisted of a blue blazer, white blouse and grey pinafore, with a blue-and-brown striped tie. Sybil's pinafore was always immaculate, unlike those of her peers. It had three box pleats at the front and three at the back, and needed careful looking after if it was to appear at its best. Sybil had found the ideal solution: as soon as she took it off at night, she placed it underneath her mattress on top of the firm base, so it was always well pressed and the pleats as sharp as knife-edges.

Every morning at six o'clock, the girls would be woken by the nuns, and after a very brief pause to yawn and stretch and wipe the sleep from tired eyes, they would rush along the smooth polished teak floor and down the stairs to the big washroom beneath their dormitory. Inside were huge barrels filled with cold water, and, after a moment's hesitation, they would jump in. Each girl had a piece of carbolic soap and her own small enamel pitcher, used to pour water over herself to rinse off the rather unpleasant-smelling soap. They brushed their teeth using their fingers and a black paste made from ground charcoal and salt. It seemed to do the trick, as Sybil's teeth were pearly white, straight and even. At half past six, the pupils assembled in the chapel for Mass, said in Latin. The two altar servers were chosen in rotation from the senior girls. At quarter to eight, a simple breakfast was served, and at half-past, classes began. As well as the academic subjects, there were periods devoted to arts and crafts, drawing and needlework. Every day, there was an opportunity to exercise, and Sybil found herself quite adept at hockey, being chosen for the first team. Lunch was at one, and this was the main meal of the day. Classes finished at five, after which the girls had an hour to themselves before a light dinner. All meals were taken in the refectory, where the pupils sat at long benches. Grace would be said, and Tamil girls, some not much older than the senior students, would then serve the food. Study began at seven o' clock and lasted for two hours.

By lights out, the pupils were exhausted. There were no complaints or dissenters, as there was a general realisation that to better yourself you had to work hard, study well, gain a higher education and thus get a good job, perhaps in the civil service or one of the key industries in Rangoon. The girls became used to the routine and the certainty it gave them. On Saturdays, the nuns would mix up large pails of Epsom salts diluted in water. The pupils scooped up a mugful each as they trooped past the pails, and in this way the nuns achieved for their charges purity of soul and of body.

Every Saturday night, the girls would entertain the nuns with short sketches and plays, which they rehearsed until they were word perfect. Sybil's party piece, which the nuns asked for with monotonous regularity, was her rendition of an amusing song called 'Stop Your Ticklin', Jock', during which she would pretend to play the banjo, rolling her eyes and laughing heartily. She wasn't sure what some of the words meant, but it was fun to sing and act, and the nuns, many of whom came from Scotland and Ireland, would laugh out loud and clap their hands in appreciation of her efforts. The school

43

also staged an annual production, and in Sybil's senior year she would play the part of Portia in Shakespeare's *The Merchant of Venice*.

When Sybil was six years old, and while the children were all at home for the holidays, Dada announced that they were to have a new brother or sister. This was an eagerly anticipated event, and the household spent some considerable time in preparing for the new arrival. A thorough spring clean took place, and many new items were bought—clothes in unisex colours, cotton nappies and new bedding. William's mother donated a lace shawl that she had had as a baby. Dada even overhauled the ceiling fans.

On the day Lucy went into labour, Eunice, Austin, Sybil and Blanche were sent out on a picnic with their ayah. They took the ferry to Rangoon and had a wonderful day playing in the park and watching the birds landing on the lake. Eunice and Austin read books while Blanche and Sybil sat and played and laughed, or when they had too much energy and needed to let off steam, they chased each other around the trees. They played happily in each other's company; it was good for them to be together again.

When they arrived back at the house, it was very quiet. Their grandparents were in the living room with William, and he called the children over to him. He looked at each of them in turn, and Sybil noticed that his eyes, which usually sparkled with fun and mischief, now appeared dull and red-rimmed. His face seemed paler, and he looked tired and in pain.

Sybil may have forgotten much about her childhood, as one does with the passing of the years, but she has never forgotten what Dada said to them on that day. The words are carved on her heart just as surely as if they had been carved on a piece of stone. He put his arms round them and held them as he said, 'My darlings, God has decided that he needs Mummy to help him look after all the poor little boys and girls, so he has taken her and the baby with him to heaven.' The tears rolled down his cheeks and dropped onto their clothes, and they said nothing as William hugged them tighter to him.

Eventually, the family all went slowly through to Lucy's room and saw her lying on the bed as if asleep. They all kissed her on her cheek, first Eunice, then Austin. Next, Sybil stood on tiptoe and put her cheek next to Mummy's. Lucy's cold skin felt like wax, nothing like the soft, warm surface Sybil was used to. She kissed her mother on her cheek and on her cold lips and felt utterly desolated. She barely noticed when Dada picked Blanche up so that she too could kiss her mother.

'Mummy will watch over us and protect us just as she has always done,' said Dada. 'We must make her proud of us. Be good and strong and always think of others. Be brave and determined like Mummy and trust in God. He has a reason for everything.'

Eunice sobbed and Austin stood tall and brave. Sybil bit her lip until it bled and dug her fingernails into the palms of her hands until the pain nearly made her scream. At six years of age, she was just old enough to understand the sadness around her. She had to remain strong for Dada. Even Blanche, who was a very exuberant and jolly child, remained quiet throughout this sad ceremony.

They slowly filed out of the room where they had slept between their parents when they were frightened, where they had sat with them as they read stories and where they had all felt as if they were so safe that nothing in the world could harm them. Sybil held Blanche more tightly than ever when they left the room.

That night as Sybil lay in bed trying to sleep, she could hear Dada weeping in his room. She was sure she knew how he felt. Mummy was the kindest, gentlest, most patient and loving person, and in their short time together they had had so much fun. She was not just their mother but their best friend too. Sybil knew she would be perfect for God and envied all the little children in heaven who would have Mummy to look after them. But why couldn't God see that they needed her just as much as He did? Sybil sobbed until her chest and stomach hurt and her pillow was soaked in tears, and finally she fell asleep, exhausted.

For days afterwards, the house was full of

people. Many friends and relatives came to call, but there was none of the laughter that used to accompany their visits. Several of the women wore white from head to toe, the traditional Burmese sign of mourning, and many arrived in tears and left still crying.

The pain of that holiday was burned vividly on their minds. William was always quiet, although he still held the children close and smiled at them with big, watery, sad eyes. Eunice spent a lot of her time in her room reading, while Austin seemed like a little lost boy, moping around the house. Blanche and Sybil were too young to spend all their time thinking about their mother and her loss. They were so full of energy and playfulness that they carried on much as before.

When Sybil did think about it, however, she had moments of unbearable sadness, and there were many painful reminders. The girls would come across William's manservant crying silently while he straightened out their father's shirts, or when they rushed into the kitchen unannounced they might find the cook standing at the sink looking out into the yard with tears streaming down her face. She would see them out of the corner of her eye and quickly wipe the tears from her face. 'It's the onions,' she would say. 'They're very strong today.' But when the children looked, they couldn't see any onions.

Not long after Lucy's death, they saw their

ayah in her room. She wasn't crying softly over strong onions or the state of the master's shirts, or weeping silently as Grandfather, Granny and Dada did from time to time, but wailing like a wounded animal, calling out loud and striking her breasts with her fists like a tortured being. This was the Tamil way of expressing the anguish of grief. Their ayah was mourning someone very dear to her and to them all. For the girls, the sight of it was both moving and frightening, and although they did not truly understand what was happening, it certainly kept them quiet for some time.

It came as a relief when the holiday ended and they went back to school. Blanche was only four, but, nevertheless, she now joined Eunice and Sybil at the convent. Sybil kept an eye on her, although for the most part she did so from a distance.

The girls were studious and diligent workers, and their teachers were pleased with their progress. Sybil did particularly well in English and arts and crafts. She worked hard so that Dada and Mummy would be proud of her. Blanche excelled at history, although if there was a test, she would write important dates on her hands and arms, just as insurance. The girls joined the Guides and went to camps where they learned how to tie knots, cook and sew. In the evenings, they would sit around singing songs.

Blanche received only one rupee in pocket

48

money each month. It was a very small amount and considerable skills were required to make it last. Sybil, on the other hand, always had money to spare, as her allowance was much bigger. Blanche discovered that one way of eking out her cash was to catch Sybil at lunchtime or after class, when she was invariably to be found outside the tuck shop with her friends. Blanche would wait until Sybil had made her purchases and then appear in front of her. Sybil knew what she wanted and would give her a few coins for a snack. She would pretend to be cross with Blanche for bothering her when she was with her chums, but secretly she enjoyed their little rendezvous. It meant she could watch over her little sister and make sure she was all right.

In the school grounds and the surrounding streets, various fruit trees grew, including mango and papaya, but one of the pupils' favourites was the cashew apple, which they picked as they walked along or ate while playing in the shaded areas in the school grounds. Sybil would eat the fruit but discard the cashew nut. When she was not in class or reading or doing her homework, she liked nothing better than to watch the multicoloured birds of all shapes and sizes diving and swooping and chasing one another through the trees. Landing in puddles, they would paddle and splash furiously, immersing their feathers before finding a sunny spot to dry and preen their plumage back into position. Sybil wondered where they went when they flew away. She envied their freedom.

Not far from the school was a soy sauce factory, and, depending on the direction of the prevailing wind, the pupils were surrounded either by the smell of the flowering shrubs in the grounds or by a strong odour of soy sauce, which served only to make them hungry. Sybil found the smell rather overpowering and preferred the sweet smell of the flowers, which reminded her of the perfumes that her mother used to wear. Lucy's favourite scent had been very expensive. William had bought it for her at Christmas 1925. It was a completely new fragrance, recently arrived in Rowe & Co. from Paris. It was made by Guerlain, and its name was Shalimar.

The more time Sybil spent in Rangoon, the more she loved it. The tree-lined streets and cultivated gardens of laburnums, poinsettias, delphiniums and bougainvillea of staggering size and beauty made for a colourful landscape, as did the bright longyis of the people on the streets. Towering over the buildings around it, the Shwedagon Pagoda, standing on a prominent hill in north Rangoon, covered in gold, shone like a bright star in the sunlight, while at dusk the cupola took on many different hues, reflecting the evening light. The sound of its bells tinkling in the breeze was, like its very presence, both peaceful and inspiring. The sight of the monks walking slowly towards their place of worship dressed in their orange robes was somehow comforting, and every day large numbers of people prayed in the pagoda. The temple provided a haven of calmness and tranquillity, a moment's respite from the troubles of life.

CHAPTER THREE

1927–39

SYRIAM AND RANGOON

Early in 1927, the children went to live with their father's parents, and from that time on they would spend the school holidays in the big colonial house near the refinery. (Although, after their mother's death, Austin spent all his time at the monastery with the De La Salle Brothers and very rarely returned to Syriam, even during the holidays. At one point, the girls wondered if he had taken up holy orders, so infrequent were his visits.) Their elder cousin Irene Le Fleur moved to Syriam to help the elderly couple look after the young girls. She had come from her father's diamond and ruby mine in the mountainous central region of Burma and was only too glad to have a reason to move to the city. Later that year, William's mother passed away, never having really got over Lucy's death, and her sister-in-law, Aunt Nellie, came to stay with them, to take care of Grandfather.

Meanwhile, William lived alone in the old family bungalow for most of the year. Only the cook remained with him, as he had long since dispensed with the services of his manservant and the ayah; even the gardener's visits had been reduced to only occasional appearances. He was still the Dada the girls knew and loved, and when they were on holiday, he would take them for picnics and play hide and seek with them, or they would fly kites in the park.

In 1928, however, William decided to take another job. For some time, he had been unhappy, not with his employers but with his own situation. With Lucy gone, William had no hope of happiness as long as he stayed in the bungalow in Syriam, and he felt it was time to move on. All the family's possessions were moved out of their old house, the shutters were closed and the gate to the compound was chained and padlocked shut. Whenever Sybil and Blanche were in Syriam, they would walk to their old house, which William had refused to part with. It was slowly decaying, the paint flaking off and the tiles slipping from the roof. It was a symbol of happiness—but the happiness of another time.

William was an ambitious and talented man, and when the Irrawaddy Flotilla Company, the IFC, had approached him with the offer of a senior management position as an engineer, along with improved terms and conditions, he had jumped at the opportunity. He would have more authority than he had had at the refinery, and the job would be more challenging. His new title was very grand: inspector of launches for the entire IFC. The job took him to Bassein, to the west of Rangoon and at the end of the railway line. The town sat on the bank of a wide and deep river of the same name. Here, his new employers had established a large engineering facility and dock for the repair and refit of their vessels, at that time by far the largest fleet of steamers, barges and ferries in the whole of Asia, and probably the largest inland water transportation organisation in the world. William threw himself into the job with enthusiasm, and he soon impressed his employers with his skill and attention to detail, becoming a popular manager with both his staff and his bosses.

Every fortnight, William would send letters to his children, telling them about Bassein, his work and his trips upriver to other locations belonging to the IFC. He wrote of journeys on the famous Irrawaddy River to places they had heard of—Prome and Mandalay and the great oil fields of Yenangyaung. He described the people he met, the strange clothes some of them wore, the buildings of bamboo and the great stone forts. He told them of the forests, birds and animals, the dank smell of the jungle and the different foods he experienced on his travels, and all these things gave his children a lust for knowledge and ignited in Sybil a desire for adventure and travel. She read the letters over and over, keeping them in a small wooden box, organised in bundles tied with ribbon.

With each letter was just enough money for their grandfather and Irene to bring them up comfortably—perhaps without the luxuries that the wealthiest families had, but they were left wanting for none of the basics of life: good food, clothes and some pocket money. In one of his letters, Dada mentioned that he had met a wonderful lady, Daisy Boyce. She was full of life, and they had spent some time together. His boss had introduced them to each other at a works function. She was very well read and amusing, William wrote, and he enjoyed her company. The next time he wrote, there were the usual stories of his trips and what he had been doing, but there was more mention of Daisy. They had been to the pictures together. This caused concern. What on earth were these two people doing going to the pictures together? They had been on a picnic to a beautiful waterfall. Sybil didn't even read the name of the place. Dada didn't seem to care that Daisy was nearer in age to Eunice than to him.

His letters were still signed 'your loving Dada', but the girls could tell that something was changing. Each missive brought more news of Daisy. Apparently, she was very popular in Bassein, and everyone knew her. As a result, she and William had been invited to the house of the IFC's district manager for a dinner party. William had bought her a new dress, and he had been very proud of her as she entertained everyone with stories of her travels. She was such a knowledgeable person, he said, and she was so good to him.

They heard less and less about their father's life in Bassein and ever more about Daisy. He and Daisy had been shopping in Rangoon, and although she was desperate to get to know Sybil and Blanche, it had been term time, and reluctantly she had accepted that the meeting would have to be postponed. They had visited Rowe & Co., and William had bought her a new dress and some jewellery. He felt sure the girls would have liked what he had chosen for Daisy. They had visited J. Thomson, the photographer, and had their picture taken. He had taken Daisy to Mogul Street, to their favourite ice-cream parlour, where he had bought her a knickerbocker glory with extra toppings. Their favourite ice-cream parlour! It was all getting too much.

Now all they heard about were the dances, the walks by the river, the picnics, the new clothes, hats and shoes. Perhaps it was time they bought a little car, wrote their father, nothing too ostentatious, perhaps an Austin 7 or a little black Ford. It would mean that he and Daisy could come to visit them more easily. 'What next?' thought Sybil.

Within a year, William and Daisy were married, and the children had a stepmother. Sybil and Blanche, still so young, found it hard to come to terms with their father remarrying. Circumstances had dictated that Daisy had been unable to meet them, although the girls felt sure she would have wanted to, if only for Dada's sake. Even after the wedding, however, William was so busy at work and Daisy seemed so preoccupied with organising her social calendar that she never had time to become close to her stepchildren. Indeed, she made little or no effort to gain their affection. The change had little impact on the girls, at least on a practical level, as they continued to live in their grandfather's house. The letters continued almost as before, although they weren't greeted with the same level of enthusiasm.

Each year when the school term ended, the sisters would meet in the grotto in the school playground and wait until their great-aunt Nellie, who lived with their grandfather and cousin Irene, arrived in a one-horse gharry. They would greet her with big hugs and load their boxes, containing their clothes, bedding and toiletries, onto the gharry before getting in. Then they would go straight to the jetty, through the crowded streets and the rickshaws, past the heavily laden bullock carts plodding slowly along the roads, past the hawkers and the naked urchins begging and playing in the streets. They would board the Irrawaddy Flotilla ferry along with many other girls from their school heading across the river to their homes in Syriam. At the far side, the Le Fleurs travelled on to their grandfather's. The big house was becoming fuller and livelier, as Irene had married Samuel

Bertram Fisher, a young man who lived a few doors away and who had become a more and more frequent visitor, and given birth to their daughter, Camellia, known as 'Juju'. Irene's husband, who worked for the Burmah Oil Company, became Uncle Bertie to all of them.

Because they had spent so much time apart at school, the girls always had a lot of catching up to do during the holidays, and they would spend long hours together. Despite the sadness they had known, they were very happy children. They would climb on the railings of the veranda and pick the delicious star fruit that grew on a tree in the back garden. When the dhobi wallah (washer man) arrived to pick up the family's dirty laundry, Blanche and Sybil would jump into his cart; the landing was always soft, as each load consisted of between two and three hundred pieces of clothing. In the evenings, the girls would put their mats out in the yard and lie under the bright Burmese moon singing songs until they gradually drifted off to sleep.

From time to time, their grandfather would spoil them and arrange for the tailor to come round and measure them for nice new clothes, or they would be taken into Rangoon to buy new shoes. It was all so much fun, and they wanted for nothing. Even they knew they were pampered. If one of them had a sore throat, she would be taken to the Burmah Oil Company dispensary, where her throat would be swabbed with iodine. Once, when Blanche had an infection in her foot, one of the servants carried her on his shoulders to the dispensary.

During the holidays, Blanche and Sybil shared a room, and when Sybil caught measles, it wasn't long before she passed it on to Blanche; when Blanche had mumps, it wasn't long before Sybil was sick as well. These illnesses were tiresome, but the sisters would play games and read to amuse themselves. One of the more energetic games involved jumping from one bed to the other under the mosquito nets. When Sybil was ten, it was discovered early one morning at school that she had chicken pox. She was immediately sent home to Syriam to avoid the spread of the illness in the school. Her father and new stepmother came to take her to the Infectious Diseases Hospital in Rangoon, but when they arrived there, Sybil flatly refused to stay in the hospital during the day, although she agreed to come back in the evening. She was a strong-willed girl, and they had no alternative but to take her home for the day and bring her back to hospital at night, when she was quite happy to remain on the isolation ward. On this occasion, however, a stern matron prevented any leaping from bed to bed.

The beginning of the new decade was marked by increasing unrest. Whoever said 'When America sneezes, the rest of the world catches a cold' could have been talking about 1930 in Burma. The Wall Street Crash in October 1929 was the sneeze, and many thousands of miles away, some of the poorest people in Burma caught a cold. In 1930, the rice market collapsed, and already impoverished farmers were left penniless. Many farmers took their own lives as they faced financial ruin and saw no other way out. Saya San, a monk and pretender to the Burmese throne, initiated an organised and violent revolt against taxes imposed by the British. The revolt quickly gained momentum, growing into an anti-colonial rebellion, but was finally put down by British and Karen troops. Despite its failure, the uprising had shown the strength of nationalist feeling throughout Burmese society; it was clear that anti-colonial ideas were no longer the preserve of the intellectuals. The revolt strengthened the power of the militant nationalist group Dobama Asiayone (We Burmans Association), formed earlier that year. There were riots throughout Burma, and the streets of Rangoon saw some demonstrations and unrest. Sybil and Blanche were in school when the riots happened, and for a short time the pupils of St Philomena's were not allowed outside the grounds of the convent because of the danger. Although Sybil didn't fully understand the situation at the time, she couldn't help but feel sorry for the farmers.

Throughout their teens, during the summer holidays the girls would make occasional trips by train to Prome, about 100 miles north of Rangoon, to visit Auntie Mary (their father's sister), Uncle Eric and their two children, Archie, who was Austin's age, and Dolly, who was the same age as Sybil. Because they spent so much time outdoors in the heat of the day, they were made to wear solar topees, more commonly known as pith helmets, to protect them from the strong sun. They made a nice change from the rather flouncy hats the Le Fleur girls were sometimes dressed in.

Eric was a chemist and owned his own shop, above which the family lived in a large, airy flat. His surname was Cameron, and his grandfather had made the long journey from Scotland to join the IFC as a ship's captain. Like many of his compatriots, he had married a Burmese woman and established himself in Rangoon, where Eric's father and eventually Eric had been born.

When the shop was open, the children had to use the back door to reach the house, but when it was closed, they were allowed to enter through the front door, past the tall jars full of herbs, past the wooden boxes and drawers containing remedies ancient and modern, past the glass bottles full of liquids of all colours and past the brass scales and weights that their uncle used to measure out the medicaments. The walls were lined with glass cabinets filled with toiletries and medicines with weird and wonderful names. Sybil loved the shop. It was a place where she could stand and wonder at the sight of the elegant glass and porcelain jars, standing almost as tall as she was. They were covered in intricate gold designs and Latin writing. She loved the smells of the soaps and perfumes, the Cuticura talcum powder and bath salts. Customers would often bring baskets of custard apples for Uncle Eric, and, although the fruit was unattractive in appearance, Sybil and Blanche loved the sweet, juicy, creamy flesh inside.

Every Thursday, groups of beggars would come to the back of the shop, and Mary and Eric would offer them as much food as they could afford to give away. When the children stayed with them, it became their job to take the food down and make sure it was all apportioned fairly. This was a task they took very seriously: Auntie and Uncle had given them responsibility for a deed that meant a great deal to people much worse off than themselves. Each of these occasions made them appreciate even more just how lucky they were, although they too had experienced tragedy in their short lives.

Sybil and Blanche enjoyed their trips to Prome, but it was always nice to return home to Syriam, where long-established traditions and habits proved comforting. Auntie Nellie had one such habit: she would often sit on her bed smoking a bidi, a Burmese cheroot, and playing pachisi, a game similar to ludo. The board was an embroidered padded cloth, and the playing area was a symmetrical cross in the centre of the board, with its four arms each divided into three columns of eight squares. A game usually involved up to four players, but nevertheless it provided endless enjoyment for Nellie as she threw her six cowrie shells and moved her larger shell accordingly. When her game was finished, she would fold up the board with the shells inside and go to sleep. Blanche and Sybil would watch this ritual with some fascination, but Sybil didn't care for the cigar smoke and would sit with a perfumed handkerchief over her nose.

The changing seasons themselves brought with them habits and rituals. In late May, the monsoons came. Preparations were made as the temperatures steadily increased to a point where they were almost unbearable, inside or out. The clouds rolled in from the ocean and the light faded as the gathering storms approached the land. The coming of the rains was a considerable relief, and the people of Rangoon would happily stroll about in a downpour as the temperatures dropped to more reasonable levels.

Even the school terms were organised around the weather. The main holiday began on 19 March, just as the heat started to become unbearable, and lasted until May, when the monsoons broke. Term always started on the same day, 23 May (unless, of course, that day happened to be a Saturday or a Sunday). This Blanche found particularly galling, as 23 May was her birthday, and almost every year it turned out to be the day when she had to go back to school. It was fine to be able to celebrate with school friends whom she hadn't seen since March, but it wasn't the same as having a proper birthday party at home with all the delights that brought.

Because the girls were in school during the monsoons, the dramatic change in weather had no great effect on them, although the classrooms of St Philomena's were a more temperate place to be, and it was fun playing outside in the rain. The heavy winds blew mangoes down from the tall trees, and Sybil and her friends would pick them up and eat them. In October, the dry weather returned again, and although the monsoon season was initially welcomed for the water it brought to the land and the cooling effect it had on the city, after nearly five months it was time for a change.

Every November the Fifth, the large British contingent and the considerable number of families of British descent would celebrate Bonfire Night. In the convent, the girls were told about the gunpowder plot. The nuns would teach their pupils the history of the conspiracy to blow up Parliament and make them learn the well-known poem:

Remember, Remember the fifth of
  November,
Gunpowder, treason and plot.
I know of no reason

Why gunpowder treason
Should ever be forgot.

The event would be celebrated with the lighting
of large bonfires topped by effigies of Guy
Fawkes, and once the fires were well under way,
spectacular displays of fireworks would take
place around Rangoon and Syriam. On 9
November, a further round of fireworks would
be set off to celebrate Diwali, the festival of
light, and children would be given sweets and
cakes. Sybil, Blanche and the family would
have their own fireworks party, complete with
sparklers.

Christmas was a time of great celebration,
with the whole family involved in decorating
the house with balloons and long, home-made
paper chains constructed from loops of brightly
coloured paper. The family always attended
midnight Mass, and before they left for church,
the main presents were given out. The girls
usually received new shoes and socks, a dress, a
coat and a hat. On returning from church, they
would eat steaming hot chicken pilau, finishing
the meal with a dessert of *dodol*, a palm sugar
and rice pudding, and *kalkal*, which was similar
to shortbread. They would then be given other
presents, which were generally more frivolous
than the main gifts—toys, games or books.

On New Year's Eve, the family would attend
their grandfather's works party, organised by
the Burmah Oil Company. They would have a

65

nice meal, followed by music and dancing until midnight. At midnight, the sound of jumping jacks (a type of firework) heralded the New Year, and everyone sang 'Auld Lang Syne'.

The girls were allowed to go with the rest of the family to dances and get-togethers, and sometimes to fancy-dress parties. They often spent their pocket money on perfume, and make-up, but if no real make-up was to hand, Sybil and Blanche used burnt matches to darken their eyebrows. Red crêpe paper was crumpled and dampened to produce enough colouring to add a flush to cheeks and tint lips. With no Pond's Cream available, they would use petroleum jelly to keep their faces smooth; it seemed to work. Their grandfather would look at them in exasperation and tell them not to put on any 'war paint', as they were beautiful enough without it.

At one of the fancy-dress parties, Blanche thought she would draw attention to the constant cessation of labour as workers downed tools in order to get better pay and conditions. She designed and made a dress with the slogan 'No More Strikes' and sewed on hundreds of matches. Sadly, it didn't fire the imaginations of the judges, and she didn't even get a consolation prize. On another occasion, she dressed up as the ace of spades and did win a prize, a box of chocolates. She had really wanted to go as Eve from the Garden of Eden, until Irene called her a stupid woman, pointed out that all Eve had had on were a few fig leaves and asked if she really wanted to go to the dance in such a skimpy outfit. Blanche was horrified and settled on the ace of spades as being safer and more discreet.

The sisters still heard from William every month, although the letters grew shorter and less happy. He was very busy at the IFC and had arranged to work extra hours to pay for all the things that he and Daisy seemed to like to do. When he wasn't working, he seemed to be caught up in a social whirl, and would go to parties, dances and out for dinner much more frequently than ever before. This was a side of their father that Sybil and Blanche hadn't seen before, and they didn't know what to make of it.

Sybil and Blanche never lived with their father and stepmother in Bassein, which was something of a backwater compared with Syriam and Rangoon. They visited only once, during the holidays in 1935, taking the train from Rangoon station on a sticky, hot and humid day. It was impossible to get comfortable in the second-class carriage. At least it wasn't third class, where the Burmans and Tamils sat. Those basic carriages, with their bench seats made of rough wooden laths, didn't appeal to the girls at all. The journey proved none too smooth, and it was a testing experience, even seated as they were on the lightly padded benches. They could imagine how uncomfortable it would be on the spine-jarring wooden perches to the rear of the train. By the time they reached Bassein, the sisters felt tired and dirty.

Their father picked them up at the station in his Austin 7, and they drove in silence to his home. The house that he had bought was fairly grand and set in a fine garden. William opened the door for his daughters, and the housekeeper welcomed them. Daisy was in a large room to the left of the hall, and she greeted Sybil and Blanche with enthusiasm, kissing them on both cheeks. Sybil didn't much care for her perfume. When the girls explored the house, they met the cook and the manservant, as well as the housekeeper who had received them at the door, but none of them looked as happy as their old friends back in the bungalow in Syriam. It just didn't feel as if they were part of the family.

Daisy had arranged for them to go to a number of functions while the girls were staying with them, but they didn't much enjoy them. Daisy was confident and comfortable in mixed company and talked in a loud voice. She enjoyed being the centre of attention. She would introduce Sybil to the men, and they would look at her as if she was a piece of prime beef. They would chat to her and ask her to accompany them on picnics or outings, but she always refused. The holiday in Bassein lasted a full week. Sybil and Blanche never went back. It was a relief to return to the convent.

The following year, William had a serious accident at work. He had been asked to assist one of his engineers with a particularly stubborn piece of faulty equipment in the engine room of one of the ships. They needed his expertise, and he gladly offered his help. During the difficult operation, much of which was done with hands and arms immersed under the filthy bilge water, William gashed his arm badly, and his blood stained the dirty water bright red. Still, they needed to change the pump, so he continued working until the new one was installed. When they'd finished, he realised the extent of his injury and went to the company nurse to have it cleaned and bandaged. As a result of the cut, William contracted septicaemia. In spite of treatment from the doctor, he made little progress, sometimes seeming to be slightly better and at other times worsening. Daisy ministered to him with great concern, changing his bandages and applying local herbal concoctions every day, trying everything the doctor suggested and some other remedies besides. Despite the love and attention she lavished on her husband, he lapsed into a coma, delirious with fever. Within a short period of time, he died. Sybil, Blanche and the rest of the family received no news of William's illness until after he had been buried in the cemetery in Bassein.

Daisy went to court to claim all William's assets and possessions, and the magistrate heard her case sympathetically. She succeeded in getting the courts to award everything to her, and the children were left without a penny. She even visited the offices of the Irrawaddy Flotilla Company, taking her brother's children with her and claiming they were the Le Fleur girls. As a result, she was given William's provident fund. Her husband's family were swiftly banished from Daisy's life, and it was to be many years before they saw or heard of her again. The monthly allowances ceased, but of course that was of less importance to the children than the death of their wonderful father and the thought that they would never receive another letter from him.

Irene and Bertie took it upon themselves to provide the children with what pocket money they could afford, and Sybil and Blanche would use this to go to the pictures at one of the cinemas along Dalhousie Street: the Odeon, the Globe, the Palladium or Sybil's favourite, the Pathé, run by the company responsible for the famous newsreels. Sybil and Blanche were able to go shopping and do all the things that young girls do almost as much as they had before the death of their father.

In 1937, Sybil was just over 17 and it was time for her to leave school. It had always been her ambition to go on to university, but two factors prevented her from this course of action. The first was the expense that further study would entail. Her grandfather could not afford it, and Irene and Bertie had little spare money, as they now had a family of their own. By this time, her two elder siblings were already independent. Austin had completed his studies to become a marine engineer and joined the Irrawaddy Flotilla Company, just as his father had done before him. Eunice had left school and married. She and her husband, Stanley, with whom she had a baby daughter, had gone to live with her uncle Mervyn Le Fleur. Sybil felt it was time she was earning a living.

The second reason was the volatile political situation at the time and the growth of the student nationalist movement. In 1936, U Nu, president of the Rangoon University Students' Union, and Aung San, secretary of the union, had been expelled as a result of a the publication in the union magazine of a controversial article. In response, the nationalist students of the university went on strike, setting up camp on the slopes of Shwedagon Pagoda. Each morning, the students would return to the entrances to the university and lie down in tight rows, a tactic that proved highly successful, as in Burmese culture it was considered so grave an insult to stand on the body of another that no one dared inflict it. The effectiveness of these pickets, along with increasingly favourable public opinion, eventually forced the authorities to give in. U Nu and Aung San joined Dobama Asiayone, becoming key members of the nationalist association, and by 1938 the movement had gained such popularity that there was widespread insurrection throughout Burma. Students remained central to the movement, and amid the violence and unrest, it was a dangerous time to attend university.

With both these factors in mind, Sybil accepted a job that she had already been offered. Opposite St Philomena's Convent was the Convent of St Vincent, a Burmese nunnery with a school attached. Because of her strong academic background, enthusiasm and ability, Sybil was asked by the sisters if she would join them next term to teach English to the Tamil primary school boys and girls. At the school, as she read reports of the escalating violence in which many students were killed or imprisoned, Sybil felt sure she had made the right choice about her future.

Although Blanche had made many friends at school in the 11 years that she had been there, she still felt an enormous sense of loss when her sister left to teach at St Vincent's. There would be no more well-timed meetings at the tuck shop, and she missed chatting with Sybil. They had grown very close over the years and had come to rely on each other's support. However, they still spent a good deal of time together during the holidays—shopping expeditions and trips to the cinema were undertaken together, and the two would often stroll down the wide streets in the centre of Rangoon sucking on pieces of sugar cane bought from a street vendor—and the reassuring routine of school and the friendships Blanche had formed with her classmates gave her comfort as she got used to the change. She threw herself into her studies, which helped take her mind off events over which she had no control. Although she couldn't know it, this was to be the first of many separations from her sister, and Blanche found the experience quite unsettling.

Although Sybil loved teaching and became very attached to her small pupils, she was restless. After a year, she went to learn to be a tailor and seamstress, working in central Rangoon in the heart of the action. She proved very adept at her new job, but still she had a desire to see more of the world, or at least of Burma.

CHAPTER FOUR

1939–41

RANGOON, MANDALAY AND MAYMYO

Sybil's next job, which she took at the age of 19, was as companion to the wife of a train driver. The Burmese railways were largely completed during the 1930s, and by 1941 they stretched from Ye, south of Moulmein, to Myitkyina in the far north, with the principal towns of Rangoon and Mandalay, and a host of others such as Bassein, Lashio, Prome, Maymyo and Shwebo, included on the expanding network. Engines from Glasgow, York and Hunslet in Leeds were shipped to this far-flung corner of the British Empire. With the locomotives came many engineers and drivers to provide training for the Burmese railway employees, and some chose to remain in this land that provided an environment and lifestyle they could not even have dreamed of in their homes in the dark industrial heartlands of Britain.

Charlie Park was one such person. He had seen the opportunities that Burma had to offer and had decided to remain. His skills as a driver were much sought after in a rapidly developing and dynamic country. Charlie was a tall, broad, handsome man with curly hair and a friendly, relaxed manner. He felt very much at home in the carefree surroundings he found himself in. It was quite a contrast to his native Midlands. In his second year in the colony, he met and married a pretty, petite Anglo-Burmese girl, Ruby, and they had three children, all girls. In those days, the position of train driver was one of considerable importance and status. Charlie had regular postings to Prome, Toungoo, Moulmein and Mandalay, and he felt it good for his wife and young children to have companionship as they travelled round, staying in each place for between a few months and a year. Sybil replied to an advertisement in the local Rangoon newspaper and met the family over coffee in the Sun Café at Scott Market. Sybil seemed an ideal companion—the girls sat quite contentedly on her knee as she and the Parks talked. She was hired on the spot, and it was agreed that she would get all her board and lodgings as well as a very decent allowance.

Their first posting was to Mandalay. Sybil was impressed by the city, founded by King Mindon in 1857 in fulfilment of the Buddha's prophecy that 2,400 years after his death a great centre of learning would rise there. She was astounded by the beauty of the Kuthodaw Pagoda, its dome covered in gold and rubies, and its walls a contrast in bright red. Behind the city's magnificent fort, once the palace of the

King of Burma, stood Mandalay Hill, where Buddhist monks had built many temples and monasteries, stretching in a line up the slope. Sybil was particularly taken with the beautiful statues of mammals, birds and reptiles to be found on the hill, representations of various incarnations of the Buddha. She found Mandalay a more relaxing city than Rangoon. It was quieter and less busy; it seemed to have retained the old values, traditions and loyalties of the real Burmese nation. The social unrest that was causing turmoil in the capital was much less evident in this part of the country.

From time to time, Sybil and Ruby took the children to the bazaar. By sunrise, the stallholders had set up their barrows and wooden shelves and were displaying their wares. The bazaar was as far removed from the large department stores in Rangoon as Sybil could imagine. Each stall had its own strong, distinctive aroma. The fishwives gutted the fresh catch with a speed that made Sybil wonder if occasionally the incredibly sharp knife might miss its target by a fraction and a small finger be found amongst the discarded entrails. Vegetables were piled high on carts buckling under the weight. Sacks of rice stood upright in rows, like miniature soldiers.

The cream of commercial society operated from narrow-fronted shops behind the stalls. The shoemaker, a small Indian with skin as dark, lined and tough as the leather he worked

76

with, sat hunched over a wooden last, cutting, shaping, bending, soaking, hammering and generally coaxing a reluctant piece of dried leather into the shape of a shoe. Once finished, he would then go through the same process again, trying as best he could in the circumstances to make a pair that almost matched. On the shelves around him hung the tools of his trade, of all shapes and sizes. Knives, needles, hammers and strips of leather hung alongside pairs of finished shoes for everyone from young children to fully grown men. Sybil had never seen anything like it. She had become accustomed from her childhood to being taken by her parents or grandparents to Rowe & Co. There, a neatly dressed salesgirl would measure each foot and bring through a selection of shoes to be tried on. They would come wrapped in tissue paper in smart boxes, and Sybil would put them on and walk round the shop feeling very grand before finally making her choice. Somehow, she couldn't help but feel that the shoemaker's shop in Mandalay left something to be desired.

Just along from the shoe shop was the butcher. Cuts of meat hung from metal hooks, and a small boy would flick a fly swat every now and then to discourage the ever-active insects from settling on their next meal. Live chickens peered out from their tiny coops and clucked with indignation. Their bright-red cockscombs flopped to and fro as they moved their heads inquisitively from side to side. Customers would observe them carefully before making their choice. With a sharp twist to the neck, the chosen bird would be dispatched to the great chicken coop in the sky and handed to the purchaser.

On the pavement a man sat, his face covered in soap lather, with a frayed towel around his neck, as another man shaved him with an ivory-handled cut-throat razor. His deft flicks of the wrist and smooth, flowing actions left the customer's face as smooth as a peach.

In the shop behind him, a man sat on a stool and beat out shapes in copper with a tiny hammer. The sound of his work echoed around the market, the sharp and rapid tapping sounding like a family of energetic woodpeckers. Bowls, cups, plates of all sizes, lamps and candleholders, some items more intricately carved than others, shone in the intensifying morning sunlight. The haberdashers did a roaring trade, with their many-coloured bolts of silk, intricately crafted lace and threads of every shade imaginable, and Sybil, Ruby and the children always stopped to purchase a few items, sometimes material to make clothes for the children, sometimes thread to darn a tear or sew on a patch. In a nearby workshop, an Indian craftsman with chubby fingers produced impossibly delicate pieces of jewellery from gold, silver, rubies and jade.

Sybil loved all these things, but she loved food even more. The sights, sounds and the strong smells of livestock, fish, herbs and spices assaulted the senses and gave rise to intense pangs of hunger. At one stall, a small Indian woman was preparing hot food for the hungry shoppers. Noodle soup with mushrooms and pieces of meat, *schwe payon hinjo* (a soup made with pumpkin, garlic and fresh herbs) and fish, chicken and lamb curries all sat next to a black pan of frying vegetables and a large pot of boiled rice. Freshly made chapattis awaited delivery to the next customer. The smell of the food filled the air and made Sybil's mouth water, drawing her and many others towards the stall. A small boy ran backwards and forwards between the cooking area and tables carrying bowls and plates of steaming hot food as the diners chatted together.

After eating, Sybil usually moved on to her other favourite stall. On it were piles of old books and newspapers in English and Indian, all discarded by the soldiers of the garrison and recycled by an enterprising businessman. Sybil had an insatiable appetite for the printed word, and she had discovered that some classics were to be found if you looked carefully.

The only stall that ever seemed to have any space around it, and one that was located with good reason at the outermost point of the bazaar, by order of the local authority, was the stall belonging to the poor man whose misfortune it was to be selling, amongst his other wares, the durian fruit.

Among all the noise and mayhem, the crowds jostling for position and waving their arms about furiously to attract the stallholders' attention, were small children, beggars hoping to be rewarded with a token offering and scavengers clearing up the rotten fruit and vegetables and the fish entrails. Dogs of all types and sizes ran playfully about, barking loudly, pausing only to gobble down any morsel of food that came their way. It was quite different from anything Sybil had experienced before, and in its own way it was truly magical.

Mandalay was a city of extreme weather. The summers were very hot, with temperatures often in excess of 45°C, while in the cold season the temperature would drop to below 10°C at night. In Rangoon, Sybil had never had to wear a coat, even during the monsoon season, and had never had to resort to quilted bedding, as they did in Mandalay.

Once, the family made a journey to Loikaw, and there Sybil was amazed to see the long-necked Padaung women. They had a custom of elongating their necks from a young age through the wearing of brass coils. The older the woman, the longer her neck and the higher her social status. They were very beautiful, all brightly dressed, but Sybil found their unnaturally long necks, encased in metal, very disconcerting.

During her time away, Sybil made the occasional trip back to Rangoon to see Blanche.

During the Diwali festival in November 1939, when Blanche was 17 years of age, she met and fell in love with a tall, dashingly handsome and witty man some years her senior. Manu Desai was working as a radio announcer for Radio Burma, as he had done for a few years, but, having graduated in electrical engineering, he also owned his own radio-repair business in the centre of Rangoon. They soon came to realise the strength of their feelings towards each other and wasted no time in making plans for the future. To the surprise of many of their friends and family, Blanche left school during the December holidays, and in January 1940 the couple wed. Blanche moved out of Irene and Bertie's home in Syriam and started a new life with her husband at 53rd Street, Rangoon.

When Sybil visited in April 1940, Blanche had discovered she was carrying her first child and she broke the news to her sister. They went to the Odeon Cinema on Dalhousie Street to see *The Wizard of Oz* to celebrate. The film made such an impression on them that Sybil went out the next day and bought enough material to make Blanche a dress exactly like the one worn by Dorothy. The pregnancy progressed without any problems, but Blanche took extra care during the monsoon. The unhygienic conditions caused by the heavy rainfall could cause such illnesses as cholera and dysentery. To avoid any risk, she limited her excursions to essential trips only and was particularly fussy about the preparation of food and the boiling of all water.

On 30 October, Blanche and Manu were rewarded by the birth of their son Leslie, a healthy, strong baby. When she and Leslie returned home from the hospital, they received many visitors as friends and family came to admire the beautiful baby and bring gifts. No visitor was more welcome than Sybil, who brought clothes she had made for both mother and baby. Life settled into a routine once again as Blanche looked after Manu and Leslie in the quiet suburb, watching in amazement as her baby son grew.

Meanwhile, after several months in Mandalay, the Parks moved for a year to Maymyo, a beautiful colonial hill town. Wealthy people from Rangoon and Mandalay often had a second house in Maymyo or in Lashio, to the north-east, where they would spend the summer, as the weather was so much more temperate and the surroundings quite spectacular. Maymyo could have passed for an English town, and Charlie Park told them that it would not have looked out of place on the Sussex Downs.

On the approach to Maymyo, Sybil was amazed to find that the train had to zigzag forwards and backwards up the track as it climbed ever higher up the steep gradient. When they reached the small station at the top of the hill, Sybil could see that the journey had been worth every minute, as the view was quite breathtaking. Tree-covered hills stretched as far as the eye could see. Near to the town were fields upon fields of strawberries and flowers, and the air was fresh and clear.

The town had well-looked-after lawns, lakes and flower gardens, and a well-stocked botanical garden. The air was heavy with the scent of magnolia, hibiscus and lilies, chrysanthemums, asters and gladioli. Trees hung heavy with large, juicy cherries and dark-red, almost black plums. Sybil had never tasted any fruit so sweet. It was an idyllic setting, and she thoroughly enjoyed her time there with the Park family and their daughters. It seemed a perfect place for young children to grow up in.

Maymyo was a garrison station, which meant that on occasion its peace and tranquillity were shattered by the most unlikely sounds and sights. On high days and holidays, such as the King's birthday or Empire Day, in a hot and humid land far from home but not far removed from military tradition, the troops would march forth from their barracks, rifles at the ready, bayonets glinting in the sun as they made their way, winding like a giant centipede, along the tree-lined roads to the parade ground. There they would march to the stirring sounds of the regimental brass band of the King's Own Yorkshire Light Infantry. As they paraded up and down in long columns of three ranks, in their immaculately starched scarlet-and-blue uniforms with polished buttons and buckles, they made a formidable sight. They were tall, much taller than Burmans or Indians, and they came in a variety of colours, from the pale white of the newly arrived to the leathery brown of the regular career soldiers. Their boots shone in the sun, looking particularly heavy against the thinness of their legs, wrapped tightly as they were with puttees. Each step they took raised clouds of dust as they pounded the earth in time with the commands. On their heads were plain forage caps, bush hats or, most impressive of all, pith helmets topped with large green pompoms. With all the pomp and ceremony, Sybil thought they were the most impressive soldiers she had ever seen, although, watching them marching in the full heat of the day, she was inclined to think of the words to the popular Noel Coward song 'Mad Dogs and Englishmen'.

There was no shortage of entertainment in Maymyo for the British officers, civil servants, company managers and land agents. The private polo, tennis and cricket clubs provided a home from home, a haven where the expatriates congregated on a regular and frequent basis to sit and talk and sip their pink gins, beers and cocktails, produced by the Tamil and Indian bar staff. The social scene was enhanced by parties and dances held by the civic, commercial and military leaders of the community. Around Maymyo, a series of horse trails and well-signposted walks were at the disposal of the more energetic, and the botanical gardens were spectacularly beautiful.

Sybil felt that her good fortune could not last forever, and indeed it proved so. During their stay in Maymyo, Sybil learned that her grandfather was very ill and had asked for her. She and the Park family made their way to Syriam, where they found that the situation was even more serious than they had thought. Grandfather was dying. Having decided that he wanted to see Sybil, he displayed his customary stubbornness to the end, refusing to die until his prodigal granddaughter had returned. Sybil stayed with him, holding his hand and telling him of her adventures and her idyllic life in Maymyo. That night, his hand clasped in hers, he finally passed away. It was with a heavy heart that Sybil returned with the Park family to their temperate haven from the busy streets of industrial Syriam.

In October 1941, just after the end of the monsoon, Sybil returned to Rangoon with the Park family and decided to pursue her previous career as a seamstress. She quickly found work—her skills were evident in the clothes she wore, all made by her own deft fingers. She created clothes for the affluent ladies of Rangoon and took in alterations for many of the large shops and department stores. It was only natural that Blanche should offer her sister accommodation until she could get herself settled and it was only natural that Sybil should be delighted to accept. The small amount of rent that Sybil paid made life easier for the young family. Spending time and eating meals together once more, Sybil and Blanche realised just how much they had missed each other in the time they had been apart. The house was filled with laughter as the girls remembered the old days and discussed their hopes and plans for the future. Christmas approached and they looked forward to spending it together.

CHAPTER FIVE

December 1941–March 1942

SYBIL

RANGOON

And then came the raid on Rangoon. It began a brutal campaign, one that saw the longest retreat in the history of the British Army. Burma was a large country with an abundance of resources (including rice, oil, timber, rubber, tungsten, lead, tin, silver, jade and precious stones) and a relatively small population. In contrast, Japan's natural resources were nearly exhausted after years of conflict with China, and its population was increasing dramatically. Japan saw Burma's resources as vital to its war effort and to its plans for westward expansion, the creation of what was called the Greater East Asia Co-Prosperity Sphere. The occupation of Burma would also protect the vast Japanese conquests in Siam, French Indo-China and Malaya, as well as providing air bases and military establishments. Furthermore, Burma's proximity to India made it an ideal launch platform for an invasion of that country.

There was another factor, some say the major

reason for the invasion of Burma. By mid-1941, the Japanese controlled all the supply routes to China except for one: the Burma Road. Material was conveyed by rail from Rangoon to Mandalay and on along the verdant, tree-lined valley to Lashio, where a sinuous, treacherous track began, stretching 750 miles east to Kunming in China. The road had been scratched out of the soil by hand and at some human cost. At many points, it was only wide enough for a single vehicle to pass. Since the beginning of the lend-lease agreement between China and America in April 1941, over 15,000 tons of war material and supplies per month had been flowing from Rangoon up the Burma Road and into China at the border town of Wanting. Without this constant supply of materials, China would be easy prey for the Japanese army and air force. From Japan's point of view, it was vital that this flow be stemmed.

For all these reasons, on 23 December 1941, during a 20-minute bombing raid, much of Rangoon was destroyed. The wooden buildings set alight by incendiary devices burned with intense ferocity. The stone buildings seemed no more immune to damage: whole walls collapsed onto the streets below, killing many while they tried to flee to safety. Still-standing structures were precariously balanced as fires raged inside the shells of buildings.

Amid this devastation, Sybil was stranded. With Bertha's decision to return to the hospital where she worked as a nurse, her small group consisted of eight people: Sybil, Mr Younis, Mrs Younis, her other three daughters from her first marriage, Ursula, Oral and Denise De Alvis, the Younises' young son and his ayah. Mr Younis was a tall, slim, well-dressed man with a very gentle and generous nature. For the office, he wore a smart dark suit and a white shirt with a brightly coloured silk cravat. His shoes, which were always polished to a high shine, were covered in dust and flecks of red brick. He was well liked in the community and was known for his kindness to those less fortunate than himself. If he could help someone in genuine need then he would do it with relish. Mrs Younis was also tall but of a more robust build; dressed in her silk sari and blouse, she made a formidable sight. The girls were dark-skinned with jet-black hair and big brown eyes, and they still had what was referred to as puppy fat. They were dressed for a day in the sun. The baby boy was plump and always laughing. He was a happy child, and Sybil enjoyed looking after him.

Having decided to get away from the city, the family made their way out of Rangoon with heavy hearts. Sybil's stomach churned with fear about what lay ahead. They encountered few people on the road. The only movement was of military vehicles in small groups and convoys. By late afternoon, they realised why the road was so empty. In the confusion, amid the destruction, they had made their way in the general direction of north, but unfortunately the road they had taken was heading north-west to Mingaladon airfield, the target of the attack by the 10th Hikodan.

Mrs Younis had a nephew, Norman, who worked at the airfield as quartermaster of the stores depot, and they were hopeful that some good might come of their mistake. The family arrived at the base, but the place was in chaos, and they were unable to find Norman. They found themselves knocking on the door of a large, imposing house a short distance from the airfield. The family who lived there took them in and gave them food and water, and there they stayed for the next two nights. Sheltering in the large house through the night of the 23rd, Sybil and her friends expected and feared further raids, but none came. Listening intently to the wireless, they were horrified to hear over Radio Bangkok that the Japanese were promising a 'Christmas present' for the people of Burma. When the air-raid sirens sounded, everyone in the house rushed into the garden and huddled under the tall, dense bamboo. On each occasion, however, it proved to be a false alarm.

The next day, Mr and Mrs Younis made their way back to the airfield and eventually managed to contact Norman, who was relieved to see them, as the news from Rangoon was dire and he had feared for their lives. They explained their plight, putting their trust in Norman's hands, as he knew the military situation. A plan was decided on. Tomorrow, on Christmas Day, Norman would take them in a military truck back to Rangoon, to the university campus, which had been commandeered as a supply depot; there, he hoped, they would be safe and secure.

That night, Sybil and the family kept their spirits up by singing carols, each lost in their own private thoughts of the joy of Christmases past, the anxiety of Christmas present and the uncertainty of Christmases yet to come. When the children were finally asleep, the adults sat quietly. Sybil looked down at her dusty, mud-streaked dress (of all her dresses, this was her favourite one, and now look at it), at her sensible shoes and her scratched legs, and she felt lost. Sybil prayed. She prayed to her mother and father for strength; she prayed for her family—her brother and sisters, her cousin Irene and Uncle Bertie. She looked at the brown parcel containing the blocks of Cadbury's chocolate, the Polson's coffee and Lyons tea that Blanche had asked her to bring home only a few hours before. She prayed for her dearest sister's safety and hoped that they would soon be reunited. It was early on Christmas morning before she slept, emotionally and physically exhausted.

*　　*　　*

On 23 December, Lieutenant General Michio Sugawara flew to Bangkok from Phnom Penh to welcome back his returning bombers and fighters. Although the raids had been a success, the news was not all good. Losses had been far heavier than anticipated. Of the 10th Hikodan, five out of fifteen of the heavy bombers had been shot down. Of the 7th Hikodan involved in the main attack on Rangoon City, two heavy bombers were shot down and a third crash-landed due to battle damage.

Sugawara was furious and wanted to attack Rangoon and Mingaladon on 24 December. However, he was unable to gather sufficient resources in time, so the decision was taken to delay the raid until the 25th. Messages to this effect were broadcast to the Burmese people by Radio Bangkok throughout the 24th in an attempt to create widespread fear and panic. Bomber and fighter formations of the IJAAF made their way to Bangkok to join in the raid and increase the strength of the much-depleted 10th Hikodan.

At 9.30 a.m. on Christmas Day, the 7th Hikodan left Bangkok. On reaching Rangoon, the planes began their bombing run, destroying the electric power plant and some of the surrounding buildings both commercial and private. The second force turned north to bomb Mingaladon airfield. Despite heavy resistance from twenty Buffalo and Tomahawk fighters of 67 Squadron RAF and the AVG, the bombers destroyed five Allied fighter planes and three other aircraft and caused damage to runways and buildings.

Four Japanese heavy bombers had been lost and a fifth so badly shot up that it was unserviceable; four fighters were also shot down. This was a considerable blow to the IJAAF, who had underestimated the anti-aircraft defences around Rangoon and the skill and bravery of the Allied fighters. As a result of these heavy losses, all daytime raids on Rangoon and the surrounding areas were stopped, and for the next few weeks, a strategy of night-time bombing was put in place.

In Rangoon, the arrival of the bombers over their target had produced the same response as on the 23rd. Although the Japanese had promised attacks on Christmas Day, the streets were soon lined with onlookers more curious than afraid. It was almost as if the raid on the 23rd had made the population even keener to witness at first hand the bombing, and no one wanted to miss the sight of the aerial dogfights played out many thousands of feet above. In the minutes that followed, almost 3,000 people were killed and a similar number injured.

This time, the effect on those who survived was immediate and widespread: every man, woman and child who could leave the city prepared to do so as there came the dawning realisation that things had changed forever. Fearful of the possibility of death within the city as tall buildings came crashing down, trapping those beneath, and wooden houses caught fire rapidly, incinerating those inside, many moved north of the city and chose to live in the open. Many thousands more, not able fully to comprehend what had taken place, loaded what few possessions they had onto hand carts or simply wrapped what they thought would be useful in sheets and tied these bundles to their backs. Those who had cows and water buffalo loaded them up. The refugees walked north to the hills, not knowing what was to be their fate. A lucky few managed to board trains heading out of the city, and a small number made their way out in trucks, or on any vehicle that could move under its own steam. Boats of all shapes and sizes with decks and superstructures covered with people left the port of Rangoon throughout the day and for some weeks and months afterwards. From the air, the pilots of 67 Squadron looked down on what looked like an endless column of ants marching determinedly, purposefully and relentlessly—but these were people striving for survival.

By the end of December 1941, over 100,000 inhabitants of Rangoon had left the city, and as Burma was overrun by the Japanese, it seemed that more than half the population was heading north. This disorganised and panic-stricken mass of humanity had more even than the might of the Japanese army and air force to contend with. Over the coming months, thousands succumbed to cholera, dysentery, malaria, fatigue and hunger. Through harsh climates, hot and humid jungles, steaming paddy-fields and freezing nights, they struggled onwards, their only hope being to reach the comparative safety of India. Only the strongest, the most determined and single-minded, achieved that goal, arriving in India as unrecognisable skeletons of their former selves, ridden with disease and crawling with insect infestations. These were the lucky ones. Many had had to leave friends, family and loved ones dead or dying by the roadside.

*   *   *

At Mingaladon on the morning of 25 December, Sybil and her friends were preparing to be picked up by Mrs Younis's nephew Norman. They gathered together the few possessions they had brought and the small amount of food and water that their hosts could spare, and they waited patiently. They were still in the clothes they had been wearing when they left the destruction at Fraser Street. It was early afternoon before the truck arrived, and they said a sad farewell to the people who had looked after them so well for the past two days. What would become of them all? Only time would tell.

Heading south-east towards Rangoon, they had travelled only a short distance when the

95

driver spotted the first group of Japanese bombers approaching from Rangoon. He stopped the truck and everyone squeezed under it for protection. From above came the roar of aircraft engines and then a distant rumble like thunder as bombs fell on Mingaladon. The ground shook, and Sybil and the family were gripped with fear. Just as quickly as it had started, the noise stopped and the sound of the planes gradually faded away. Emerging from beneath the truck, they looked up at the dogfights taking place to the east of the airfield and counted their blessings.

They set off again and managed to cover a few more miles before the driver brought the truck to a halt. A second group of bombers, an even larger formation, was heading towards them. Better aware of the danger this time, the group dived into the dense cover at the side of the road, sheltering under bamboo and bushes. Again they heard the drone of the bombers, the high-pitched sound of the fighters and the rumble in the distance as the second wave of bombs hit the airfield. It seemed like an eternity before all fell silent. The truck still stood where they had abandoned it. The journey to the university was completed without further interruption.

The compound was located on the shore of Victoria Lake at the corner of Prome Road and University Avenue Road. The grounds were carefully maintained, with immaculately manicured lawns and well-stocked flower beds tended to by an army of local gardeners. Tall trees cast their shade on the rich green grass. To Sybil and her friends, it was an oasis amidst a desert of destruction. The main building was a large colonial-style administrative centre, built in red brick with arched windows and balconies on every floor. A series of satellite buildings and lecture theatres lay scattered around the grounds, with paths leading to each one. Off to one side stood a semicircle of small bungalows built to house the professors and other senior academics in some degree of style and comfort. Within the campus was the Judson Baptist Church and Judson College, which was a separate institution founded by missionaries and housed in an imposing building. This had been converted into an army field hospital prepared to deal with the expected military casualties. A row of ambulances carrying Red Cross markings on the roofs and sides were parked outside. The main buildings on the campus had been commandeered by the armed forces and housed a mixture of combat troops and supplies. The perimeter was well guarded and defended.

On arrival, Sybil's group was taken to the central administration block, where they spent the first night. The building had never been designed to provide accommodation and was short of basic facilities, but the family were to be moved to a more suitable location. On the following day, they were taken to one of the bungalows. It was a well-kept home, complete with a modern kitchen, a sitting area and three bedrooms, and it was a welcome sight to the frightened and tired travellers. Norman had managed to obtain sufficient food for the next few days and showed them the location of the recently finished air-raid shelters before he departed. They were all extremely grateful to him and wished him well, as they knew the fighting and bombing were becoming more intense.

The night of 25 December 1941 was a quiet one. Christmas Day was over and neither Sybil nor her friends knew what had happened to their loved ones. There had been no peace and goodwill to all men, no singing of carols and no opening of presents, no Christmas lunch, no games and no familiar traditions. Sybil tried not to wonder what the new year would bring, whether she would spend next Christmas with her family, but she was very afraid.

The morning of 26 December dawned bright and warm. No one was to leave the compound, so the day was spent exploring the grounds, relaxing on the grass and watching the clear blue sky. Later that day, Norman returned with a radio, which the family would listen to as often as they could. He also brought some old newspapers and magazines, which everyone read from cover to cover.

On 28 December, the air-raid sirens sounded and fear took hold of them all once again. They dashed across the compound to the shelters and took refuge. These shelters were particularly well equipped, with carpets and mats on the ground for sleeping on. Norman had told them that the majority of people in Rangoon had to make do with trenches dug in the ground covered by makeshift roofs constructed from bamboo poles, the ubiquitous Burmese building material, on top of which were laid corrugated iron or tin sheets. On top of those sheets were piles of earth designed to slow the progress of any pieces of shrapnel. These shelters were basic, often damp and of no use whatsoever against a near miss or direct hit. The shelters in the university compound were unashamed luxury in comparison.

When the all-clear sounded, they simply picked up what belongings they had taken with them and walked calmly back to their bungalow. The next day, the Japanese threw another group of bombers and fighters against Rangoon, and the sky above seemed full of aircraft. This time, they watched from the doorway of the shelter as enemy planes swooped and swirled about the sky, chased by Allied fighters. They saw a handful of bombers trailing plumes of smoke and diving out of control as streams of bullets from the fighters repeatedly hit them, and they heard the explosions when these planes finally hit the ground.

On New Year's Eve, the bombers were back,

but, on this occasion, Sybil decided she would no longer cower underground waiting for the all-clear to sound. She would remain in her room and listen to Radio Java, which had all the latest news and music, reading her books and magazines. Rangoon and Mingaladon were bombed virtually every night between 3 and 8 January; however, Sybil remained in her bed calmly listening to Radio Java, earning herself the nickname 'Radio Missie' from the Younises' ayah. She had always had a defiant and stubborn streak.

From the 8th, sporadic strikes by small numbers of bombers took place around Rangoon, and the family remained on constant alert. From time to time, Norman would appear unannounced, carrying supplies, ensuring the family were reasonably well catered for. So far, the many raids had failed to damage their area of the compound, although some of the administrative and storage buildings had been reduced to rubble.

Around 20 January, Norman arrived with more supplies and the news that the Japanese had pushed north and east into Burma and that Tavoy had been taken. His superiors had told him that this was a temporary setback and the Allies were preparing a counter-attack to drive the enemy back over the border. About a week later, he returned with more news: the Japanese had taken Mergui airfield, and the town had been evacuated. The fall of Tavoy and the loss of Mergui gave the Japanese command of an important port, as well as land, sea and air control of the entire southern coast, from Malaya to Moulmein. But all was still not lost, Norman assured them—as he himself had been assured by his superior officers.

From 1 to 4 February, the family were constantly moving between the bungalow and the shelter as the Japanese flew 17 separate missions against Rangoon and its airport. The sirens sounded almost constantly, and wave after wave of bombers and fighters flew overhead. This was one of the most frightening periods of their stay in the compound. The constant threat meant there was no time to relax or prepare oneself mentally for what was to come. But still Sybil continued to listen to Radio Java, escaping through the music they played.

In early February came the news that Moulmein had been taken by the advancing Japanese army despite a heroic defence by the local garrison and remnants of the 17th Indian Division. Life went on in the compound. Sybil had begun to help out at the field hospital, caring for wounded who now arrived in a constant stream. By the end of the month, there was frantic activity on the campus as supplies were moved out and combat soldiers arrived and departed. It appeared from the chalk-white complexions of these young soldiers that they had just arrived in Asia. They spoke English but with strong dialects and using phrases that Sybil had never heard before. They were full of hope and the confidence of youth. They arrived and almost immediately were mobilised to the defence of Burma, and particularly Rangoon. Sybil prayed they would be successful.

On 24 and 25 February, the Japanese renewed their air assaults against Rangoon, and such was the ferocity of those raids and the strafing of the streets by fighters that Sybil stayed close to the bungalow or sheltered under the canopies of the nearby trees. It had been some time since Norman's last visit, and when he came to see them at the end of February, he was less convinced that the British could hold on to their positions. His news was bad. The 17th Indian Division had gradually been pushed back to the wide Sittang River. The 500-yard-long bridge across the river had now assumed vital strategic importance and the troops defending the bridge were coming under increasing pressure. The commanding officer had to make a difficult decision, and in the early hours of 23 February, he had the bridge blown. Over half the division was trapped on the Japanese-held side of the river. Many men died at the hands of the Japanese or in attempting to swim across the swollen river, and much of the division's equipment was lost to the enemy.

Mr Younis knew that the Sittang River should have been a strong defensive position, and he had a terrible feeling of foreboding as they settled down that evening to listen to Radio Java. Norman also told his family of the looting and destruction that had devastated Rangoon. He said that the prisons and asylums had been opened, releasing criminals and lunatics onto the streets, where they had gone on a rampage of drinking and desecration. He warned them to stay well inside the compound where they would be safe. Still more troops arrived at the university compound and this lifted the spirits, but by day and night, Sybil could hear the sound of explosions and gunfire getting nearer. She made herself busy helping out around the university, as an extra pair of hands was often required for clerical as well as basic nursing duties.

On 1 March, Sybil heard on her small radio that the Japanese had invaded Java, but broadcasts continued as normal. Early that month, the remnants of the British defensive forces, reinforced by the 7th Armoured Brigade and the 1st Battalion The Cameronians, had taken up positions around Pegu. Gallant though the actions of these troops undoubtedly were, and although there were some local successes, it became obvious that sheer weight of numbers on the Japanese side would overcome whatever resistance there was. What was more, the Japanese soldiers were perfectly at home in the jungle. They were able to encircle the defending troops and trap them in a pincer movement, necessitating a retreat and subsequent battle just to regroup. Inevitably, large numbers of soldiers and significant amounts of equipment were lost.

By 6 March, the Japanese had taken control of all roads and railway stations to the north of Rangoon and had ambushed several parties of Allied troops. The Japanese were well entrenched and prepared for a long fight, but they were short of food and supplies, including ammunition, and, on hearing to their surprise that units of the British garrison were withdrawing from the city, Colonel Takanobu Sakuma ordered his men to break off contact after dark and make their way to Rangoon to capture the port, which was vital for the resupply of his troops. This, as fate would have it, left the roads and railway lines to the north open for the Allied troops to retreat and for refugees from southern Burma to flee.

On the morning of 7 March, Norman arrived at the bungalow in something of a panic. This in itself was alarming, as he was normally a very calm person. He informed Sybil and the family that the Japanese were advancing on Rangoon. It was only a matter of time before the army arrived, and they had to go immediately to the railway station. They hastily gathered up their possessions and what food and water they had before getting into Norman's army truck to head for the station. They drove through deserted streets and scenes of devastation. Buildings were destroyed, reduced to rubble, the trees that had lined the roads were splintered like matchsticks and over the city hung a dark cloud of acrid smoke. Norman told them that the British planned to blow up the power station and the oil terminal that afternoon, so they wouldn't fall into the enemy's hands, and that the smoke was coming from the systematic destruction of the port, where buildings and equipment were being sabotaged.

There were other civilians at the station, but the bulk of the evacuees were military personnel. The noise was dreadful, with much shouting and people pleading to be let on the trains. They soon learned that their best chance of escape was to take the train to Shwebo, 400 miles north of Rangoon, and get onto one of the regular evacuation flights that were leaving the airfield there for India.

The first train to leave was full of wounded combat troops, sick civilians, doctors and nursing personnel. Huge red crosses had recently been painted on the roofs of the carriages, and these still-wet markings glistened in the sunlight as Sybil's group crossed the bridge to the platform. With a roar from the steam engines and a squeal from the wheels as they fought for purchase on the rails, the first train drew out of Rangoon station. God willing, it would soon be their turn. As soon as the first train departed, a second drew alongside the platform. It was now mid-morning, and the heat of the day was beginning to cause tempers to fray. There were some minor skirmishes as desperate people clamoured to get onto the train. These were isolated incidents, however, and the majority of the refugees simply waited with a calm air as if resigned to their fate.

The second train was eventually packed full of young children who had been sheltering in their schools and colleges. Their teachers, many of whom were nuns, accompanied them. They formed orderly lines and patiently waited to board the train in an organised manner, coming forward in groups as they were called by a bearded Indian railway official dressed in an immaculate uniform topped off by an impressive turban. The children ranged in age from around four years old to early teens, and many were still dressed in their school uniforms. Their train pulled out of the station at around midday, and still Sybil and her friends sat on the platform.

A third train slowly pulled in to the station and drew to a halt. The number of people on the platform and around the station seemed not to have diminished despite the departure of two trains loaded with evacuees. Once again, the railway official supervised the loading of the train, and this time the passengers seemed to be mainly women and children or families. Eventually, the official asked Sybil's party to board the train, and the small group stepped forward. Sybil and the ayah carried the three young girls, while Mr Younis carried his son and helped his wife on board. It was then that the Younises' ayah decided to remain behind, refusing to get on the train despite the best efforts of the family. She passed the little girls up to Mrs Younis and then she was gone, swallowed up in the crowds that still lined the platform.

It seemed like an eternity before the train was finally ready to depart, and when eventually it pulled out of the station, accompanied by huge plumes of steam, the family could do nothing but sit back in their overcrowded carriage and pray for safe deliverance. Their thoughts turned to their faithful ayah, who had stayed with them since the start of the conflict; she had been so good at looking after the children, keeping them calm and occupied during the worst of the raids. They thought of Norman, who had remained behind with his fellow soldiers, and of Bertha, who was determined to minister to the sick and wounded. Sybil prayed for their safety and for her own family.

As they reached the outskirts of Rangoon, they heard several enormous explosions, and, looking back towards the city, they saw huge plumes of black smoke rising up into the sky, forming dense clouds. Flames shot up almost as high in huge columns. The oil terminal in the port area had been blown up, and in one hour more than £11 million worth of Burmah Oil Company property and fuel had been destroyed, including the building in which William Le Fleur had once worked. More explosions followed throughout the city as the army implemented a scorched earth policy. From their carriage, they could see fires spreading freely. This, surely, was the end of Rangoon.

BLANCHE

FLIGHT FROM RANGOON

When night finally fell on 23 December, Blanche and her family loaded as many of their essential belongings as they could onto a bullock cart, taking with them all their gold, diamonds, rubies and emeralds, and a bag full of silver rupees bearing the head of George V, and went to the monastery where Austin had studied. There, on the outskirts of the city, the monks provided them with shelter. News had come during the day that the Japanese had entered Burma from all sides, so there was no hope of escape; all Blanche's family could do was keep running. At around midnight, when there were few people on the streets and all had become silent, they loaded up a car, and Blanche, her son, her husband and his brother and sister-in-law slowly made their way out of the city.

They drove all night and well into the next day, until the car's engine finally stuttered and coughed, caught once more and lurched forward before cutting out for the last time, out of petrol.

108

Blanche, heavily pregnant, and her family loaded what they could manage onto their backs, and, carrying baby Leslie, they set off along the track. The heat was intense as the sun beat down on them, and after a short while they had to rest under a banyan tree. For the first time in her life, Blanche was truly terrified—for herself and even more so for Leslie and her unborn child.

When the heat of the day had died down, they continued their journey, and by the end of the second day they came to a small village of round bamboo huts raised a few feet off the ground. The roofs were made of attap, a thick palm leaf, and the houses were one-roomed dwellings, small in comparison with her house in Rangoon. The villagers greeted them warmly and were able to settle them in two of the huts, as the previous owners had already fled in fear.

It was Christmas Day 1941. Blanche thought of her house in Rangoon, all decorated for Christmas. The presents they had painstakingly bought over the last few months were all wrapped up and lying beneath the tree in their front room. Of the gifts, they had taken only a few new clothes that they had bought for Leslie. Most of the food had been brought with them, but the toys and games they had purchased were left undisturbed on the floor. This alone was enough to make Blanche sad, but her despair became deeper as she kept asking herself over and over, 'Where is Sybil? Where is Sybil?'

until the tears fell down her cheeks.

That day, they made the best of what they had. They shared their food with the villagers, who produced a simple but splendid meal. As night drew in, they sat in their new home and sang Christmas carols. It raised their spirits and made them think of happier times.

Over the next weeks and months, life went on in the village. The family found they could make do without the relative luxury they were used to. They had no running water, but the well was nearby. There seemed to be no real shortages: fruit and vegetables were abundant, and there were even chickens and wild animals with which to supplement their diet. Day after day and night after night, for what seemed like months, they could see and hear Japanese planes heading for Rangoon and other parts of Burma, and Blanche prayed each day for the whole family but especially for Sybil. Certain that the enemy were getting ever closer, Manu announced his intention to go and fight for the freedom of his country, and he and many others like him took up arms against the Japanese. He returned only infrequently, with whatever supplies he had managed to acquire to help his family.

During the day, most of the men and women in the village foraged for food and cultivated the small amount of land they had cleared in the jungle, while a few of the older women looked after the children and prepared the meals. For

110

the most part, they seemed a contented group, and Blanche would join in their singing to keep her spirits up.

As time went by, the sounds of war seemed to be getting closer, and aircraft regularly flew directly over the village. They could hear fighting, gunfire and explosions, and they could see the occasional cloud of smoke rising high into the clear sky. Fear gripped Blanche as she remembered 23 December and the sights that had greeted her when the bombing had finally stopped and she had plucked up the courage to leave the safety of the house. In her mind, she could see again the mutilated bodies at the end of the road, the young women with limbs blown off, body parts scattered randomly here and there, small children looking for all the world as if they were peacefully asleep, a twisted and battered pram lying on its side. Then she had found her friend. She and this woman had shared stories of their children, confided in each other all their doubts and fears, and exchanged tips on parenting, just as all young mothers do. She had been lying on the ground, her clothes covered in dust and blood and shards of red brick. She looked quite beautiful, and Blanche had held the dead woman in her arms, cradling Leslie and her together. There was no sign of her baby.

Blanche tried to push these thoughts to the back of her mind, and during the day, when there was much to do, it seemed easier to forget.

111

It was only at night, when the village was silent, that she began to have nightmares, often awakening in the early hours of the morning, afraid to go back to sleep for fear of resurrecting the demons that tormented her.

On 26 February, all Blanche's fears and bad memories were temporarily driven from her thoughts. Her waters broke that morning, and she knew it was time. The village was deserted; everyone was away from the huts, carrying out their usual tasks. When she went into labour, only one old blind woman was there to help her, but Blanche had no time to care about the strange set of circumstances she found herself in. Back in Rangoon, many months ago, they had made plans for the birth. It was to have taken place in one of the hospitals run by British nuns, and Blanche had been to see the room where deliveries took place. She had met some of the nurses and the midwife who would attend the birth. It was a clean, bright and friendly place, and everyone had seemed very efficient. Now here she was on the hard floor of a bamboo hut with an attap roof in the middle of a jungle, with a midwife who was too old and blind to be of much help. The labour seemed to go on forever, and there were times when Blanche thought she would never make it, but she clung to her faith and prayed for the ordeal to end.

When the child was born, the blind woman discovered that the umbilical cord had been wrapped around his neck. Blanche had lost a lot of blood, and she felt an overwhelming tiredness wash over her. When she finally heard the sound of the baby crying, she felt her strength returning. The blind woman cut the cord with a rusty old razor blade, the only thing she could find. None of it mattered now, as Blanche held her second son in her arms and he began to feed hungrily. When the villagers returned that evening, there was great excitement and happiness at the birth of a healthy boy. They all came to the hut with little gifts and admired the handsome baby, and some felt it would bring luck to the village. Blanche chose the name Raymond. He came into a world in turmoil, with an uncertain future ahead of him.

When Raymond was only six days old, a dramatic change happened in the village. It was 4 March, and as usual the men and women were working in the fields, when the first wave of Japanese troops entered the settlement. These were no ordinary Japanese soldiers: these were the 'wild ones', as they came to be known by the villagers. They were soldiers of the Manchukuo Imperial Army. Manchuria, a province of China, had been established as a puppet state by the Japanese in 1932. These men earned their nickname. They would frequently march down the road dressed only in loincloths, and the village girls would run terrified and screaming into their huts. It became common practice for the Manchukuos to enter each hut on a regular basis and take whatever caught their eye. They even took Leslie's nappies, thinking they were handkerchiefs.

Finally, the Manchukuos came to the hut occupied by Blanche and her two sons and stole all her jewellery, her rings, her gold bangles, earrings and necklaces. Like many Burmese people, Blanche, rather than having a bank account, invested her money in gold and precious stones, and this was the last straw for her. For weeks, she had endured constant harassment and the stealing of food and clothes, but now her savings had been taken, and enough was enough. She picked up her two boys and marched to a nearby house where she knew a wounded officer of the Burma Defence Army was recovering. (The BDA, initially the Burma Independence Army, was a nationalist force formed with Japanese support shortly before the invasion and led by former student leader Aung San.) She complained to him and gave a description of the items that had been taken from her. She told him that it was simply not right for the villagers to be treated in this way. He in turn went to the Japanese officer in charge and explained the situation. A few days later, the Japanese officer turned up at her hut with all her stolen jewellery and asked her if she would know the criminals who had taken it. Blanche, fearing that the thieves would be punished too harshly, even killed, said she would not be able to recognise them.

The fighting was right on their doorstep, and artillery shells often exploded nearby. One day, the Allies bombed the village. The first planes flew low, dropping flares, and then came the second wave. The Japanese were shooting at the planes from the ground, and Blanche had to hide in a drain with Leslie and Raymond as the explosions came nearer. One landed close to the end of the drain and sent showers of earth over Blanche, who was shielding the boys. Their hiding place filled with dust and smoke, and then the shelling suddenly stopped and they returned to their hut unscathed. Across the road were a number of other small houses. A bomb had scored a direct hit on one, and it had been destroyed. Everyone inside had been killed.

As the days passed and the Japanese pushed north, the sounds of the fighting grew more distant and the bombing raids became less frequent.

CHAPTER SIX

March–April 1942

SYBIL

NORTH TO SAFETY?

Sybil had never seen or experienced anything like it. Every part of the train was packed. Each seat had at least one person on it, as mothers and relatives held children on their laps. The floor was covered with people squatting or standing wherever they could. Some of the smaller children and babies were put in the overhead luggage nets to enable more people to crowd onto the train. It seemed that they were probably the most comfortable, slung in mesh hammocks, swaying gently with the motion of the train. There was no possibility of movement, and Sybil and the family were glad they had at least managed to visit the somewhat dilapidated toilets in the station before boarding the train. Others were not so lucky and simply had to relieve themselves with as much privacy and decorum as a packed train would allow, using whatever receptacles they could get hold of. The stench of fear and sweat and bodily fluids filled the air, and Sybil held her clean handkerchief over her nose and breathed through it, as she had done when Auntie Nellie was smoking her cheroots, hoping the cloth would filter out the smells, which were almost overpowering.

The rocking motion of the train and the heat lulled many of the refugees to sleep. When Sybil awoke, the train had stopped. She was hot, hungry and very thirsty, but little could be done to alleviate this sorry state because rations were short and what little they had needed to be eked out. The train started moving again but at little faster than walking pace. How were they supposed to outrun the Japanese if they kept travelling at this speed? Sybil had heard that the troops had little in the way of tanks and big guns but that they did have bicycles, and during one dream she imagined whole hordes of Japanese soldiers overtaking their sorry little train while pedalling furiously. She awoke with a start and glanced sideways to see if it had been more than a dream. Thankfully, no Japanese were to be seen, with or without bicycles.

The train stopped overnight, giving an opportunity for the occupants to stretch tired, cramped legs. As the sun came up, it resumed its journey north. From the window of her carriage, Sybil could see mile upon mile of paddy-fields leading to dense green forests and faraway mountains. She remembered travelling on this very line a few years back, when she had been working in Mandalay and Maymyo. Those journeys were carefree and fun, all part of her big adventure, her journey of discovery. Now she travelled in fear of her life.

The journey seemed to go on forever. There were no signals, those having been destroyed by the retreating forces. In some places, the points had to be changed by hand or rudimentary temporary repairs made to damaged tracks. Those on board the train had lost all concept of time and had no idea where they were. How long should a 400-mile train journey take? With the Japanese advancing close behind, it seemed that they would never make it. There were frequent stops to take on any available water; from streams and lakes at the side of the track, the boiler was replenished and the engine given new life. At the end of the long day, as the light began to fade, the train came to a stop and the passengers alighted to relieve themselves, stretch their legs and collect brushwood for cooking.

It was mid-afternoon on the third day when the train crawled into Shwebo, and there was a huge sense of relief. Soon everyone would be flying out to the safety of India. Sybil and her adopted family alighted from the train with their fellow travellers in a fairly orderly fashion. Despite the numbers of people on the train, the level of overcrowding, there remained an air of dignity, and people seemed conscious of the need to behave in a well-mannered way. Their grubby clothes stuck to them and made them itch unbearably. They had last had a bath back at the university compound, and how they longed for another. They felt so dreadful they would have given almost anything for a hot bath and a change of clothes. The first stop was the station toilet, and luckily Sybil and her friends did not have to queue long before it was their turn to enter. What a relief to be able to wash in cool, clean water. The bath would have to wait, but just to feel the splash of water on their faces was refreshing enough.

They headed for the station exit and joined the long columns of people walking out of Shwebo on the road to the airfield. They had been assured that the camp was just a few miles from the station, but they seemed to walk for an eternity. People dropped by the wayside, utterly exhausted, succumbing to the effects of dysentery, dehydration and simple lack of food. A few died on that road, in sight of possible salvation. Onwards Sybil and the family walked, praying and putting their faith in the God who had seen them through to this point. By early evening, they had reached the evacuation camp, situated next to a disused airfield. It had been opened up by volunteer workers when it became obvious that an escape route to India was called for. They hoped that because the airfield had been inactive, it might not appear on enemy maps. So far, it had remained unscathed.

There was an orderly line of people standing outside a building clearly marked 'Office'. The camp was full of people. The majority were Anglo-Indians, Anglo-Burmese and Indians; comparatively few Burmans and only a small number of Europeans were to be seen. In one corner was an enclosed storage area surrounded by barbed wire. In it were the everyday belongings of families from all over Burma. It was obvious from the heaps of abandoned personal items that the camp had already been the departure point of many hundreds if not thousands of people. Battered suitcases, bundles of clothes, pots and pans, bedding, even the occasional mattress, and more personal items such as photographs, shattered in their frames, lay on the littered ground. There were hundreds of small but priceless items, memories from happier times. Sybil could see a violin case and nearby a wind-up gramophone surrounded by broken records; she wondered what had become of their owners. Not far off were row upon row of abandoned cars. For some time now, people had been arriving at Shwebo in cars packed with every item they thought might prove useful in their new life in India only to be informed that they had to leave all their belongings behind.

Inside the office, each person was given a ticket and told to find a bed in one of the two long Nissen huts nearby. The first was full, but in the second there were unoccupied beds, and the party were only too glad to lie down for a few minutes before making their way to the kitchen for what was their first proper meal in days. Up until this point, their fear had kept hunger at bay, but now they were starving. In the kitchen, they were given cutlery, a plate and a tin mug, and they dined on tinned beef, mashed potatoes and tinned fruit, all washed down with a mug of hot sweet tea. Exhausted but feeling at least reasonably well fed, they made their way back to the hut, and, settling down on the mattresses, they fell into a deep sleep.

Throughout the day, a number of lists of names were posted on a notice board. These were the people who would leave on the next flight. Naturally, these lists were scrutinised carefully. The first thing everyone did as soon as they awoke was go and check the board. The names of Sybil and her friends were not on the list that morning. They spent the day wandering round the camp, queuing to use the primitive toilet facilities and the bathroom, which was a piece of pipe running from an old tap and attached to a wooden stake driven into the ground. The pressure was so low that it took forever for the bucket to fill with enough water to wash hands and face. They were aware that they smelled bad, but then so did everyone. After a while, they became used to it.

It was during that first day at Shwebo that they heard the news about the train packed with schoolchildren and their teachers that had departed from Rangoon station just before them. Travelling slowly north, it had been spotted by a flight of Japanese fighter planes and strafed repeatedly with machine-gun fire from end to end. Inside the packed compartments, there was nowhere to hide, and although the train kept moving, the trapped passengers could not escape the hail of bullets. Only a few survived.

Much later, news of the hospital train, the first train out of Rangoon on 7 March, filtered through. It was another tragic story. It had been fired on by Japanese Mitsubishi Zero fighter planes. The airmen ignored the large Red Cross markings on the roof of each carriage and the train was strafed relentlessly. When it stopped, the doctors, nurses and orderlies carried the wounded to the side of the track, where they began to attend to them. Then the fighters returned and sprayed either side of the train with machine-gun and cannon fire. Only those who managed to dive into the shelter of the jungle survived.

The next rescue plane might arrive at the airfield at any time of day, and if your name had appeared on the list of evacuees for that particular flight, it was simply a case of stopping whatever you were doing and making your way quickly to the side of the plane and up the steps. Even at this point, when they had already given up almost everything, the refugees had to leave any belongings that weren't considered absolutely essential. These unnecessary items were simply thrown on the ground. Even small, lightweight things might suddenly be tossed on the ground, with no regard for their worth or meaning. It was obvious that reducing weight was critical. The rescue planes were designed to hold around 26 to 30 people, but in the rush to evacuate the crowded camp, each one left with 70-plus people crammed into every available space. Once loaded up, the planes, mainly American C-47s (or, as the British came to know them, Dakotas), would lumber along the runway, and eventually, as everyone on the ground held their breath, the plane would become airborne at what seemed like a dangerously slow rate. Luckily, the planes had been built with a very high operational safety margin.

On the second day, Sybil's group were sheltering under a clump of trees, shaded from the sun and in a quiet spot at the edge of the camp, when Japanese bombers and fighters appeared overhead. It wasn't the first time that the alarm had sounded, but on the other occasions the planes had flown over at a great height, ignoring the camp and clearly with another objective in mind. Now, however, the fighters came in low and strafed the camp. A flight of birds took to the skies with cries of alarm. Men, women and children ran in every direction. There was very little shelter or protection. Panic set in, and screams of anguish were heard as women lost sight of husbands and children. When all went quiet, the family emerged from the trees into the devastated camp. The dead and dying lay strewn in unnatural positions, and the huts and office had been shot up. Within minutes, however, it was business as usual. The survivors emerged from the buildings, from under the parked cars and from the toilet block, which was unscathed, and started to clear up the debris.

Then came the news that they had all been dreading: following the fall of Rangoon, the Allies had been forced northwards, allowing the IJAAF to use the forward airfields in central Burma and giving them control of the skies to the north of Shwebo. Burma had to all intents and purposes capitulated, and the remaining evacuees were told that there was little hope of any more planes attempting to get through. The danger that they would be intercepted by Japanese fighters on their way out was too great. The only options were to walk westward and try to make the Indian border on foot or to try to catch a train from Shwebo station to Myitkyina, where, it was believed, the airfield was open and rescue flights were still going in and out.

With three young girls, a baby son, Sybil, Mrs Younis and himself to think of, Mr Younis felt sure that they would not all survive the walk to India, and so once more circumstances dictated their plan of action. Along with many of the other refugees, they started the long trek back to the station, leaving behind a small number of people who were determined to stay and trust to their fate. The rest prepared to make the long trek west by road and rough jungle tracks, unsure of what dangers might lie ahead. An estimated one million people attempted the journey from Burma to India on foot. There are no accurate figures for the numbers who died on the way, but the death toll was undoubtedly very high.

At Shwebo station, they waited patiently for a train to Myitkyina, and, to the surprise of many, one eventually turned up. It was already fairly full, but by the time it pulled out of the station, every seat was occupied, every inch of floor space was covered and the view from the windows was blocked by people hanging on to the outside. The roofs of the carriages provided seating for many more.

Myitkyina was some 200 miles to the north-east, at the end of a single-track line that passed first across flat plains to reach Wuntho before beginning the climb to Indaw and on to Mogaung. There was little beyond Myitkyina except two distant outposts on the Chinese border, manned by only the hardiest of guards. Surrounding the remote town were fast-flowing rivers, snow-covered mountains, dense jungle and roads that were at best treacherous and winding and at worst became thick mud, causing people and even the most sure-footed pack animals to slide over the edge into deep gorges. If only they had another option available to them; but there was none, so it was to Myitkyina they travelled.

Even on the plains, progress was slow. When faced with any kind of an incline, the train seemed to move at a snail's pace. In the sweltering heat and the filthy, packed carriages, however, this seemed unimportant. It was survival that concerned everyone. Water was rationed to small amounts of tepid liquid from the boiler of the train or begged from any person who could be persuaded to spare a drop. Food was scarce but the passengers shared it out among themselves as best they could. Two days later, they rolled slowly into Myitkyina, exhausted and starving.

The occupants of the train disembarked and began the three-mile walk to the camp next to the airfield. Sybil, carrying one of the girls in her arms, was too worn out to do anything more than put one foot in front of the other and pray that she would remain strong. The new camp was even busier than Shwebo. Long queues of people stood waiting patiently for the next plane, determined not to lose their places. The new arrivals registered at the office, and their names were put on a list. Again, they were given tickets and billeted in long, narrow army huts. It was around the middle of March, and they had no idea how long they would remain at the camp.

126

Myitkyina was similar to Shwebo but on a larger scale. Many hundreds of evacuees had already left from the airfield, and here too there were the great heaps of discarded possessions and ranks of abandoned vehicles. Sybil rarely talked about her escape from Rangoon and loss of contact with her family, but other refugees told her heart-rending stories of having to leave their hill-station homes in considerable haste. They talked of rushing away from their beautiful, tranquil surroundings, leaving their clothes hanging neatly in their wardrobes, cosmetics and jewellery boxes on dressing tables. They spoke of books left on shelves, family photographs and mementos in cabinets, and of simple things like china and cutlery, wedding gifts, abandoned where they had been set out for a meal that was never eaten.

One distraught woman told Sybil of her son, a small, sickly child, who cried at having to leave behind his toys, and especially the large wooden rocking horse that had been made for him by one of their servants. It was a magnificent animal with pricked-up ears and a real mane and tail, and it had pride of place in the nursery. The boy would only let go of the horse's neck when his mother promised he could have a real pony when they reached India. She allowed him to take one item, a soft teddy bear, and they set off in search of safety. After many days without adequate food or clean water, the boy had fallen ill, succumbing to one

127

of the many illnesses that thrived in jungle conditions. They had done everything they could to keep him alive, but he was too weak and he died in his mother's arms. As she told her story, the woman sat and sobbed, clutching the small blue teddy as tears rolled down her cheeks. The story left everyone feeling drained and deeply saddened. Many began weeping as they relived the horrors of their own experiences.

Sybil knew how these people felt, having to leave behind almost all their belongings and choose only a few of the most loved or valuable ones. How did they make that choice, when suddenly everything became precious, evoking sometimes long-distant memories? Photographs of long-dead relatives and recent pictures of loved ones; heirlooms that had been handed down from generation to generation and more recent acquisitions, some brought from far-off homelands; personal papers, birth certificates, tiny curls cut from a baby's hair and kept safely: which should be taken and which left behind? Having made the difficult and heartbreaking choice, the evacuees found that their carefully selected mementos had to be left at the camp, abandoned with the treasured possessions of strangers in a dump in the north Burmese hills.

Sybil felt a deep sorrow for the others and for herself. She wondered if her experience had been less painful. She had not even been given the opportunity to choose from her precious

128

possessions, to go through the wooden box containing letters and photographs from her father, each pile tied together with a silk ribbon, and feared that she might never see any of them again.

It was the mother's story of the death of her small child that affected her more than the loss of any material possessions. What could be more precious than the life of one's own son or daughter? It made her think of the death of her mother and father, and she feared for the lives of her brother and sisters. She could not even begin to imagine how the young woman felt holding her son while he lay dying. Sybil bit her lip until it bled as she fought back her own tears. It was a tragedy in an endless ocean of tragedies.

The group grew silent, and Sybil was soon lost in her own thoughts and memories. After a while, she got to her feet and started walking slowly around the camp, as if to escape the stories. Past small groups of people telling their own heartbreaking tales, past people sleeping on the ground, occasionally flicking flies away with a twitch of a limb, past queues of people waiting to use the latrines and washing facilities. Sybil needed to be alone, and she walked with her head down, keeping to herself.

A routine had been established at the camp and life followed a pattern. At least there were limited toilet and washing facilities, a luxury after the long train journeys of the past week.

There was a great deal of sickness, particularly dysentery and cholera, and despite the best efforts of the medical staff many died. Everything was in short supply. Not just life-saving medicines but also basic food items were being rationed. Meals were rudimentary, consisting mainly of small amounts of rice, a few vegetables, fresh fruit and bread, which was more often than not stale—but at least it was food. She remembered watching the beggars in the streets of Rangoon eating just such food as this and despaired. Sybil missed her ayah's cooking, the spicy curries, the sweet dodol and the endless amounts of fresh fruit, some picked from their own garden. At the camp, luxuries such as sugar, tea and tinned milk were to be savoured, for they were not available often. If she ever escaped from this nightmare, Sybil promised herself, she would never allow herself or her family to go hungry, no matter what the circumstances.

Books played a significant part in the life of the camp. Among the abandoned possessions were novels by the Brontë sisters, Dickens and Agatha Christie and poetry by Burns, Keats and Shelley, books that once adorned the shelves of wealthy teak-plantation owners, oil-company managers, officers quartered in their hill stations and well-to-do tea planters, all left behind in the rush to safety. These books were more precious than their distinguished authors could ever have believed, as they were one of the few means of escape from the fear, drudgery, dirt, squalor, sweat and sickening odours that pervaded the camp. With every page, their readers could shake off the reality of their circumstances. Sybil read passages over again, the events of the novels becoming vivid in her imagination. She replayed scenes in her mind, putting her own interpretation on them.

When Sybil had been at the camp for a few days, an announcement was made that no Burmans would be evacuated; they would be left behind to suffer whatever fate would befall them at the hands of the fast-approaching Japanese soldiers. It was then that Sybil found a use for her skills as a seamstress: she was asked by many of the Burman women to convert their traditional dresses or longyis and the clothes of their children to Western-style clothing, in the hope that they could pass as Anglo-Burmese or Eurasian. This Sybil did, spending from morning to night unpicking, cutting and remodelling beautiful silk dresses into equally beautiful blouses and fashionable skirts. She changed the children's clothes into colourful shirts and blouses, little shorts and skirts. Who knows how many women and children were saved as a result of this innocent deception? It at least gave them a chance of getting their names on the lists of evacuees.

When she wasn't occupied in the time-consuming and tiring task of altering clothes, Sybil, like many of her companions, took her turn helping to attend to the sick, wounded and dying. She carried out simple nursing duties and cleaned up after the patients, doing what needed doing and not complaining. What right did she have to complain when by the grace of God she remained fit and well, while those around her suffered so terribly? Sometimes, when a patient's condition worsened, all that Sybil could do was to sit with them and hold their hand, talking or singing softly to them until, slowly but inexorably, they slipped away. It broke Sybil's heart when this happened, but she remained strong on the outside, always presenting a cheerful disposition to those who remained in this world. The number of children who died in the camp was particularly saddening. Despite the best efforts of the medical staff, there was often little they could do to prolong the lives of already weak, sick infants and children. Sybil felt it unjust that parents should be subjected to the loss of a child; she witnessed this situation too frequently and knew how devastating it was.

As she spent more time looking after the sick and wounded, Sybil began to notice that it was not always the most frail or seriously ill who died; sometimes a person who was apparently less dangerously ill than others would simply pass away, deteriorating much more rapidly than those around them. She saw this almost daily and began to feel that survival was dependent on more than just one's physical condition. While physical strength was important, mental strength, inner strength, was equally if not more vital, as was the desire, the will, to live. Sybil herself was determined that she would get out alive, and her belief in herself was bolstered by an undying faith in God, who had protected her thus far in her journey.

Life in the camp was for the most part a series of distressing scenes, and however hard Sybil tried to replay these scenes in her mind, searching for a happier outcome, however hard she might hope for an end to the stench, the disease and the deaths of her fellow refugees, from the very young to the very old, she could do nothing to change the reality. Even in her dreams she found no escape. People slept, cooked, read, gave birth and died all around her, and when she awoke, she found that the reality matched the dream, but mixed in was the smell of sweat, human waste and putrefaction, the circling of carrion, the swarms of flies, the armies of white maggots making every dead body seem alive with movement and the ever-present leeches, bloated by the ready supply of human blood.

Sybil watched birds flying around the camp, flitting from tree to tree, chasing one another in unfettered flight. How she wished she were one of those birds, flying high above the troubles and sadness below, far removed from the predicament that faced the refugees, free to escape the approaching threat of the Japanese

133

forces. At night, the camp became quieter, and Sybil could hear the sound of crickets and the rustling of small lizards as they roamed the undergrowth. She would look up at the clear sky, at the moon and the stars, and wonder if her family were still alive and if they too were looking at that same moon and stars. She missed them all the more at night, when the hard day's work had been completed and her thoughts turned to her personal loss and sadness. Often, she would wake in the early morning and wish she could see her brother and sisters, and she missed Blanche especially. She tried to picture them in her mind and to keep that picture bright and clear. She tried to keep her memories sharp and reflect only on the happiness they had once shared. It all seemed so long ago.

By early April, Sybil's group were still at the camp, although flights did continue to transport the refugees to India. The Japanese invasion had severed the Burma Road supply route, and an alternative means of supplying the Chinese forces had to be found. A daring plan was hatched: American transport planes loaded with military hardware for the Chinese army would fly from India across the Himalayas, a route known as 'the Hump'. With sheets of ice forming on the wings and fuselage, the planes faced a constant struggle to remain airborne. The heavily laden aircraft had to contend with extreme turbulence and violent thunderstorms.

The route was so dangerous that pilots called it 'the Aluminium Trail' because of the amount of wreckage scattered over the most difficult parts of the flight path. The planes flying the southern route over the Himalayas passed over Myitkyina before crossing the Chinese border and landing at Kunming. Having unloaded their supplies and refuelled, these planes touched down at Myitkyina and picked up evacuees for the trip back to India. Ordinary transport aircraft also landed at Myitkyina to fly out the camp's inhabitants when possible. Despite these flights in and out of the airfield, the numbers of refugees were so great that many people were stranded in the camp and surrounding areas.

Thus, in early April, Sir Reginald Dorman-Smith, Governor of Burma, cabled the British ambassador in Washington to find out whether it would be possible to receive US aid in evacuating Myitkyina. The response was positive, and civilian Pan American Airways pilots joined the fight to rescue the trapped men, women and children. More than 14,000 people were airlifted to safety by the Americans. Once a plane had landed in Chittagong or Dibrugarh, it would be turned around rapidly and a return flight undertaken. These planes flew continuously back and forth over inhospitable terrain, with loads far in excess of their usual limits and under constant threat of Japanese fighter attack. There was little doubt that this saved many lives, and evacuation from

Myitkyina by plane was certainly infinitely preferable to the long and dangerous walk to India.

Early in April, Sybil heard the news that Mandalay, the country's second city, the seat of Burmese kings and once her home, had been razed to the ground during three days of bombing with incendiary devices. Many hundreds of people had lost their lives.

On the 8th, it was Sybil's 22nd birthday. She and her friends celebrated, even managing to get their hands on some extra rations. The family had made many friends during their stay in the camp, but still they had a fear of becoming really close to anyone because of the uncertainty that surrounded all of them. They had to remain detached to a degree or risk the anguish of a close friend dying or being left behind when it was time to depart. They had enough to worry about without that additional pressure. That didn't stop them all celebrating Sybil's birthday, though, and indeed it was a relief to have a reason to be joyful.

Two days later, the names of Sybil and her small party appeared on the list of evacuees, and, as so many had done before them, they took their place in the long queue and waited patiently, not daring to move from the line lest they should lose their place. Planes were flying in and out in what seemed an endless stream, as the desperate attempt to save the endangered and terrified inhabitants of the camp was in full flow. When each empty plane arrived, it was loaded up with refugees as quickly as possible, as it was known that Japanese fighters were operating in the area, encountering only minimal resistance from the Allies.

It was late afternoon before Sybil, Mr and Mrs Younis and the children were called forward to board. Each person's belongings were checked at the door of the transport plane, and all non-essential possessions were simply dropped on the ground before the refugees were packed into the spartanly equipped fuselage. The books that Sybil had come to love were left behind, passed on to someone who would fly out later and who would then pass them on to someone else. By this time, Mr Younis was extremely thin, his cheeks sunken; Mrs Younis too was thinner, and the girls had lost their puppy fat. They had all suffered dysentery or some form of illness. Sybil had not seen her own reflection in the mirror for some time but she knew that she too had lost a good deal of weight. Already thin, she often had to make small tucks in her clothes so they fitted her. The baby was still smiling, but he had grown quite thin and weak. Their evacuation had not come a minute too soon.

Inside the plane, there were metal benches against the sides, and an additional row of seating had been placed along the centre. The evacuees sat down, tightly packed together, and were told to hang on to the webbing straps attached to the roof. The plane started to roll forward, and eventually the engines began to roar and it gathered speed, bumping along the uneven ground. Suddenly they were airborne, the bumping stopped and the plane ascended into the clear blue sky.

Their destination was Chittagong, just inside the Indian border and across the Bay of Bengal from Calcutta. Shortly after take-off, however, they heard that the plane was being diverted to Dibrugarh in the far north of India, near the Chinese border. Rumour had it that Japanese planes now based in Burma were bombing Chittagong and their fighters were controlling the airspace between Myitkyina and the Indian border. The distance to Dibrugarh was much shorter, and to those inside the plane, which had become very cold because of the altitude at which they were flying, the change of destination came as a relief. Now Sybil understood why the crew wore sheepskin-lined flying jackets and warm boots, clothing that had seemed incongruous down on the ground where it was hot and humid. The drone of the engines was comforting and many tried to sleep in defiance of the constant vibration. The flight crew handed out small paper bags, and, with the turbulence, the constant motion of the plane and the smell of their bodies packed together in the enclosed space, it soon became apparent to everyone what the bags were for. All they could do now was pray that they reached safety.

BLANCHE

NORTH-EAST OF RANGOON

The Manchukuo troops did not stay in the village long. They moved north to continue the drive that would push the Allied forces out of Burma. Behind them came the Imperial Japanese Army. The troops were highly disciplined, and they left the villagers alone, as they were too preoccupied with the nearby fighting and rounding up stray British soldiers. The jungle was an even more frightening and dangerous place than before. Wherever one went there were the bodies of dead British and Japanese soldiers. Swarms of flies and bluebottles descended on the carcasses and large white maggots dined on the putrid flesh. The smell was unbearable. Nothing could have prepared Blanche for the sight of so many young men who were never to return to their families.

On 8 April, when the children settled down to sleep and only the sounds of the jungle could be heard, Blanche thought of her sister and of all the birthdays they had celebrated and shared together. For all Blanche knew, her sister, always her best friend, might never have reached her 22nd birthday. It was with a heavy heart that she finally slept.

At this point, the villagers were more afraid of the dacoits than of the Japanese. They roamed with impunity around the area, taking anything of value and sometimes killing those who resisted or who witnessed their crimes. They carried a long-bladed, machete-like knife called a *dah*, which could inflict terrible injuries with just one blow. Blanche, her brother-in-law and his wife feared for their lives and stayed close to the village. She decided it would be safer to bury all her jewellery, and took it to a spot near a bridge over a small stream. She dug a deep hole and placed all her rings, bracelets and jewels in it before covering it all up. She fully intended to go back and rescue it all when it was safe to do so.

In the meantime, she kept 25 diamonds in a small velvet pouch in case of emergency. One night, a rumour spread that dacoits were coming and that they were killing their victims. Blanche panicked and reluctantly threw the diamonds down the latrine. She watched as, one by one, they sparkled in the moonlight before slowly sinking out of sight. The bandits never came.

Gradually, as the Japanese troops established themselves in the area, they restored law and order and suppressed the dacoits, and when everything calmed down, the villagers began to feel safer in their homes.

A short distance away from the village was a small hill station where the Japanese officers were quartered. In one of the houses on top of the hill was a geisha house, established by the senior officer, a general. The women had been brought over with the troops to provide entertainment for high-ranking soldiers. The general and his most senior officers each had a favourite geisha. The usual working day for such an officer could not have been more different from the conditions experienced by his troops: a leisurely horse ride, followed by a meal, work, another meal and then a short stroll to his accommodation at around 5 p.m. before relaxing in the company of his personal geisha. For a fortunate few, life went on as if the war were far away, rather than on their doorstep.

Occasionally, the geishas would walk down to the village, and they soon befriended Blanche, who was of a similar age. They would play with the children and often they took Raymond up to their house, where they bathed him, powdered him and dressed him in beautiful silk clothes before feeding him. He was a strikingly handsome boy and his ever-smiling face proved irresistible to the girls. The geishas were very good to Blanche and the children, and they would bring her food and clothing.

The villagers had established a reasonable relationship with the occupying forces. The Japanese claimed to be liberating the Burmese from British imperialists, and indeed many Burmese nationalists welcomed the invasion, at least to begin with. For the troops captured by the Japanese, however, things were very hard. The soldiers of the Japanese Imperial Army had total and utter contempt for the men they captured. To the Japanese soldiers, it was more honourable to die for the Emperor than to surrender. They therefore found it hard to understand how these giants of men, who in some cases stood more than a foot taller than their captors, could allow themselves to be taken prisoner.

As there was no provision for the holding of these prisoners and their treatment was brutal, their fate, more often than not, was death. The fortunate ones were simply shot; the unlucky were captured. Prisoners of war in Burma might be tied to posts in the ground and used for bayonet practice, receiving one thrust to the throat followed by several to the abdomen. Death was long and lingering. Punishments and interrogation techniques were sadistic. Nails were ripped from fingers and individuals were suspended upside down in the full heat of the sun. Men would be beaten to the ground with blows from rifle butts or bamboo poles. Sometimes soldiers would have their legs tied together and would be dragged along the rough roads behind any form of transport that could be found. Even if a man was dragged only a short distance, the skull could be shattered on boulders and internal bleeding could be fatal.

Blanche witnessed some of the treatment meted out to the POWs and became more reluctant to wander around the village. Life was monotonous. Every day, the same routine: awaking to the constant pangs of hunger, cooking rice for breakfast, washing and dressing the children, trying to keep them amused and take their minds off the diet of endless rice and vegetables, or occasionally rice with some kind of meat in a curry. The meat came from skeletal cows and water buffaloes and the odd chicken or goat. This was supplemented with wild fowl, snakes, baboons and any other creatures that could be caught. No one asked what kind of meat they were eating or where it came from; they were just thankful for what they had.

Sometimes, although they did not always have much to spare themselves, the Japanese soldiers would bring food to the villagers: tinned fruit, condensed milk and Marmite from captured British rations, as well as extra bags of rice. Some of them were kind and did what they could to make the lives of the local inhabitants more bearable.

Another hazard faced the villagers as they tried to make the best of their lot: the Kempeitai, the military police, moved into the area and were making life difficult, especially for the men, whom they spied on constantly. An atmosphere of distrust and fear pervaded, and Blanche began to feel uncomfortable. 'We talked less and worked hard, because we did not know who was watching or listening.'

CHAPTER SEVEN

April 1942–June 1943

SYBIL

INDIA

As they travelled away from Myitkyina, the engines droned in a rhythmic flow of sound, filling the packed fuselage with noise, and the plane vibrated and creaked in sympathy. The metal seats became incredibly cold as the plane gained height, but the children in Sybil's arms seemed unaffected by the whole experience and didn't appear to notice the drop in temperature. Many of the other passengers were violently sick, and Sybil watched one woman clutch her small paper bag as if it were a lifeline. For most of the flight, she just sat still, growing paler and paler as the colour drained from her cheeks, but after a particularly bad period of turbulence, the lady suddenly vomited, completely missing her paper bag and covering another passenger in the meagre contents of her stomach. After a brief flurry of activity, the passengers returned to normal, and again Sybil did her best to hold her handkerchief over her nose to help filter out the smell.

The landing at Dibrugarh was bumpy but welcome. Once they had alighted, they were taken to a holding point and eventually processed by an extremely efficient and sympathetic British official. Finally, they were moved to the dock area, where they walked along a jetty to board a small steamship. They had no idea what lay in store for them, but at least the bombing seemed to have been left some way behind. For the next two days, they travelled down the great valley of the Brahmaputra River. The food and accommodation were very basic, and the ship was packed from stem to stern with refugees travelling south, but the atmosphere was friendly, and a great sense of camaraderie built up, as if to say, 'We have survived a living hell together; now we can survive anything.'

At the end of the second day, they disembarked and were escorted to a railway station the location of which was a mystery to them, as all identifying signs had been removed. A further two days of travel on a dusty, hot and rather well-worn train ensued before they finally arrived at their destination: Calcutta. They had been travelling non-stop for almost five days now in the most difficult of conditions, and everyone was exhausted. The children were almost literally dead on their feet. At the station, they were loaded into army vehicles and transported to different destinations. Sybil and her group were taken to an Indian college on the outskirts of the city. Some were taken to Fort William, the second fort of that name in the city, the first being the site of the 'Black Hole of Calcutta' incident. Others were transported to schools and military establishments throughout the city.

At the college, they were once again processed in an orderly fashion, before being given clothes and shoes donated by the people of Calcutta for the refugees. This was the first change of clothes they had had since they had left Rangoon on 7 March, more than five weeks earlier. Everyone took turns having a bath, and it was the most luxurious experience to soak in clean water that actually managed to cover one's legs, instead of trying to wash in a rusty bucket with dirty water only a few inches deep. There was even soap—carbolic, as opposed to the delicate, scented kind that Sybil loved, but at that point in time, it was the best soap she had ever seen. Once they were washed and changed into clean clothes, even the children perked up and the mood became much more positive. Because of the generosity of their Indian hosts and the charitable collections made by the local memsahibs, they now had a change of clothes, a change of undergarments and new shoes, and they were clean and tidy. They were conscious of being a lot better off than those left behind.

Sybil, Mrs Younis and the children were allocated to one dormitory, formerly a classroom, along with a number of other women and children, while Mr Younis slept in another with the other men. They all met up during the

146

day and at mealtimes and spent their time walking around the campus, trying to get back to some sense of normality and coming to terms with what they had been through.

Mr Younis had been talking to some of the other refugees and had discovered why their plane had been diverted to Dibrugarh from Chittagong. The plane that had taken off before theirs had been flying to Chittagong, but as it approached the Indian border, it had been intercepted and shot down by Japanese fighter planes operating from recently occupied airbases in northern Burma. The airspace from just south of Myitkyina to Chittagong was effectively now controlled by the Japanese air force. They had had another extremely lucky escape.

For a week, they remained at the college, and during that time Mr Younis managed to contact business associates of his from Meerut, India. In Burma, Mr Younis had been a well-to-do silk merchant, and he traded with other businesses in countries to the east and west. One of the organisations he dealt with was a firm of scissors merchants in Meerut, and over the years Mr Younis had become very friendly with the owners. They had stayed with him in Rangoon and had often asked him to visit them, and now seemed the ideal time. Mr Younis's friends were delighted to hear from him, as the news from Burma had made them fear the worst. When he told them of his and his family's situation, they insisted that he make arrangements to travel to Meerut immediately.

The Younises, the De Alvis girls and Sybil packed up their new belongings, meagre as they were, collected some rations and were picked up by a military vehicle and transported to the railway station. After spending a very pleasant week in the college, the thought of once more travelling a long distance to an unknown place was rather unsettling, and everyone was tense and a little on edge. As they made their way through the busy streets of Calcutta to the station, they thought of the journey they had made when they left Rangoon. They were homesick, and Sybil ached for the family she had left behind.

This time, however, the train was rather different. Gone were the crowds taking up every seat, the floors and corridors packed to overflowing with people. Their previous journeys had been spent in cramped and unbearable conditions; now they were given four-berth compartments, one for Mr and Mrs Younis and the small boy, and another for Sybil and the three girls. There was a washbasin in each compartment, and a toilet, which they shared. Compared with the train from Rangoon and the one to Myitkyina, this was sheer luxury. As well as the rations they had been given at the college, they were able to buy fruit and chocolate at stations along the way, and they could not believe their good fortune. It seemed that life was taking a turn for the better.

The journey to Meerut was a long one, a distance of almost 900 miles, and Sybil enjoyed one of the best nights of sleep she had had in months as she was rocked gently by the movement of the train and the regular clickety-clack of the wheels on the tracks. The familiar and soothing sounds were punctuated only by the occasional noise of the steam whistle blowing up ahead to warn others of their approach. Sybil found the high-pitched whistle strangely comforting. For 12 hours, they slept, awakening considerably more refreshed, and in the daylight they sat and looked out at the green landscape and cultivated fields of their new home. After travelling for almost two days, they finally arrived at their destination and were met at the station by Mr Younis's friends, who made a big fuss of them all, but especially of the children.

Meerut was a big city, packed with people and very busy. The heat was intense as they made their way through the crowds in a very plush car, a Wolseley 25. It was a complete contrast to the type of transportation they had become used to, and it seemed very strange after all they had been through. The house was big and of typically British colonial construction. Wide verandas went round the house on the ground and first floors, providing shade and a quiet place to sit and relax in the fresh air. The gardens were large and well laid out, with wide lawns, well-established trees and small ponds. In the evenings, they were the perfect place to walk with the children before putting them to bed. Servants looked after all the domestic chores and ensured all their needs were catered for. During the day, it was too hot to venture into town, and they all stayed indoors, looking after the children, teaching them to read books and playing games with them, keeping cool beneath the large electric fans suspended from the high ceilings. Sometimes, in the early evening, when the temperatures had dropped sufficiently, Sybil and Mrs Younis would go out to the busy market to shop for clothes and food for the family, and they always enjoyed haggling with the traders for fresh fruit, spices and vegetables, material for dresses and sandals to keep tired feet cool. They managed to overcome the language barrier, and it was almost like being at home.

The sun beat down on Meerut, and this took its toll both physically and mentally on the inhabitants. Tempers were short, and the heat was so intense that by late April Sybil's skin had broken out in large heat boils, and only prompt action by the local doctor saved her from any permanent scarring. By the end of May, when the cooling rains would have arrived in Syriam, there was still no respite. Through June, the heat intensified, and when at last the rains appeared at the end of the month, their effects were so insignificant that Sybil barely noticed the infrequent showers or the very small drop in temperature. How she wished for the monsoons of her past to clear the air and bring life to the parched countryside.

Having left Burma with only the clothes they stood up in and with very few personal possessions, their only source of income was a regular weekly allowance from the Indian government. This was given on the strict understanding that once a person was employed, they would pay all the money back. This funding was a tremendous help to Sybil and her friends and was greatly appreciated.

From April to August, they remained with the scissors merchant's family, until finally they were allocated a house in the military cantonment in Meerut. It was sad to leave their friends, but they felt that to stay longer would be to take advantage of their kindness. In late August, they moved into their new house. Outside the city, the temperature seemed lower, the days cooler, and the occasional breezes were a very welcome respite from the burning sun.

Word finally reached the inhabitants of Meerut, including the significant number of Burmese refugees, of the many thousands of people who had had no alternative but to attempt the walk from Myitkyina to India, a distance of more than 200 miles over inhospitable country. They had to make this journey in the most difficult weather, as the monsoon arrived early that year. Their route took them over the Myitkyina Plain, through the foothills of the Kumon Range and across the Hukawng Valley. This was known as 'the Valley of Death' after the massacre of many of the local population by Naga headhunters, who continued to inhabit the area and still collected heads. All this had to be achieved in temperatures of over 40°C and humidity in excess of 80 per cent, with inadequate clothing and on a diet consisting of rice and more rice, with the addition of what little could be foraged along the trail. Once across the Hukawng Valley, there was still the barrier of the Patkai Hills to be faced. The refugees had to traverse the Pangsoi Pass, at a height of more than 4,000 ft, before crossing the Indian frontier and dropping down into Ledo.

Of some 50,000 civilians who set off from the area around Myitkyina, full of hopes, prayers and fears, more than 26,000 died on the trek out of Burma. One of the many tragic stories concerned the children of the Bishop Strachan Home for Girls. Those who had survived the bombing and shelling of Rangoon, around 40 in number, with several members of staff, attempted the Hukawng Valley route, with little in the way of supplies. Still dressed in their white school uniforms, they must have been a ghostly sight as they made their way along the trail. During the journey, exhaustion, disease and starvation took their toll, and only four pupils made it to India.

For Sybil, such news was heartbreaking, and it underlined to her how lucky she had been: her escape, difficult and full of tragedy as it was, had not even begun to approach the hardships endured by many thousands of others.

In the cantonment, Sybil saw the young men and women in military uniform going about the camp with an air of purpose and decided that she wanted to contribute to the war effort. In November 1942, as the weather began to turn cooler, she finally plucked up the courage and joined a queue of girls enlisting at the recruitment office. They were all chatting excitedly, and one girl, who appeared more streetwise than the others, said, 'Don't give your correct age.' Why this should make any difference to the recruitment process was a question that puzzled Sybil, but she would have to think it out later, as she was next in line. She entered the office and the short interview began. Mrs Hemingway, the subaltern, asked her questions about her health, the skills she had and what work she would prefer to do. Another woman, Mrs Duckworth, made copious notes. Sybil answered all the questions truthfully, except for her date of birth, which she gave as 8 April 1921, knocking a year off her age. The words of the girl in the outer office had clearly made an impact on her, but she still wasn't sure why she was supposed to give the wrong age. It was only later that Sybil realised the girl had been underage and had assumed, because of Sybil's youthful appearance, that she was too.

Sybil said she would do any job, and Mrs Duckworth mentioned a few of the available positions. Again, Sybil said she didn't mind; she just wanted to help in any way she could. Mrs Duckworth told her that the telephonist in the ward master's office had put in a request for a transfer to driving ambulances and that she would fit the vacancy perfectly. She was given a thorough medical, issued with a uniform and started work the next day at the British Military Hospital, Meerut. So it was that Sybil joined the Women's Auxiliary Corps (India) and went to war.

The British Military Hospital was housed in a large stone building. At the grand central entrance, two heavy wooden doors led to a tiled hallway. Through a set of swing doors, you entered the hospital proper. From a central hallway, two large corridors branched off to the left and right. Along these were the wards and administrative offices, the ward master's office and the dispensary. At the end of the right-hand corridor was a wide staircase leading to the second floor. Near the entrance, on the left-hand side, was a lift for patients who could not manage the stairs. Despite the heat outside, the building remained relatively cool and pleasant because of the thickness of the walls. It was the sort of hospital you would find in any sizeable British town in the 1940s. There were additional buildings dotted around the grounds, mainly wards and storage areas.

After a short period of training, Sybil proved a very competent and meticulous worker. Her job was to take incoming calls, log the time of call and who it was for, take any message and ensure that the correct person received it. She also had to operate the switchboard to place external calls. She liked the job and the camaraderie of her colleagues in the office, and she took pride in becoming increasingly efficient. She was methodical and precise, and the recipients of her messages always knew she had written them because of her neat handwriting. It was a very busy environment, and there was rarely any time to relax, although occasionally they managed to grab a quick tea break. Sybil was conscious of her appearance, and her uniform was always immaculately pressed, her brass buttons polished to a high shine and her shoes gleaming. She had been taught the benefits of spit and polish: with a brush, a bit of regulation boot polish, a bit of spit and a serious amount of elbow grease, the results were amazing, and her shoes shone brilliantly.

It was around this time that the office began to receive a steady stream of young soldiers, often coming to the door with the lamest of excuses for being there. Word had gone round the camp that there was a new girl in the ward master's office and she was very pretty.

Understandably, the young men wanted to see for themselves. Soon, Sybil was being asked out by quite a number of these soldiers, and when they had time off, they would walk in the gardens. Those who had cameras would have photographs taken of Sybil and themselves in the gardens of the hospital, or she would take photographs of them. It was fun, but she made sure they all realised that it was only her friendship they would get.

Things were getting hectic in the hospital as more and more wounded were being transferred from the Burmese front, where casualties were high. Mrs Duckworth suggested that Sybil move into the hostel, which was based near the main hospital building. It would mean she was nearer her work and would no longer have to pay rent to stay in the cantonment. It would give her more money to spend, too. Sybil was also paying back the money she had received from the Indian government. By the time she paid her rent and her government loan, she had very little left for herself. It was a wrench to leave the Younis family, and especially the children, but Sybil could see the advantages of the move, and, with no little sadness, she made it. The hostel was always kept clean and tidy, and Sybil had her own room near to the shower block and bathrooms. It was full of young women about Sybil's age who worked in and around the military hospital, and they all were determined to work hard but also to enjoy themselves as

156

much as possible. Sybil started to be asked out to the pictures by the young soldiers, and at last she began to feel she was leaving the horrors of the war behind her.

Three of the soldiers were pursuing her with dogged determination and declarations of undying love. The first was Corporal William Macaulay, known to everyone as 'Mac'. He was in the Royal Army Medical Corps and worked in the hospital. Originally from Glasgow, he was tall, handsome and red-haired, with a broad accent and a dry sense of humour. The second was an Anglo-Indian soldier, little more than a boy. The third soldier was a man named Flory, like the protagonist of Orwell's *Burmese Days*. Would he triumph in love, where the fictional Mr Flory had been soundly defeated?

Lance Corporal Reid Flory was considerably shorter than Mac. He had blond hair and hazel eyes, but it was his smile that made him attractive to Sybil. He always seemed to be happy, telling stories and singing as he worked. Each time he saw Sybil, his smile became even wider. Reid worked in the dispensary next to the ward master's office. On leaving school, he had commenced his studies in pharmacy at Robert Gordon's Technical College in Aberdeen, and that was where he had been when he'd joined a long queue of civilians and enlisted at the start of the war. He and his friends were looking for adventure, and in Reid's opinion there was precious little of that in Aberdeen.

Joining the 154th Brigade of the 51st Highland Division, he fought in France at the beginning of the conflict. His regiment became known as the 'Highway Decorators', as everywhere they went they painted their 'HD' insignia on walls, buildings and anything that stood still. Reid had been one of a group of soldiers from the division who had been ordered to fight a rearguard action to delay the German troops long enough for the army to evacuate Dunkirk. They achieved this aim, but only a small number were able to evacuate from a small fishing village to the west of Dunkirk. Reid witnessed many of his boyhood friends being killed in the action as they fought heroically to prevent the Germans from advancing before the evacuation had been completed. After a brief period of leave, he was placed back on active service and moved to the Royal Army Medical Corps, where they could make better use of his pharmaceutical training. He was then transferred to India.

It was during his initial service in France that Reid started smoking, a habit that would stay with him all his life. His comrades would often stop during the long marches for a breather and a cigarette, and eventually Reid was persuaded to try his first Woodbine, which made him sick, much to the amusement of his pals. However, Reid came to appreciate the short breaks and found that the cigarettes steadied his nerves. He even managed to acquire some evil-smelling

French smokes that kept the bugs away a treat. In India, the habit proved effective at keeping the voracious insects at bay and could even be used to get rid of leeches. The simple application of a lighted cigarette to the head of a leech would cause it to give up its tenacious grip on the flesh and drop off.

Sybil's initial contact with him began with a commercial arrangement of sorts. All the military personnel at Meerut received weekly rations, which included green tins of Maconochie's beef stew (which was delicious and which they both enjoyed) as well as cans of bully-beef and beans. Reid had developed a hatred of the pink, mottled, fatty slab of meat; Sybil was none too keen on the baked beans. It seemed only natural that an exchange of tinned foods should take place, and a mutual convenience quickly grew into a close friendship. It was not an exclusive friendship, however, as Sybil liked all three of her suitors, and wanted to be friends with all of them. But for Mac and Reid, friendship was not good enough; their intentions were more serious than that. The Anglo-Indian boy, faced with such determined opposition, eventually gave up.

The two friends were getting increasingly protective of Sybil and ever more jealous of each other. An agreement was reached, and one of the older, married soldiers, Mr Denman, who was a father figure to Sybil, was roped in to help. No single suitor would be allowed to take

159

Sybil out on a date without the presence of the other, or, if the other was on duty or unavailable, Mr Denman was required to act as a chaperone. So whenever Sybil went on a date, there were always two men on her arms. When she went to the pictures with Mac, Reid would often sit behind them. When she went on a picnic with Reid, Mac or Mr Denman would tag along.

This went on for some time, until finally Mac reached the end of his tether. He desperately wanted to be alone with Sybil. He was very much in love with her and found the constant presence of a chaperone somewhat restricting and rather off-putting. He conspired with Sybil to travel separately and in secret to the cinema, where they would meet up, but Reid had spies in all camps and was waiting for them when they arrived. This subterfuge was contrary to all the agreed rules of engagement formulated by the three men, and so a mock court martial was held, with Mac found guilty of the charges laid against him. His sentence was to be denied contact with Sybil for two weeks, a punishment that caused him great anguish.

The course of this ongoing wartime romance could have taken quite a different turn, as Reid was promoted to sergeant and transferred to a military hospital in Delhi. However, he could not bear to be parted from Sybil and requested a transfer back to Meerut, even taking a drop in rank back to lance corporal. Reid pursued the

St Philomena's School for Girls, Rangoon, where Sybil, Blanche and Eunice were educated.

AR RIGHT: Sybil wearing the uniform of the Women's Auxiliary Corps (India) in the grounds of Meerut Military Hospital, 1943.

RIGHT: Reid in his Royal Army Medical Corps uniform, summer 1943.

Reid and Sybil on their wedding day, 17 August 1943.

A view of Rangoon from the Custom House, with the Sule Pagoda to the right, 1945. In the distance left of centre, the Shwedagon Pagoda is just visible. The fine buildings almost look untouched by war, but closer inspection reveals that incendiary devices have destroyed the interiors, with only the walls remaining intact (photograph by Glenn S. Hensley, held by University of Chicago Library, Southern Asia Department).

ABOVE LEFT: A young Blanche photographed in Rangoon, 1946

ABOVE MIDDLE: Manu just after the war, looking thin and gaunt, with Blanche to his left. Happier times are ahead.

ABOVE RIGHT: Austin after the war in his naval uniform.

The MS *Batory*, the 'Lucky Ship' that transported Sybil and her children Ian and Flora to their new life in Scotland.

Brackenridge, Ellon, Aberdeenshire: Sybil's first home in Scotland.

Reid, Evelyn, Ian, Flora and Sybil outside 22 Park Crescent, Ellon, in 1950. A home of their own for the first time.

Sybil holding Derek in the summer of 1952.

Sybil with her young family in 1954. From left to right: Flora, Sybil, Derek, Ian, Evelyn.

ABOVE LEFT: Manu and Blanche at a dinner party in Rangoon, 1958, not long before they left for Calcutta.

ABOVE RIGHT: The SS *Santhia*, the liner that transported Manu, Blanche and their children from rapidly changing Burma to the bustling city of Calcutta (courtesy of simplonpc.co.uk).

LEFT: Blanche in the late 1960s. This picture was taken by her daughter Anita a professional photographer in her Calcutta studio.

ABOVE LEFT: The *Sybil M*, summer 1976, named in tribute to the woman Reid fell in love with in India. The small boy is their grandson Ian.

ABOVE RIGHT: Reid and Sybil in their pharmacy shortly before their retirement in 1988.

RIGHT: Reid and Sybil in 1988, at the retirement party held for them at their son Ian's house.

Blanche surrounded by family at her 85th birthday party, 23 May 2007. Chicku has her arm around her great-grandmother's shoulders.

Blanche's daughter Yvonne and her dear friend Hilda Soord, during her visit to Calcutta in March 2006. One month later, Hilda posted the website notice that would lead to the reunion of Sybil and Blanche after almost 66 years apart.

RIGHT: Sybil and Blanche, together at last, Calcutta airport, October 2007.

BELOW: 'That's my little sister.'

RIGHT: The family from Scotland seeking shade by the Oberoi Grand pool. From left to right: Evelyn, Sonny (behind Evelyn), Ewan, Sybil, Caroline, Nicola, Rebecca, Flora and Derek.

BELOW: Sybil and Blanche at Blanche's home in Calcutta. The years just slipped away.

Some of the family at the Novelty Hotel, Calcutta, November 2007.

Blanche and Sybil singing at the party organised by grandson Peter to celebrate the sisters' reunion – a moving, memorable and joyous occasion.

girl he loved with determination, persistence and persuasiveness. He would write her long love letters, send her poems he had written, make her laugh with his antics and sit singing songs to her, songs like 'A Bird in a Gilded Cage', 'Come into the Garden, Maud' and, most frequently, 'Yours', a Vera Lynn song.

Vera Lynn had visited India in the spring of 1943, and had performed, from Calcutta to the mountains of the north, her extensive repertoire of songs. Huge audiences of troops would gather for her concerts, and Lynn would sing to them until she could sing no more. Members of the audience were often moved to tears, as her beautiful voice would melt even the most battle-scarred heart. She made many hospital visits and would sit with the injured, chatting and answering questions about home and the war in Europe, which was uppermost in the soldiers' minds. They had left family, friends, wives, sweethearts back home, and they were anxious for any news. Sybil and Reid had attended one of her concerts, and Sybil would always remember the words of each song. The one that Reid sang to her, 'Yours', a quite beautiful love song, was her favourite. She thought it was the most romantic song she had ever heard, and even Vera Lynn would have been hard pressed to match the love and passion with which Reid sang it. She often sang the song to herself, and she began to feel that maybe she would be Reid's 'till the stars lose their glory'.

One day, as Sybil was out walking in the gardens with Reid, her old boyfriend Theo De Alvis turned up at the hospital. He too had made his way out of Burma, and eventually he had managed to locate his family in Meerut. When he arrived to visit them, he immediately asked where Sybil was and set off to find her. When he found her walking in the gardens with Reid, he exchanged polite conversation with them for a short time before wishing them well and saying his goodbyes. Sybil never saw him again.

Reid would take her for drives around the streets of Meerut in one of the ambulances, although, as he'd never actually had a lesson, his driving was a little erratic at first. The streets were very crowded, and there was little or no adherence to any Highway Code, but driving a very large army ambulance gave Reid a considerable advantage. Pedestrians would scatter, other road users would move swiftly to the side and Sybil would hold on tight to her seat, feeling a mixture of fear and amazement that he managed to avoid everything—or perhaps it was more the case that everything managed to avoid him.

They would talk for hours, he of his childhood and life with his sister, mother and many uncles and aunts in Ellon, near Aberdeen. Sybil knew a little about his country because of the numbers of Scots settled in Burma. He talked about his hopes and dreams, his love of the sea and boats. He never mentioned his part in the war in Europe or the deaths of his best friends 'Saucers' (so-called because of his big ears) and 'Beets' (a tough country boy whose nickname came from the 'tackety beets', big metal-studded boots, he had worn all his life). They had grown up together, started school together, played cowboys and Indians, pretended to fight battles from wars long ago and played football in the streets of Ellon. They signed up together for the big adventure in a shabby recruitment office in Aberdeen. As part of the British Expeditionary Force, their division was ordered to support the French at the Maginot Line. They managed to escape the initial horrors inflicted on the BEF to their north and south, but were eventually surrounded and had to fight their way west towards the coast. Beets had been a few feet away when he was hit by machine-gun fire, and Reid had held him in his arms as the life drained from him. Reid wept for Beets and for his family and for himself. While he told Sybil that if it hadn't been for the bravery of his friend Saucers, they would never have made it to the coast, he never talked of seeing his comrades being machine-gunned to death on the beaches or of his evacuation from northern France on 4 June, when he had survived because he was a strong swimmer. Many around him drowned before they reached the evacuation boats.

Sybil talked to him of her life in Burma, of an

idyllic childhood in a beautiful country, of her school, her family, the jobs she had done and the places she had visited, from Maymyo to Moulmein to Mandalay. She never talked about 23 December 1941 or her experiences as a refugee in Shwebo and Myitkyina. Those were conversations for a much later time, and it would be many years before either of them shared with anyone else the horrors they had experienced.

BLANCHE

RETURN TO RANGOON

News of the war came daily, but it was hard to know what to believe. Rumours abounded of atrocities against Karen soldiers loyal to the British. As the British Army had retreated, they had discharged the Karen troops and sent them home. Many took their weapons with them and joined with Indian troops and civilians to carry on the fight for their country against the Burma Defence Army. According to one story Blanche heard, the Japanese had recently ordered the BDA to destroy two Karen villages, and every man, woman and child had been put to death. Blanche remembered her fiercely pro-British Karen grandfather and mother, so gentle and loving. How could this be happening to her people? In fact, the BDA waged a war against the Karen that resulted in almost 2,000 dead and some 400 villages destroyed.

In June 1942, the monsoons came. Slowly, the incoming clouds rolled relentlessly north. That spring, the heat had become unbearable as day after day brought the unforgiving glare of the sun. It was so hot that there was very little activity during the day. Even the desire to eat was dulled, although the lack of variety in the diet probably contributed to the loss of appetite. The Japanese soldiers, resting after returning from the front, did not venture out until early evening when the temperature was more bearable. At first, only a few large raindrops fell, making a pattering sound on the broad leaves. These first drops were gratefully received, as all knew that there would at last be some relief from the high temperatures. The villagers stood outside and enjoyed the feeling of water trickling over hot skin. The children danced around and jumped in and out of the rapidly forming puddles.

The clouds piled high upon one another, stretching as far as the eye could see, and the days became darker. After those first few light drops, the rains came with a vengeance. 'It is hard to describe monsoon rain to someone who has never experienced it,' says Blanche now, 'but it is rain like no other. It is heavier than any normal rain. It is unrelenting, and after a short time, you feel like it will never end.'

The village became a sea of mud, the flat

ground taking on the appearance of a great elephants' watering hole. The *chaungs*, or streams, turned into torrential rivers, crashing over rocks and waterfalls, bringing teak logs, branches and small trees cascading down. Woe betide anyone caught in the onrushing water: it would bring instant death. From time to time, the bodies of dead soldiers would come tumbling down in the swollen waters; British or Japanese, the foaming water made no distinction as they drifted south to the open sea.

The attap roofs of the houses began to reveal their weak spots, and the rain dripped slowly and monotonously onto the floors inside. There was water above and water below and no escape from it. To venture outside was to become drenched in minutes, the water flattening one's hair, running in rivulets down the front of the face and the back of the neck and eventually trickling down the torso. Mud oozed up between bare toes, and feet and legs were soon caked in it. There was no break from the rain. Even when there was a brief pause in the downpour, there came only the realisation that the monsoon was simply gathering its strength for another prolonged assault. In these conditions, leather rotted, metal rusted, equipment failed, and there was mildew and the smell of damp everywhere.

During the monsoon, the rainforest took on an even more dangerous persona. The rotting bodies, the poisonous snakes, the vermin and the mass of insect life were still there, but the jungle itself became deadly and malarial. Ticks, which caused scrub typhus and carried dysentery, were more plentiful than before, and leeches penetrated even the thickest clothing. Soldiers coming out of the jungle found that when they removed their shirts, they were covered in fat wriggling leeches. Mosquitoes brought dengue fever and malaria. Lung flies would attack exposed flesh, the bite turning into a large, hard septic lump, which would soon ooze pus and begin to smell of rotting flesh.

These things were bad enough, but cholera was the worst killer. Many Japanese soldiers lay weak and dying in their own watery faeces, occasionally vomiting and slowly but surely dehydrating. After a short time, the skin would lose its elasticity and the eyes become sunken and lifeless. The voice would became weak, with a characteristic high pitch, and relief came only with coma and death. Try as they might to contain the spread of the disease, it was not long before the death toll mounted up and funeral pyres were lit all around the village. There was no other way to prevent the disease spreading, as burial would just compound the problem. Although Blanche, the children and the villagers remained largely isolated from the soldiers and ventured out only occasionally, to forage for fruit and vegetables to supplement their rice rations, a number of Burmese did succumb to the illness, and they too joined the

175

piles of bodies awaiting cremation. Blanche was extremely careful (as she had been when she was pregnant with Leslie during the monsoon), boiling all the water she used and cooking the daily meals until they were steaming hot. She would accept no extra food from the soldiers or from the other people in the village unless she could cook it herself. Some of the others told her she was being overprotective, but she was determined to safeguard her children.

How many hundreds of soldiers died in that first monsoon season of the Burma campaign? Certainly, far more died of diseases such as dysentery, scrub typhus and cholera than died in action. The Japanese soldiers near the village had come for rest and recreation after months of bitter fighting, and here, many miles behind the front line, many died a terrible death. It made Blanche cry with pain: she cried for her children, and she cried for the mothers of those Japanese and Allied soldiers who died deaths not of heroes but of strong men reduced to mere skeletons. She had seen the Japanese troops overrun her country, and, despite herself, she had admired their bravery. She detested their cruelty but tried to understand the reasons behind it all. In the end, as the soldiers lay dying and she was forced to help nurse them, they did not call out to the Emperor god for whom they had blindly given their lives. When they finally reached the point where death was inevitable, they cried out for their mothers.

In late September, after many long months, the monsoon was over. In time, the mud would change to hard-baked earth and the chaungs would return to slow-moving pleasant streams meandering along under the hot sun. Blanche was restless. There had been no possibility of travel during the monsoon, but now, unable to bear any longer the treatment meted out by the Kempeitai to her fellow villagers, she made the decision to return to Rangoon and attempt to rebuild her life. Her in-laws tried to persuade her to stay, but Blanche had seen too many horrors in the village and felt that the only way to escape her nightmares was to get away from that place. It was with a heavy heart that early one morning she said goodbye to the local people who had become her friends. She became tearful as she left her in-laws, and, carrying her belongings on her back, tied tightly in a blanket, she set off with Leslie and Raymond for the railway line, with her brother-in-law to guide her. There was no opportunity to retrieve her buried jewellery, and indeed there was no guarantee that the monsoon hadn't simply washed it away. Blanche and the children had held on to their lives and their health, and that was worth more than all the jewels they were leaving behind. She worried, however, about leaving the place where Manu had last seen her, and made her in-laws promise to let him know of her return to Rangoon if he managed to make contact with them.

It was late in the day by the time they reached the station, and there were no passenger trains. The only vehicle standing at the platform was a goods train full of undernourished livestock. One wagon was empty of animals, its sliding doors ajar. A small number of people were already sitting in the straw, trying to make themselves as comfortable as possible. Blanche put her children in the carriage and climbed in beside them. Minutes later, some Japanese soldiers appeared on the scene and started shouting at the occupants, waving rifles and bamboo sticks at them. Then they attacked Blanche's brother-in-law, beating him with bamboo poles and rifle butts until he lay unconscious on the platform. The soldiers did not try to hurt anyone else. It was as if they were satisfied that someone had paid the price for these civilians travelling on the train. Blanche didn't know what to do. The soldiers would not have allowed her out of the carriage to help him, and at any rate she was too terrified to leave her children. When the train started to pull out of the station, she could only stare in horror at the sight of the curled-up body and wonder what would become of the man who had been so kind and helpful to her and the two boys. She watched for any sign of movement, but soon the platform was out of sight, and she could only pray that he was still alive and would survive. Blanche never saw her brother-in-law again.

So it was that Blanche, Leslie, Raymond and an assortment of strangers began their journey to Rangoon. At night, the carriage was very cold, even with the door shut, and they all shivered and huddled closely together. During the day, the heat inside became intense, and although they opened the doors wide to try to encourage a flow of air, the temperature never seemed to drop. The heat was exhausting, and there was nothing to be done but to try to drift off to sleep. When they reached Rangoon station, they had been travelling for two days, and Blanche was relieved that, after that first, horrendous incident, they had been left alone by guards and railway officials. Even as they left the train, no one made any move to detain them—perhaps they looked too exhausted, grubby and tired to bother with.

Blanche and the children made their way back to their house on 53rd Street to find that it had been thoroughly looted. The Christmas presents were gone, which was only to be expected, but everything that could be taken had been removed, and the house was as bare as the day when Blanche had first moved in. Yet it was home, and as soon as she stepped inside the front door, she felt a weight had been lifted from her shoulders. She had brought some food with her, and after she'd cleaned the house as best she could, she and the children sat down to eat their rice and vegetables. They slept soundly that night.

The next day, Blanche planned to begin searching for her family. But before she could venture out into the streets, her brother Austin turned up at the door. For months, he had been regularly visiting the homes of all his family members in the area in the hope that someone might turn up, and his delight at seeing Blanche and the children alive brought tears of joy to his eyes.

Austin had remained in Rangoon during the worst of the bombing and had seen the triumphal march of the Japanese army down Dalhousie Street. Few Rangoon residents had remained to witness the arrival of the victorious Japanese troops, led by General Sakurai on horseback, but from the shelter of a nearby building Austin had seen the grand spectacle and wondered if his home would ever be the same again. The impressive procession moved north, and some hours later Sakurai had set up his divisional headquarters on the shore of Victoria Lake. The clubhouse of the Rangoon Sailing Club, also situated at the lake, was turned into a convalescent home for wounded Japanese officers. Later, Burma Area Army, formed in the spring of 1943 under Lieutenant General Masakazu Kawabe, located its headquarters at Rangoon University. The campus, Sybil's home in the immediate aftermath of the bombings, became the administrative, tactical and strategic base for the Japanese army in Burma. Many of the officers chose to set up home in the magnificent private properties around Rangoon, while others stayed on campus in the bungalows that dotted the grounds.

Austin had to find a way of making money in this new Rangoon. He had acquired a cycle rickshaw, abandoned by its previous owner, and established a nice business transporting civilians and occasionally Japanese officers to and from their places of work. Although his first instinct was to refuse to take Japanese troops, he realised that this would result in his death. He knew that his only course of action was to accept them as passengers, although he defiantly took longer for each journey and charged considerably more. It was his only way of fighting back.

With the children to feed, Blanche and Austin had to do additional work. Each morning, Blanche would get up early with the children, and with Austin they would search the streets and surrounding areas for wood. Finally, when they had amassed all they could carry, they would make their way home. Austin would then cycle to the centre of Rangoon to pick up passengers. At the house, Blanche would chop the wood into small, manageable pieces of firewood and tie them in bundles of six pieces. In the evening, Austin would return home and then load up his rickshaw with the results of her labours, selling the wood for kindling or bartering it for food and other essentials. 'That was how we managed,' Blanche says simply.

Through the cooler months from October 1942 to February 1943, this was how they got by, scraping a living, with just enough food for all of them. By March, the warmer weather had rendered kindling unnecessary, and things had again begun to change, as Allied prisoners were being moved en masse to unknown destinations south of Moulmein. The shipping lanes from Japan were controlled by the US Navy, and Japan was suffering increasing losses: much-needed men and materials were being lost at sea. The solution that was decided upon was an ambitious project to build a railway line connecting Rangoon and Bangkok. The link was seen as vital for supplying troops and preparing for an invasion of India. Native Burmans were being offered three-month contracts at very reasonable wages if they agreed to work on the construction of the railroad. Many signed up for what was to be the longest three-month contract in history, for once you started work on the railway there was little chance of escape other than in death.

Blanche and Austin knew many men who went to work on the railroad. Some took their wives and children with them, as they had been promised excellent working and living conditions and plentiful supplies of food, something most of the population could only dream of. They never saw any of these men again, and they began to hear rumours about

182

'the railway of death'. Austin began to suffer harassment from the Kempeitai, who thought he should volunteer, but of course he wanted no part in the scheme. 'After that,' Blanche recalls, 'we had to run from Rangoon again. We ran to a village—not far but out of the city.'

CHAPTER EIGHT

1943–46

SYBIL

INDIA

In the summer of 1943, Reid proposed on bended knee, and Sybil, finally won over by his relentless pursuit, said yes. The date was set for 17 August, and the happy couple set about making the occasion as special as possible. Mrs Hemingway, the subaltern, gave the tiered wedding cake; her assistant, Mrs Duckworth, organised and paid for the reception. Reid organised the drinks, of which there was no shortage, and proved a generous host, a trait that was to remain with him for the rest of his life. A local tailor made a beautiful white dress, and the Indian-gold ring was purchased for the princely sum of 13 rupees, about £1.60 in those days. Mr Denman, Reid's great friend, was asked to be best man, while Sybil asked a friend from the hostel, Shireen Mall, to be her bridesmaid. The chaplain was organised to carry out the ceremony, and all was set for the wedding to take place in the large hall in the hostel. Well almost set, for it is traditional to have entertainment after a wedding, and in the end one of Reid's friends, George Barclay from Motherwell, an NCO in the Royal Army Pay Corps, stepped in. The corps had a military band of some distinction, and those highly skilled musicians could be relied upon to play any tune that was in fashion at the time.

In attendance were all Sybil's friends from the hostel and hospital, Mrs Hemingway, Mrs Duckworth, the colonel of Reid's regiment and a few of the captains, along with all Reid's friends and colleagues. They danced the night away with foxtrots, waltzes, military two-steps and Canadian barn dances to the lively sound of the Royal Army Pay Corps band. During that tense time of war, the 50 or so guests found themselves in a strange moment of normality, and they were going to make the most of it. The party went on long into the early hours, and many of the guests were extremely fragile when they reported for duty, some still wearing their wedding outfits.

The only sadness was that the Younis family were unable to attend, and shortly afterwards Sybil lost touch with them. Mr Younis, like many men and women who had first-hand experience of Burma and the Burmese people, was using his knowledge of his country to help the army in their preparations to retake it. This took him away from Meerut for long periods of time, and with Mrs Younis looking after her family and Sybil becoming increasingly busy at the hospital, their meetings were more and more infrequent. Although they had always intended to remain in contact, such were the speed of events and the pace of change taking place around them that it was all they could do to plan their own lives in a situation of turmoil. They had been through so much together since that fateful day in December 1941; they had shared so many experiences, so much sadness and joy. Sybil was sure that had it not been for her second family, and Mr Younis in particular, she would not have survived.

Reid and Sybil moved into the barracks' married quarters—simple but adequate accommodation, with all the amenities that anyone could want. Meals were still taken in the mess, and for a short time Sybil continued to work in the ward master's office, but by the end of November, after a year in the army, she decided to become a full-time wife. In late 1943, her doctor confirmed that Sybil was pregnant. Sybil and Reid looked forward to becoming parents, and plans were made in preparation for the happy event. On 5 March 1944, Sybil gave birth to a son, Ian. He was two months premature, a tiny creature with a shock of black hair. It was several weeks before Sybil was allowed to leave the hospital with Ian, as he had to gain a considerable amount of weight, but he proved more than up to the challenge. Parenthood suited them well, and Ian was a good baby, inquisitive but quiet and calm.

While Meerut was a safe haven, at the front, hundreds of miles to the east, the war was taking a different turn. The Allies had been making successful forays into the territories occupied by the Japanese, with the main offensive starting in Arakan, Burma, in January 1944. Despite strong opposition, the preliminary stages of the attack were very successful, and by late February the Allied troops had inflicted the first major defeat on the Japanese in Burma. This was perhaps the turning point of the campaign. The Japanese, unable to capture much-needed enemy supplies, found themselves short not only of military material but of more basic requirements such as food.

Over the coming months, a series of Japanese offensives intended to gain a foothold in India failed to achieve this result, and they continued to suffer high casualties and loss of vital equipment, with little prospect of reinforcements and materials arriving to alleviate the desperate situation. During April, one of the decisive battles took place at Kohima, where Allied forces were outnumbered by ten to one. The situation looked hopeless, but airborne supply drops and the timely arrival of reinforcements resulted in defeat for the Japanese. At Kohima garrison stands a war memorial of native stone on which is inscribed the famous and poignant epitaph:

187

When you go home,
Tell them of us and say:
For their tomorrow,
We gave our today.

Then came an event that helped the British forces: the monsoon broke. While the Japanese supply lines were stretched to breaking point, with the roads and tracks turned to quagmires, supplies were delivered to the Allies by air. With the monsoon came dysentery and other illnesses, and the undernourished Japanese troops were forced to withdraw. Although they continued to make sporadic attacks south of Imphal, they were unable to make any progress. This did not mean they were a beaten army retreating in disarray, however. The Japanese continued to fight to the death, inflicting high casualties on the Allied forces and causing large numbers of wounded to be withdrawn from the front to military hospitals near the Indian border. It was this rapid increase in wounded that would affect the lives of Sybil and Reid as they moved through 1944 and into 1945.

For the time being, their lives were reassuringly stable in comparison with the uncertainty of the past. In the summer of 1944, Reid was transferred to Agra, and he, Sybil and Ian moved to married quarters in the barracks there. In May 1945, a daughter, Flora Ann, was born in Agra Military Hospital, this time a healthy baby delivered at full term, and with a loud and demanding voice.

By a strange coincidence, while in Agra, Sybil was invited to a tombola, where she met her cousin Irene Fisher's in-laws, who had also fled Burma and were living in the city as refugees. Irene and her husband, Bertie, had been like a mother and father to the Le Fleur girls after they had gone to live at their grandfather's house. They had some good news for Sybil: Irene was alive and living near Calcutta.

In June 1945, shortly after Flora was born, events took an unexpected turn. With the war against the Japanese succeeding and the Allies slowly advancing against determined resistance, the numbers of casualties were reaching a peak, and Reid was transferred to a military hospital near the front to help tend to the increasing numbers of wounded and sick. Although he was working in a hospital and supposedly protected by the Red Cross insignia, it was nonetheless a dangerous environment, and the number of casualties and the nature of their injuries left the medical staff constantly exhausted. Reid was surrounded by wounded boys no older than himself whose lives had been changed forever by the conflict. He had to remind himself that these were the lucky ones, that many would never return home. He received regular letters from Sybil and wrote back to her as much as time permitted. It was those letters that kept him going, along with the thought that it couldn't last forever and he would soon be reunited with his beautiful wife and his son and daughter.

Sybil had her hands full, looking after two small children, but each day they gave her indescribable joy. She would sing them to sleep the way her mother had done for her, and when she trimmed their nails, she would recite the same poem that she had listened to as a child. Holding the tiny hand and beginning with the thumbnail, she cut each in turn, finishing with the little finger.

This is the father, good and kind,
This is the mother, gentle and mild,
This is the brother, grown so tall,
This is the sister, never seen without a doll,
This is the baby, still to grow,
And that's the whole family, standing in a row.

In one of her letters, Sybil told her husband about the excitement of discovering a large snake, some 4 ft long, in the bathroom of their house. She called for their servant to come quickly, and he was shocked to see a krait lying comfortably in the bath. Its scales were black and a drab light brown, and it seemed to be drowsy. He warned Sybil to keep the children out of the way because the snake was deadly poisonous—its venom could kill within a short period of time. He picked it up just behind its head and took it outside, where he hit it repeatedly on the head with a heavy stick until it was dead.

On 1 May, after years of fighting in Burma, Rangoon was at last recaptured. It had taken more than three years, but the city was finally free. The fighting was brutal. The Japanese refused to be taken prisoner, and with the fall of Rangoon their retreat became more disorganised. Without strong leadership, lacking food and ammunition, and with monsoon rains making movement difficult, the Japanese forces were pursued mercilessly by Allied troops led by the Gurkhas. On 6 August, Lord Louis Mountbatten, Supreme Allied Commander South East Asia Theatre, declared the campaign to be won. The Japanese army had lost almost 200,000 soldiers.

Since March, the Americans had been firebombing Japanese cities, causing immense destruction and loss of life. Then, on the day the Burma campaign was won, an atom bomb was dropped on Hiroshima by the United States. Three days later, a second nuclear attack targeted Nagasaki. On the 14th, Japan surrendered unconditionally.

After the war's end, Reid had remained at a forward hospital helping with the sick and wounded. Normally, Sybil received several letters each week, although they invariably took some time to reach her. She looked forward to these letters, keeping them and reading them over and over. She would reply with enthusiasm, for she loved and missed Reid and his silly humour that made her laugh even when times were sad. But some months after the end of the war, she stopped receiving replies from him. The fact that his letters had been so regular and always positive, asking about life at the barracks, the children and his friends, gave Sybil even more cause for concern, as she knew he enjoyed writing to her and loved receiving her letters even more.

In November, nearly sick with worry, Sybil confided her worst fears to her neighbour, and she suggested that Sybil go to the main office to ask the military for information. Not wasting any time, Sybil went straight away, leaving her neighbour in charge of the children. There, she blurted out her concerns for her husband to the officer in charge, and such was the level of her anxiety that the officer agreed to put through a call right away. It was, however, some time before they received an answer to the question of her husband's whereabouts.

The reply was not encouraging. All the officer was able to tell her was that her husband had been invalided back to Britain because of the nature of his injuries. She later discovered that his condition had been very serious. He had been bitten on the leg by a poisonous snake. He had fallen into a coma and been taken to a hospital in Bombay and then shipped back to Britain. For several weeks, he had not been able to communicate because he had been delirious, fighting to stay alive. The hospital ship had docked at Southampton, and he had been transferred immediately to a military hospital in

Surrey, where he began a slow recovery. The officer reassured Sybil that she would be reunited with her husband and that he would begin to make the necessary arrangements. She was asked to return to the office the next day.

For the first time since she had come to India, Sybil was filled with foreboding and uncertainty. Suddenly, the reassuringly settled life that she had grown to love was thrown into turmoil, and her emotions almost overwhelmed her. She was afraid for her husband, afraid for her children and afraid for herself, but, as she always tried to do, she maintained an air of calmness and strength. Her neighbour told her to ask for as early a return date as possible: previous experience had shown that if you said you wanted to travel in February, it was often March or April before you actually set off. Such were the logistics of wartime transportation. With everyone at the barracks office doing everything possible to reunite the family, it simply became a matter of waiting.

Christmas 1945 was a lonely time for Sybil and the children. Although friends surrounded them and everyone did their utmost to keep her spirits high, she wondered what would become of her young family. The events of Christmas 1941 had caused her to reflect on the happy Christmases of her childhood, spent with her parents and grandparents, with Austin, Eunice and especially Blanche. Christmas 1942 had brought home the realisation that she had survived a truly terrible ordeal. Christmas 1943 had been undeniably happy: it was the first with her new husband, and they had a baby on the way. Christmas 1944 was another joyous occasion, which she and Reid had celebrated with their small son Ian and their many friends, with Sybil again pregnant. Now, with the war over, after thinking that all her unhappiness had been left behind, Christmas 1945 had brought all the uncertainty back. Hogmanay, which Reid always made a significant event in the family calendar, passed with little joy.

In early January, Sybil was called to the office to be told that her travel orders and papers had come through. She was to go with her children to Bombay and join her ship, MS *Batory*, on 19 January for the voyage to Britain. With their departure less than two weeks away, there was much to do. Everything essential was kept near at hand while other items were packed in a large trunk ready for shipment. By 16 January, all the arrangements had been made, and Sybil had packed everything carefully. They were taken by car down to Agra station, and when all their possessions were loaded into the goods van, they said their farewells to the small group of friends who had accompanied them. Sybil was a wanderer with an adventurous nature, and this looked like being the start of an even more exciting journey; nonetheless, the passage to a new life was a daunting prospect, one that filled her with uncertainty.

The two-day trip to Bombay was completed without a hitch, and it proved a pleasant start to their adventure. The four-berth cabin was clean and more than spacious enough for Sybil, Ian and baby Flora, and food and water, including an abundance of fresh fruit, were available to buy at all the stations en route. On the afternoon of 18 January, they arrived in Bombay and travelled to the docks, where they boarded the MS *Batory*, a large, two-funnelled luxury liner with a black hull and grey superstructure, and were shown to a cabin on the lower deck. Two other girls joined Sybil and the children in their cabin, but there was plenty of room for everyone. Their luggage was soon stowed, and Sybil was able to relax and take in their new surroundings. The *Batory*, named after a sixteenth-century Polish king, was an ocean-going liner of over 14,000 tons. During the war, it had taken evacuees from Britain to Canada and Australia, acted as a hospital ship and transported troops, sailing in the dangerous waters of the Baltic and Barents seas, the Atlantic, Mediterranean, Indian and Pacific oceans. Although by no means a fast ship, it had proved utterly reliable. The *Batory* had been part of many a convoy targeted by bombers and submarines but had never sustained as much as a scratch, earning the nickname 'the Lucky Ship'. Despite the six years of military service, it remained a luxurious liner, with fine cabins, wide decks for sunbathing, smart decor and remarkably good food.

They set sail on 19 January as planned, and Sybil and the children were content. It was nice to walk on deck and feel the wind in your face. She would often sit out and watch the white caps of the waves and the swell of the sea. The food was excellent and included traditional dishes prepared by the Polish crew. The children behaved themselves well during the trip and were popular with the crew. Sybil would read to her children from the books she had found on board, and at night she would sing them to sleep, just as her mother and generations of mothers had done.

One of the others in their cabin, an Anglo-Indian girl, was not having such a good time of it. From the moment they cleared the harbour at Bombay, she was seasick, and this continued for the whole journey. The poor girl was only able to take fluids, and much of what she did get down found its way back up again. Sybil worried that she might not even have the strength to get to her feet when they reached their destination.

The first leg of their journey took them west across the Indian Ocean to the Gulf of Aden and thence into the Red Sea, a journey that took the best part of seven days. The weather was perfect, and the evenings were pleasantly cool, which meant that Sybil and the children slept well. To add icing to the cake, the sea was flat and calm all the way to Suez, where they travelled along the 101 miles of the canal. Sybil would sit for hours watching the camel, oxen, goats, dogs and their owners going about their business at the edge of a desert that seemed to stretch forever into the distance. The ship stopped at Port Said to take on provisions, stores and parts to ensure the smooth running of the ship. Some of the passengers went ashore briefly, but Sybil stayed on board with the children. She thought the canal was quite incredible, an amazing feat of engineering cutting straight through the desert. The sight of land on both sides was comforting. At Port Said, she saw the statue of Ferdinand de Lesseps, the French engineer whose vision and skill led to the creation of the canal. He stood proudly on a column with his right arm extended and his hand pointing to the east, the direction from which she had come. She hoped it wasn't an omen telling her to turn back.

The ship sailed on, south of Malta, along the coast of North Africa and through the Strait of Gibraltar, getting a good view of the Rock from the deck. The further west they travelled, the rougher the seas became, and the weather turned noticeably cooler. Still Sybil enjoyed the fresh air and the freedom of walking around the deck with her children. Still her cabin companion was sick, lying on her bed looking deathly pale and growing weaker by the day. The ship headed north, and Sybil heard from a crew member that, because of worsening weather, the ship was not going to go across the Bay of Biscay but instead stick more closely to the coastline. This would make the journey longer, but it was by making decisions such as this, Sybil presumed, that the captain ensured his ship remained lucky.

On 19 February 1946, exactly a month after they'd set off, they docked on the Clyde in Glasgow. The plan had been to come into Southampton, but the captain's orders had been changed, so they sailed north to Scotland, which suited Sybil very well. Her first day on Scottish soil was to be postponed for a short time, as the medical officer who had joined the ship when it entered Scottish waters had found a number of children with suspected chicken pox, and so the *Batory* lay at anchor by the quayside with its quarantine flags flying, and no one able to get on or off. It was snowing heavily and of course rather chilly, but to Sybil and the children, this was magical. She had never seen or felt snow before, and it was better than she had ever imagined from the books she had read or Christmas carols she had sung. She didn't feel the cold at all, and in fact she already felt quite at home.

When the quarantine was eventually lifted the next day, Sybil was amazed to see her seasick friend get straight off her bed and walk off the ship carrying her belongings. It was an amazing recovery, and Sybil stared in disbelief.

She was to be met in Glasgow by her mother-in-law, Flora, and Reid's sister Janet, and although she was apprehensive, she was looking forward to getting to know them. She was also excited at the thought of being reunited with Reid, who by this time would have been discharged from hospital and sent home. It was mid-morning when Sybil and the children, with their few possessions, walked down the gangplank and into the arms of their new Scottish family.

BLANCHE

NORTH OF RANGOON

In the village to which Blanche had fled in the spring of 1943 was a house owned by an Anglo-Indian woman named Mrs Innes. She took Blanche and Austin in and helped to look after the children. During the day, Austin was forced to work for the Japanese rebuilding bomb-damaged roads and railway lines nearby. From early morning until darkness fell, he would carry earth in wicker baskets, or sometimes on stretchers made of two bamboo poles with a hessian sack suspended across them, a method that required two people and a certain degree of coordination. Sometimes Austin would be given a chunkle, an Asian hoe. This was a wooden-shafted implement with a sharp metal head that was used to break up soil. It was backbreaking work, and even rough, calloused hands would be covered in blisters by the end of the day. Occasionally, they had to remove stands of bamboo by digging with picks and shovels, and if that didn't work, the last resort was blasting them with dynamite.

Austin would return home exhausted, covered in earth and mud. After a meal consisting of rice and whatever else they managed to get their hands on, they would sit out on the veranda and sing to keep their spirits up. 'The food was not so bad,' recalls Blanche. 'We had wild pigs and ducks, and we had fresh duck and hens' eggs. We did have some meat, although the cows and water buffalo were a bit thin. There was plenty of fresh fruit on the trees and bushes, and we picked what we needed.'

The Japanese soldiers made the villagers clear their gardens; there was to be no grass or shrubs of any kind, only bare earth. They were also made to catch rats. Both tasks were probably intended to prevent the spread of disease, although the Japanese never told them why they had to do these things. 'We were all given rat traps, and they gave us a coupon for each rat we caught. We could exchange the coupons for extra rice. If us women didn't catch enough rats one day, we were just threatened and warned to do better tomorrow, but the men were given terrible beatings.' For day after day, they caught rats for the Japanese, and Austin worked until he was exhausted and his ribs were clearly visible. The skin of his face was stretched tight over his cheekbones, and his arms and legs were as thin as sticks.

'We made a shelter under the house, and we felt very safe in there because it was surrounded by lots of tall trees—bamboo, banyan. One day, British planes came. We thought we would be bombed. We went to our shelter, but nothing happened. They only flew low over the village, so we came out again and pretended we weren't afraid. They returned the next day, flying low, and they dropped bombs nearby, close to the road and the railway line. I prayed Austin would be all right.'

These raids continued from March until June, and the damage caused to railways, roads and bridges meant that the workers were under constant pressure to repair and reconstruct. Working alongside the Burmese were prisoners of war, held in a camp close to the village, and it was impossible not to be moved by the sight of these men. Blanche could see that many of them were little older than her. Some looked like walking skeletons. One day, she heard a voice coming from the barred window of a prison building. It was an English voice, so she stopped and talked for a short while. The next day, she brought Burmese cheroots and matches and passed them through the bars before walking quickly on.

'They used to talk to me through the bars,

and I didn't know how dangerous it was. I used to buy them bidis and put them through the bars or throw them across the wire, and they were very happy. Whenever I could give them food, I would throw that over too—a sweet potato, some vegetables, some extra rice. They would smile and be very polite and well mannered. It made me weep to see them so thin. They always had so much work to do, and they were beaten a lot by the guards.'

These prisoners suffered the same tortures and beatings that she had witnessed before, and sometimes she would see a prisoner standing to attention, with the sun beating down on him, being forced to hold a large boulder above his head or at arm's length. If he dropped it, he would be beaten with bamboo canes. Few prisoners tried to escape: the camp was surrounded by dense jungle with its own dangers, and many Burmese were still sympathetic towards the Japanese and would not aid any escapees. Those who did escape and who were recaptured were returned to camp and some were beheaded as a warning to the other prisoners.

The Japanese spotted Blanche giving food or bidis to the POWs on several occasions, but other than making threatening noises and gestures, they did nothing to stop her. She would often walk slowly past the compound, talking to the soldiers, and they would tell her where they came from: England, Wales,

Scotland, Canada, Australia, New Zealand, Holland—names of places she had read about as a schoolgirl. Blanche was intrigued by the tattoos that covered many of these men: dragons, snakes, crucifixes and hearts, with the names of wives or sweethearts entwined. She came to know their names. Some she knew by their proper names, while others called themselves by their nicknames: Chalky, Nobby, Taff, Mac, Jock. These men looked so fragile but so proud. She promised herself that in future she would do all in her power to help them, no matter how small or insignificant her efforts might prove.

The monsoons came again, bringing with them death and disease. The rain turned the earth into a morass, and despite the exhortations to '*Hayaku, hayaku!*' (often anglicised to 'Speedo, speedo!'), progress on road and rail repairs slowed down. Beatings were more frequent, and Austin would often return home with cuts and bruises. There was no point in complaining, though, for tomorrow would no doubt bring more of the same.

No bombers came over during the monsoon, and it seemed as if the war had gone quiet. Now it was simply a case of surviving. Blanche made sure she boiled all their water, cooked everything extra carefully, kept the children inside and abandoned the search for rats. If the Japanese wanted rats, they would have to catch them themselves. Blanche knew that the vermin, like the monsoons, carried disease, and she wasn't going to let anything happen to her children.

Even in the worst of weather she would walk to the POW camp if she had anything to give and felt it was safe to do so, and the prisoners would blow her kisses. Conditions were appalling. The rain had rotted the tattered uniforms until most of the POWs had only shorts or a loincloth that they referred to as a 'jap-happy'. Leather boots had long since disintegrated, and some men had fashioned footwear out of pieces of old tyre. Others just put up with the feeling of mud on their ulcerating limbs. Some had legs and feet so swollen it made movement almost impossible. This was a symptom of beri beri, which more often than not proved lethal: the body drowned in its own fluid.

The incessant rain turned the area into a swamp and the prisoners looked more exhausted than ever before. Each time Blanche went to the camp, there seemed to be a few faces missing. Disease spread, cholera, dysentery and malaria took their toll and some finally succumbed to the beatings they received. The graveyard beside the camp seemed to be the only thing that was thriving.

A handful of elephants had been brought in to do some of the heavy work. The animals had been used in the Burmese teak plantations for hundreds of years. Each one was brought up by a handler, called an 'oozie'. The more docile and easily handled elephants had wooden bells around their necks, while the more volatile and aggressive creatures had large iron bells, so that they could be heard from a long way off. The bells had their own distinctive tones to enable each handler to recognise his elephant's sound. A strong bond grew between an elephant and its oozie, and they depended on each other to get the job done safely. Not all the handlers survived the outbreaks of disease, and when an elephant's oozie was gone, it cried and bellowed with anguish or rage and would do no more heavy lifting.

Time passed, but life in the village was monotonous. Even the regular sing-songs failed to lift the spirits. The rain fell in endless torrents and the season seemed to go on forever. Blanche counted the days. And then, in early October, it was as if someone simply turned off a tap. The rains stopped, and they had survived another monsoon. Work was stepped up a gear and 'speedo' was the order of the day. The Japanese redoubled their efforts with the rat traps, encouraged the villagers to reach their quotas once more, with failure to do so bringing more beatings for the men.

Blanche continued to make her journey to the camp, occasionally managing to smuggle a pumpkin or marrow to them along with the usual cheroots. Sometimes, if new guards were on duty, they would fire shots in her general direction, and although at first she would duck in fright and shock, she came to believe that if the soldiers really wanted to kill her, then they would have no trouble doing so. She admired the men behind the wire. No matter how appalling the conditions or how ill they looked, they still smiled at her. 'The war truly brought out the best and the worst in mankind.'

By December, some prisoners were being moved to other areas and the remainder were forced to work longer and harder, until they dropped. They would then be prodded with bayonets or beaten to make them start again. Austin was barely able to continue, and after he received a particularly harsh beating, Blanche decided it was time she, Austin and the two boys returned to the city. That night, they crept silently out of the village and, travelling only by the light of the moon, made their way south towards Rangoon. When the sun came up, they slept in the shade of a dense thicket of bamboo, waking only to eat what little food they had and drink fresh water. Another night of travelling and they were on the outskirts of Rangoon. When daylight came, they made their way, trying to look confident and purposeful, to the house of their father's brother Mervyn and his wife, May.

When Aunt May opened the door, she was surprised to see Blanche, Austin and the children, and shocked by their bedraggled and emaciated appearance. She welcomed them in, and they all sat together in the front room while Blanche and Austin told of what had happened to them since the bombing of December 1941, almost two years ago. May gave the boys two pieces of chocolate she had saved. It was the first time they had tasted anything so delicious.

Mervyn had fled to Prome after the invasion, but living with May were several of their relatives, and they all worked for the Japanese as forced labour. Some laboured at the docks, loading and unloading large cargo vessels; others repaired roads or worked in demolition, making bombed-out buildings safe. It was agreed that, to avoid suspicion, Austin would join the gang of workers at the docks with Eunice's husband, Stanley. In the immediate aftermath of the December bombing, Stanley had sent Eunice and their infant daughter to her Uncle Eric in Prome. He had remained behind to help look after Mervyn's house. By the time he had decided he ought to flee north, it was too late and he was unable to escape.

That Christmas, the family celebrated together. Perhaps the decorations were not as grand as before, and perhaps the laughter and singing were not as loud or as hearty, but at least they felt they belonged together. On 31 December 1943, they saw in the New Year and prayed that the war would end soon.

'I thought of the previous two years, running from place to place, singing and dancing to make ourselves happy. And then we all spoke of the rest of our family, and we became sad wondering where they all were. It made our hearts weep to think they might be dead—Irene, Eunice, our uncles and aunts and their children. I wondered what had happened to Sybil, why she hadn't come home that day. Why couldn't she have been more organised and finished her Christmas shopping earlier? It made me so angry and so very sad.'

From the kitchen of the house, a large military establishment could be seen quite clearly. Many of the buildings had been bombed, but the parade ground was intact apart from a few craters. From time to time, Blanche and Aunt May were able to see soldiers carrying out their drills, marching in step across the concrete. One day in January 1944, there was a much larger turnout of troops than usual. The soldiers of the Indian National Army, a force supported by the Japanese and initially recruited from Indian prisoners of war, stood to attention in the centre of the ground. A military vehicle arrived, and an officer began his inspection, walking along each row, occasionally pausing to talk to an individual. Blanche recognised the man as the leader of the INA, Subhas Chandra Bose, a major figure in the movement for Indian independence from Britain.

Days became warmer and nights were hot and sticky. The men would return from work exhausted, and, after a wash, they would have a meal of rice—always rice—and whatever else they had. After their evening meal, the family would sit out on the veranda, and in the clear moonlight they would sing their favourite songs. Austin played the mouth organ and Stanley the guitar. One night, as they sang and strummed, a Japanese officer came up to the house. His presence made everyone nervous, but he gestured for them to continue and sat for a while before taking his leave. He returned several nights later, and this time he stayed longer, just listening and smiling. After that, he became a fairly regular visitor to the musical sessions on the veranda. Sometimes, when he knew the songs, he would join in. He had been educated in America, he told them, and had returned to Japan in 1939, just before the outbreak of war in Europe. He was the eldest son of a *shishaku*, a viscount, and he told them that if he made it through the war, he would inherit the title on the death of his father. He seemed most uncertain of his chances of survival.

'He was a very nice man, very quiet and well mannered. He would show us pictures of his family and grow sad. He had a letter from his son saying that he was top of the class now and that he was doing his best for the family and for the Emperor. He asked his daddy to come home soon because they all missed him. He became very quiet when he showed us that, and I think he felt lost, just as we felt lost. He knew no more about what his fate would be than we did

209

about ours. He missed his family just as we missed ours. He had a broken heart just as we had broken hearts. Sometimes I could see tears in his eyes. Then he would get up and leave, and we all felt a great sadness for what the world had become. He was a good man.'

The officer made regular visits, bringing little treats for the children and food for everyone. It was almost as if he had adopted another family because he could not be at home with his kin. He stopped coming when the monsoons arrived. There was a rumour that many Japanese soldiers had been sent north to the Indian front.

Throughout the city, parties of Allied soldiers from the prisons were forced to work repairing bombed buildings, roads and railways and unloading grain from the few ships that entered the port. Blanche always gave them cigarettes and any food she could spare.

This monsoon was the same as so many others: days of endless rain and interminable boredom. When the workers returned in the evening, they were soaked to the skin, and many had fevers. Blanche thought of the prisoners she had helped back in the village to the north and wondered if she had betrayed them by leaving them for the comparative safety of Rangoon. She prayed that they would survive.

News came that the British had re-entered Burma and were advancing south, but it might all be just rumour, and work went on as before.

The only evidence for a change in the tide of war was that fewer ships were entering the docks to be unloaded.

As 1944 drew to a close, Blanche and her family were no nearer to discovering their fate. Then the air raids started in earnest. 'It was very monotonous, dull, sickening. Every time there was a raid, it was the same old routine: put your lights out, close your doors, and don't run out into the road. We used to hear them, the planes. The Japanese planes, the drone was very light and high-pitched; the British planes, the drone was very deep and heavy like a throaty roar. We knew which were which. We had a big house, and in the yard was a huge banyan tree. When the raids came, I used to run around the banyan tree, to the opposite side from the planes. Auntie May would sit on the porch smoking her cigar. I used to shout at her, "What are you doing? I am safe. You are not safe sitting there smoking. They can see the light of your cigar." So dangerous, she was . . . she never stopped smoking her big long cigars.'

One night during a raid, Blanche ran out of the house and made for her banyan tree only to get a terrible fright when she nearly tripped over an emaciated cow, which had evidently also decided that under the banyan was as good a place as any to be at a time like this.

That spring, the bombing raids intensified and the family, with the exception of Auntie May, who continued to sit on the veranda defiantly

211

smoking her cigars, took to the shelters for longer and longer periods of time. 'I used to smoke. I was so afraid, I took to smoking. I would go down to the trench, with the milk tin with a candle in it that we used for a light, and I'd take a cigar with me. When it rained, the trench filled with water, and we'd have to put the children in a cot just above the level of the water. Then we'd settle ourselves down, and I would smoke. Once there were Japanese in our trench. They were spies, I think. They knew that our spies used to show torches during air raids to help guide the bombers, so the Japanese would send their people to the shelters. These Japanese told me to put out my cigar, but I told them, "What harm am I doing? I am doing nothing, leave me alone." They shut up after that. I had suffered so much for so long, and I couldn't take any more of their comments.'

The bombing affected the family's lives more and more. 'We stopped going to the market. There were no radios, no newspapers, but there were always lots of rumours: "There's going to be another bombing raid." Well, that was no surprise—they happened so often. "The Japanese are going to shoot so-and-so." The rumours went on. The British kept advancing, and the Japanese couldn't believe it. The bombers kept coming, wave after wave, wave after wave. There was no time to cook or eat or do anything. We were always in the trench. The minute we got out, there would be another air raid, which showed they were getting very near. We used to watch the dogfights, when the searchlights pierced the night sky. It was so beautiful, the planes caught in the searchlights. They would dive and weave and climb, trying to escape the beam of light. Puffs of smoke would appear in the sky around the planes. We used to watch, never thinking of the danger.'

Towards the end of April, the streets of Rangoon became dangerous as looting and lawlessness broke out. Blanche and the children remained indoors until things quietened down. In early May, the Gurkhas entered Rangoon, and Blanche witnessed the ferocity with which they fought. She watched as with one blow of his kukri a Gurkha severed the head of a Japanese soldier. Blanche was sickened by the sight.

'The Japanese were terrified of the Gurkhas. They were excellent jungle fighters and very ruthless. We would hear stories of thousands of Japanese soldiers being killed each week. The Gurkhas always looked so happy. I was given a kukri by one of them. It had a short, curved blade, and it was razor sharp. I don't know why he gave it to me. I said, "No, I don't want it, it's dangerous," but he insisted, so I took it. I used it to chop firewood later on, after the war. I still have it.'

By the middle of May, the city was once more a safe place to be. Rangoon was back in Allied hands. The troops marched smartly down Dalhousie Street, and it was a magnificent sight.

'When the British came in, it was wonderful. They used to march down the streets singing "It's a Long Way to Tipperary", but they would change the words and sing "It's a long way to tickle Mary", and they would laugh and tell us not to mind their words because they were just for fun. Some of the songs had quite rude words—I don't think they were the original ones!'

Although the sight of the Allied soldiers was one that gladdened the heart of Blanche and her family, she couldn't help but pity them. 'I felt so sorry for the soldiers. They looked so tired and dirty. Their uniforms were caked with mud and their faces were grubby and streaked with rain. They wore battered bush hats with rips and tears in them. I don't suppose they could wash or change their clothes when they were fighting, and they'd had to fight through the worst of weathers. They were very nice to us. There were English and Scots and many, many Indians, and of course there were Welsh, lots of Welsh. The British taught us a lot of songs: "Lili Marlene", "The White Cliffs of Dover", "It's a Lovely Day Tomorrow", "When They Sound the Last All-Clear". We all used to sing them together. Such beautiful songs they were. We were very happy. But even then, just as we thought it was over, the young Burmese boys had to get ready to go and fight the enemy and drive them out of our country.'

Not all the news was good for Blanche's

family. The monsoon that year was particularly bad, and it proved one rainy season too far for many of the starving and undernourished. Two of the regulars at their evening sing-song passed away, victims of cholera, dysentery and fatigue. One was Stanley, Blanche's brother-in-law. He was a mild-mannered, gentle man who had endured three years of hardship, inadequate food, forced labour and beatings, and he succumbed to illness with the end of the war only a matter of weeks away.

As the war had drawn on, Aung San had become disillusioned with the Japanese. He had formed the AFO (Anti-Fascist Organisation) and had led an insurrection in the Burmese forces. Now those troops, renamed the Patriotic Burmese Forces, were fighting with the British and Aung San was negotiating with them for freedom from colonial rule. On 19 June 1945, in the liberated city of Rangoon, his wife, Daw Khin Kyi, gave birth to a daughter Aung San Suu Kyi, who would become a political leader in her own right.

By June, the Japanese forces were in disarray, but they continued to put up resistance. 'Then, one day, we heard that Hiroshima had been bombed. It was 6 August, I think. Three days later Nagasaki was destroyed, almost half the city was flattened. Winston Churchill was a good man. When they dropped the atom bomb, we were so happy because it brought an end to the war.'

The terms of the surrender agreement were decided on and it was signed at 1.42 a.m. on 28 August in Singapore; symbolic ceremonies were held thereafter. On 12 September in Singapore, General Seishiro Itagaki signed the surrender of the Southern Army; the following day, Major General Jiro Ichida signed the surrender of Burma Area Army; and on 20 October, a formal surrender ceremony took place at the Judson Baptist College on the University of Rangoon campus. At this ceremony the commander-in-chief of Burma Area Army at the time of the surrender, General Heitaro Kimura, and his senior officers handed their swords to Lieutenant General Montagu Stopford and other senior officers of the South East Asia Command.

CHAPTER NINE

1946–58

SYBIL

ELLON, SCOTLAND

On the quayside at Glasgow, Sybil, Ian and Flora were greeted by a girl a little younger than Sybil and a woman with a wide smile and arms held open to hug her and the children. They were Reid's sister Janet, a medical student at Aberdeen University, and their mother, Flora. Once introductions had been made and Sybil had asked about her husband and how he was recovering, they hailed a taxi to take them to the railway station for the trip north to Aberdeen. The huge steam locomotive was hitched to six dark-blue-and-maroon-liveried coaches, and it hissed and puffed gently as it lay at rest. The occasional escape of steam produced a white cloud in the cold winter's air. It was late afternoon when they set off. Once they were out of the city, the landscape was covered in snow. It looked like the Christmas cards Sybil had seen in the shops in Rangoon. The compartment was warm and snug, and she looked around at the wood panelling, the well-upholstered seats, three to each side, at her new sister-in-law and mother-in-law and wondered what new adventures she would have. They had brought sandwiches for the journey north and prepared flasks of tea, and in their comfortable surroundings they settled down to a tasty spread. Soon after they'd finished eating, the children drifted off to sleep with their heads on Janet's and Flora's laps, and they looked so peaceful and safe. It wasn't long before Sybil dropped off to sleep herself.

It was the early hours when the train pulled into Aberdeen station. There to greet them on the platform were Reid, his cousin Pat and another cousin by marriage, Willie, who owned a taxi firm in Ellon. He had come to give them a lift—quite a kindness in that era of petrol shortages. It was a moment of great excitement as Sybil and her husband were reunited after nine months apart. The journey to Ellon, through deep snowdrifts and along roads reduced to a single lane, was completed slowly and safely, and soon they had arrived in the drive of the family home, Brackenridge. The children were asleep, so Reid and Janet carried them into the house and up the stairs to the beds that had been prepared for them. Pat and Willie said their goodbyes, Flora and Janet went off to bed, and Reid and Sybil stayed up and talked, as they had much to catch up on. Reid explained what had happened to him. Although he had been unconscious for much of the time, he had been able to fill in the gaps from what he had been told. Sybil told Reid about their friends, what the children had been doing and her journey on the MS *Batory*, and by the time they fell asleep, it was late morning.

When the couple awoke in the afternoon, the children were downstairs playing with their granny, her sister Mary Ann, always known as Great-Aunt Tan, and Janet. There were toys and books everywhere, and they all seemed to be having a wonderful time. The rest of the day was spent talking about the time Sybil and Reid had spent apart, as well as entertaining the children, who had really taken to their new relatives. That night, Sybil had an introduction to Flora's cooking, with a wonderful spread of roast beef, Yorkshire pudding and all the trimmings. It helped that the family were farmers and butchers in and around Ellon, although this did make her husband very fussy about his meat, which explained his hatred of bully-beef.

The next day, Janet went back to university and Reid went to work part time with his cousin in the butcher's shop until he too would resume his studies at the end of the summer. Leaving the children with Flora and Aunt Tan, Sybil went off exploring her new home. Brackenridge was a fine house situated on the outskirts of Ellon and accessed by a private road. On the right-hand side of the circular gravel drive was a large garage. At the end of the drive stood

Brackenridge, a large white house set in two acres of woodland and lawns. As she walked round the outside, feeling the snow scrunch beneath her shoes, Sybil thought the surroundings were perfect. The front of the house overlooked fields, hills and the River Ythan, where Reid had played as a child. A formal flower garden and a rockery stretched from the path at the front of the house down to the boundary wall, where large rhododendron bushes and rowan trees stood. The imposing front door was flanked by windows, and on the gravel path a wooden bench was covered with pure white snow.

The gravel path continued round to the side of the house, where Sybil found two dark-green doors next to the back door. The first opened to reveal heaps of glistening lumps of coal, and behind the second door was a storage shed for bicycles, badminton sets, croquet equipment and other games to be played on the lawn. There was also an outside toilet, which was used mostly by the gardener but also came in handy for those playing outside. With the shortages of war, the most notable feature of the toilet was the paper: neatly torn squares of newspaper were threaded on a loop of string and hung on a nail. A formal lawn stretched between the house and the garage, and beyond it stood woodland of tall trees, with paths and walks set into the rocky and hilly landscape. To the rear of the house was a huge expanse of wild garden, which included a bamboo patch. The ornamental bamboo, slender and attractive with small delicate leaves, was tiny in comparison with what Sybil was used to, but somehow it made her feel more at home. She walked slowly down the front steps to the path by the flower garden, listening to the snow under her feet and appreciating for the first time the reassuring sensation of walking on compacted snowflakes. She carefully made her way down to the rhododendron bushes and back up to the side of the house before returning via the lawn to the back door. It was so quiet and peaceful, and at that moment she felt strongly the contrast with her previous life.

Inside, the large inviting lounge, dining room and sitting room were delightfully furnished, with antiques and soft, warm carpets. The dark wood reminded Sybil of home, but she had never seen a house with so many paintings hanging on the walls. In the sitting room was a highly polished Broadwood grand piano, and from the windows the views were of woodland and beautiful rhododendron bushes. Upstairs, there were four bedrooms, and Reid, Sybil and the children shared Reid's old bedroom, large enough to accommodate all in comfort. It was all very welcoming, although it was quite different from any home she had known in Burma.

Sybil spent the first few days exploring the grounds and relaxing listening to the radio. Reid was just as amusing as ever and life was fun again. The arrival of Sybil, an exotic war bride, in a small Scottish town generated some interest and it wasn't long before a reporter from the local newspaper came to interview her for an article they wanted to publish, asking her what she thought of her new country and how the children were settling in.

Although she was a skilled seamstress, an ability she shared with her mother-in-law, Sybil had only very basic culinary skills. In her childhood and youth, her meals had been cooked by servants, and after her marriage to Reid the family had eaten in the mess. In Scotland, however, she would have to cook for her husband and children. Flora was a superb cook and baker, and so the tuition began.

During the next few months, Sybil learned to make sponges, shortbread, Scotch pancakes, trifles and two treats made almost entirely of sugar and guaranteed to rot your teeth: tablet and fudge. She was taught to cook mince and tatties, Irish stew, steak-and-kidney pies and puddings, roast beef and Yorkshire pudding, roast lamb, boiled and baked ham, liver and onions, soups, sauces and Reid's beloved porridge. Eating porridge was something of a ritual with him, and Sybil had to soak the oats overnight and get up early to cook it the next morning. Being near the coast, they also had an abundance of fresh fish, and Sybil learned to bake, boil, poach, fry and grill every fish available from the small van that

222

came every Thursday. That first summer, the fruit and vegetable crops were abundant and Flora taught her daughter-in-law how to make jams and jellies, preserves and pickles, compotes and chutneys. Afternoon teas were a very grand affair, with scones, pancakes, rock cakes, sponges and all kinds of jams, as well as thick clotted cream. Gradually, Sybil learned to cook at least as well as her teacher; sometimes, Flora would let Sybil do the cooking and baking for them all, and no one would notice the difference. Flora had lots of friends, and they were never short of company. The kettle was always on the range so a cup of tea could be brewed instantly. The two women had in common a great love of dressmaking, sewing and knitting, and they would sit together for hours in companionable silence, working on new clothes for the children or on a particularly complicated piece of embroidery. Between them, they created a wardrobe of skirts and dresses for Sybil that were the envy of their friends, combining the current fashions with practical materials, such as bright tartans, that Flora had kept for emergencies.

Flora also taught her daughter-in-law new songs and little distractions to amuse the children. One of the lullabies was 'Coulter's Candy', an old Scottish lullaby that Flora had sung to her children when they were babies. Sybil would make Ian and Flora laugh when she played with their fat toes and recited one of her new rhymes:

223

This little piggy went to market,
This little piggy stayed at home,
This little piggy had roast beef,
This little piggy had none,
And this little piggy went wee, wee, wee, all
the way home.

By May 1946, Sybil was carrying her and
Reid's third child. During that hot summer,
when she wasn't cooking, baking and sewing
and Reid wasn't working, they would travel to
Aberdeen on the bus from the stop near the end
of the road leading to Brackenridge. It was an
Alexander's bus, cream-coloured with a blue
roof and a picture of a bluebird in flight on the
side. They would go shopping or sightseeing,
and sometimes they would take the tram to
Codona's Amusement Park on the wide Beach
Boulevard. Sybil loved the waltzers and the big
dipper, the ghost train and the haunted house.
They would treat themselves to candyfloss and
toffee apples, and life didn't get much better
than walking arm in arm among the attractions.

Sybil also enjoyed her shopping trips to the
department stores in Aberdeen. On Union
Street, she went to Falconer's and Esslemont &
Macintosh and then she walked to Isaac
Benzie's on George Street and to Boots the
Chemist, where she could buy the perfume that
reminded her of her mother, the one her father
had bought for Lucy at Christmas 1925,
Shalimar. The highlight of each visit was a trip

up Union Street on one of the electric trams. She marvelled at the way they made their way silently along the streets while cars, buses, pedestrians and traffic of all descriptions moved out of their way. The tram took her up to the top of the street to Reid & Pearson's.

The shops she visited were so similar to Rowe & Co. and Whiteway, Laidlaw & Co., and yet the setting was so different. Union Street was narrow in comparison with broad, tree-lined Dalhousie Street. There was no pagoda with gold and jewels sparkling in the sun, and the bright outfits of the Burman people were replaced by the austere clothing worn in post-war Britain—blacks, greys and browns. There were no groups of Buddhist monks passing by in their dark-orange robes, no oxen roaming the streets, and the temperature was decidedly chilly. However, what there was gave Sybil comfort. There was permanence and strength in the grey granite buildings, a feeling of solidity and substance, and at that time, that was exactly what Sybil needed.

Sybil's introduction to Scottish culture continued. Reid would take her to football matches, and she soon became a keen follower of Aberdeen Football Club, 'the Reds'. They would get tickets to the big games against Hibernian and Rangers, and Sybil was watching at Hampden Park in Glasgow when her team beat Hibs for the Scottish Cup in 1947. She would cheer her side on with a gusto that belied her diminutive stature.

Each Sunday, Flora and Janet would attend the service at St Mary's on the Mount on the Ellon-to-Aberdeen road, and occasionally Reid would join them. Sybil, however, attended the Roman Catholic chapel in Ellon. It was little more than a small house converted for the purpose of holding Mass. A visiting priest gave the sacrament once a month.

On 15 December 1946, a second daughter was born to the Florys at the small maternity unit in Ellon. Christened Evelyn Mary, she was a cheeky, healthy baby girl with a good nature and a strong pair of lungs, which she was not afraid to use. Sybil was given a government maternity payment of £13 towards essentials for the new baby, but when she gave Reid the money he went out and bought a radio for her, knowing how much she liked listening to music. Evelyn's grant was to give them many years of entertainment.

The winter of 1946–7 was a particularly harsh one, with hard frosts and heavy snowfall lasting into the spring. Reid would take Ian and Flora out to build snowmen with stones for the eyes and mouth and a carrot for a nose. They would have snowball fights, and Reid would take them on hair-raising trips on the smart wooden sledge that he had used as a child. Sybil thought winter was a wonderful, magical season and loved the cold crisp mornings, the clear blue skies and the pure white snow. She would take the children out to play and for short walks. It felt so healthy. In the evenings, she gazed up at the clear northern skies and her thoughts returned to the family she had left behind. Were they still alive? Did they wonder about her whereabouts?

Space at Brackenridge was now a bit tight, and the couple needed their own home and room for the children to grow up. As soon as he could, Reid had put down for a council house, and eventually their name arrived at the top of the list. The family moved to 22 Park Crescent in March 1947, just as the winter was coming to an end. Their new home was part of a development of houses built in a revolutionary new manner: they were prefabricated and transported in sections to the site. The prefabs were designed to alleviate the housing shortage. Number 22 was a small bungalow consisting of two bedrooms, a sitting room, a bathroom and a kitchen. They also had the luxury of their own small front garden with a well-kept lawn, and there was a vegetable garden at the back of the house. There was a drying green with metal poles and rope on which to hang washing, and Reid put up a swing for the children. It was their first real home together, and they settled in well with their new neighbours. The family made weekly visits to Brackenridge to see Flora, Tan and Janet, so the children continued to enjoy the delights of their own private woodland playground.

Every November the Fifth, the family would gather with their friends to light a small bonfire and set off an exciting display of rockets, Catherine wheels, bangers, sparklers and a variety of other pyrotechnic devices. Reid took charge, and everyone was kept well back as he placed and lit each firework very carefully. It must have been something of a surprise for their Scottish neighbours to discover that Sybil not only knew the story behind the celebration but also remembered the famous poem better than they did.

In 1948, Reid finished his studies and registered as Reid Flory, MPS (Member of the Pharmaceutical Society). His next step was to find a job, and he was fortunate to gain employment with David Allan, who owned D.S. Allan Chemists in Holburn Street, Aberdeen. They hit it off right away and would become firm friends. D.S. Allan's was a traditional chemist, fitted out with dark mahogany display cabinets with glass tops. Along each wall was a row of small drawers, each displaying on the front a colourful porcelain label with such exotic descriptions as PULV:ERGOTAE:PREP, Latin still being used daily to describe medicaments. The shop had a unique aroma. It was a clean smell, slightly chemical in nature but mixed with soaps, spices, herbs and perfumes. It took Sybil back to her uncle Eric's shop in Prome, some 6,000 miles away. Reid loved working there, and as well as practising his dispensing skills, he was able to expand his interests into photography, building up a significant amount of business.

Reid was an expert at what would now be called networking and developed many contacts in and outside of the pharmacy business. He was even able to obtain for his family fruit and other treats, even peaches, which were in very short supply. When Sybil took the children to Aberdeen, they would visit him at the shop and arrange to meet at Holburn Ices, an Italian ice-cream parlour just up the hill towards Union Street. They served the most delicious knickerbocker glory, a tall glass filled with fruit, ice cream and red strawberry or raspberry sauce, topped with cream and a cherry. There were also wonderful banana splits when bananas were available. At Holburn Ices, Sybil always remembered her childhood visits to Mogul Street and thought longingly of her family.

Sometimes Sybil and Reid would take the children to the amusements on the beach, and when Chipperfield's circus visited Aberdeen, Reid made use of his contacts and always managed to get tickets. They gasped out loud with the rest of the audience at the high-wire acts, laughed at the clowns and looked in wonder at the exotic animals. The elephants reminded Sybil of her trips north of Rangoon, where she'd seen elephants moving timber in the teak forests.

Reid was gaining his independence and splashed out on a motorbike, which he used to commute from Ellon to his work in Aberdeen in all but the worst weathers.

In the summer of 1950, Arthur, Reid's uncle, took time off from his business in Los Angeles to make the trip to Scotland, a country he had left as a young man. He was a gentle, quiet man and he reminded everyone of his sister Flora in his calmness and even his appearance. He was easy-going and made friends with many of the people he met during his trip. Sybil and Reid were to get to know him well, and when his visit was over, they drove him down to Southampton to see him off. That was the last time he saw his homeland, although his daughter Florence would often visit in the years to come.

The year 1952 was a time of change for the whole country. On 15 February, the funeral of George VI took place. It was the largest outside broadcast ever undertaken by the BBC, and it even reached parts of Scotland, although there were few privately owned television sets. On 14 March, while snow lay thick on the ground, the Kirk o' Shotts transmitter started broadcasting television to Scotland. In the nearby village, meanwhile, there was no electricity supply. That year, there was a change to the Flory family, too. Almost six years after Evelyn was born, Sybil gave birth to another boy, Derek Reid Flory. I was a chubby-faced boy with big brown

230

eyes and jet-black hair, born, like Evelyn, in the maternity unit of Ellon Hospital, which is now the clubhouse of Ellon Golf Club. Shortly after the birth, Reid's uncle Alfie visited from America with his wife. He was a serious and studious man with a more reserved disposition than Arthur, ideally suited to his profession of banker.

In 1953, technology reached Brackenridge: a new television set was delivered in May, bought specifically to view the coronation of Queen Elizabeth II. The whole family gathered round to watch the grainy black-and-white images on the screen, and the excitement was palpable. When the new queen travelled north to Aberdeen a year later, her cavalcade went down Holburn Street and passed by the shop. Reid climbed the shop's tall wooden stepladder with the baby, while Sybil stood on the pavement with the children, and they waved their flags as the young queen went past.

The business was doing well, and when David Allan decided to retire, Reid bought the shop from him and began to devote more time to building up the dispensing, cosmetic and photographic sides of the small pharmacy. He became knowledgeable about make-up, as Sybil used her expertise to teach him.

One day at their home in Ellon, Sybil noticed that Ian, Flora and Evelyn were huddled together whispering in a conspiratorial manner. She asked them what they were doing, and, with

231

some trepidation and guilt, they showed Sybil the shoebox they'd sneaked into the house. Inside it, nestled in some tissue paper they'd spirited out of the cupboard, was a tiny chaffinch with a broken wing. Sybil fed him and gave him some water. When Reid came home that night, he made two tiny splints and set the bird's wing. One of their neighbours donated an old birdcage, which was cleaned up and placed in the living room. Every day, Sybil would feed and water the little bird, which had been given the rather unimaginative name of Chaffy by the children. Every day, he became stronger, and finally the splints were removed. Chaffy wouldn't fly, however. When the cage door was opened, he would jump onto Sybil's hand, and when she put him on the floor, he would follow her around, hopping after her and cheeping as loudly as he could. For more than two years, he kept her company, and she grew increasingly fond of her little bird. She had often, from early childhood, wondered what it would have been like to be a bird, with the freedom to fly, and now she felt very close to the little chaffinch who longed to take to the air but was unable to do so.

In 1957, the Florys moved to 6 Modley Place, a three-bedroomed, traditionally built semi-detached house, with a garden shed for Reid's motorbike. It was soon after the move that little Chaffy died. His death affected Sybil very badly, even more than the tragedies she had witnessed over the years. Perhaps it was a long-overdue release of all the heartache she had experienced in Rangoon, Shwebo, Myitkyina and India. Maybe it was to do with her own desire to fly like the birds; perhaps, with the death of Chaffy, she saw the death of her dream. Undoubtedly, much of her grief was simply the result of the fondness she had for Chaffy. She had admired his bravery in adapting to a strange environment, a new family and a totally different life—something she knew only too much about. She wept inconsolably and was upset for several weeks. She was completely heartbroken and vowed that the family would never again have a pet of any description—a promise she kept.

For Reid, the motorbike had lost its appeal, and he bought a Buick, a huge lumbering relic probably brought to Britain as an American army staff car, as it had an olive-green finish. The car had wide running boards, and it could have come from an American gangster movie with its garish whitewall tyres. The passenger area was vast, with leather bench seats that could seat at least six.

One day in March 1958, Reid drove the Buick to work and parked near the shop. He opened for business as usual and did a brisk trade. At lunchtime, he closed the shop, and as always he walked up to the café near the top of Holburn Street. He had only been sitting there for a short time when sirens started blaring and fire engines raced down the street. Reid finished his lunch and was walking slowly back when he was confronted by smoke and flames and firemen keeping the public back. When he could go no further he realised that the building on fire was his shop. It was totally destroyed. The next day, after the shop had been made safe, he was allowed back in. The smell of burnt wood hung in the air and what Reid saw depressed him: charred wood, broken glass, sodden shelf displays, ruined products. The contents of the pill bottles were dissolved and joined together in solid lumps. The huge china medicine jars of which he was so proud had been shattered by the intense heat. Water lay in pools on the floor and everything was thoroughly soaked. For weeks, his clothes reeked of burnt wood and smoke, and no matter what Sybil did, she couldn't get rid of the smell. An investigation revealed that the large chrome drum used to dry recently developed photographs had developed an internal electrical fault and started the fire.

They had spent so long building up the business, Sybil helping with the accounts and ordering make-up and perfumes, and now it had literally gone up in smoke. Everyone was very supportive, but Sybil and Reid knew they had to put the setback behind them and move on. Reid always looked to the future, saying that the past was past and nothing could be gained from dwelling on it.

To take their minds off the disaster, Reid took

Sybil and the family to see the recently released film *South Pacific* in Aberdeen. The Rodgers and Hammerstein musical is set on a small Pacific island during the Second World War. Sybil found the tale of love, faith and survival very moving, and Reid took her on her own to see it once again during its run.

In early May, Reid's attention was drawn to an advertisement in the *Pharmaceutical Journal*. A pharmacy was for sale in Huntly, some way west of Ellon, on the way to Inverness. Reid showed the advertisement to Sybil, although he was afraid of raising her hopes. The very same day, he arranged to visit the shop and meet with the owner. The business had potential, and Reid liked the location. After consulting Sybil, and assured of her support, he went back to Huntly armed with the necessary funds and purchased the chemist's shop and the adjacent house. He persuaded the owner not to shut the shop, as he knew this would damage business, and made plans to start work there immediately after the purchase was concluded.

By June, the business was his, and Sybil and the family made plans to leave Ellon for a new future. It was a difficult day when they left. Sybil had settled in well with Reid's family, and they'd all made a great number of very dear friends. There were lots of tears when they had finally loaded up the car and the small van they'd borrowed and set off to start again.

BLANCHE

RANGOON

With the war officially over, Blanche and her family began to rebuild their lives. Manu returned to Rangoon to search for his wife, and the couple were reunited. It was a highly emotional time. The war had changed everyone both physically and mentally. Once well-built men were gaunt, haggard and exhausted by their experiences, and Manu was no exception.

'After the war, it was very difficult. We had no money left. I managed to get a job in the British Army officers' shop selling shoes, socks, blankets, battledress, regimental ties, medal bars. Then some of the prisoners from the village found me. Don't ask me how. They were going back home, and they brought me clothes and food and thanked me. For what were they thanking me? I had done nothing, no more than anyone else would have done. I just wished I had been able to do more for them. I didn't recognise them at first. They had put on weight and they were no longer the skeletons I had prayed for in their camp; they were big, strapping young men, some with such baby faces. They had neat haircuts and healthy complexions. All the scars had gone from the outside; I prayed that given time the scars on the inside would heal also. It was very moving.

I knew all their names and we laughed and hugged. I only remember one name now: Leslie Greenhouse. I remember thinking it was an unusual name. He told me when he was in the camp that he was from Dover. When he came to see me I remembered and started singing "White Cliffs of Dover", you know, the Vera Lynn song. "There'll be bluebirds over the white cliffs of Dover tomorrow, just you wait and see. There'll be love and laughter and peace ever after tomorrow when the world is free." I had a beautiful voice then, not like now. He held my hands and sobbed until the tears fell down on my shoulders, and I held him, too.'

Manu restarted his business. Little remained of the infrastructure that had made Burma one of the leading nations in Asia, and it was time to rebuild and make the country prosperous again. In January 1946, Aung San became the president of the newly formed Anti-Fascist People's Freedom League, and by September he was effectively prime minister, leading the Governor's Executive Council. 'We started to get the newspapers again and we would read about the plans for Burma's independence. They were exciting times, and we had such high hopes for our once strong country.'

Blanche began the search for the missing members of the family. 'We started searching for all our family, and we found my sister Eunice and our cousin Irene. My brother had been with me for some time now. So we were left with Sybil. We used to say, "How are we going to find Sybil now? Where has she gone?" I told them the story of the Christmas shopping trip. She just walked out on 23 December 1941. After that, no trace of her. We thought, "She may be dead, she may be somewhere else"—we just didn't know. When we all got together we used to wonder all the time where she was. Irene didn't know if she was alive or dead. She used to cry for hours because she brought us up and she missed Sybil.'

Not everyone in the family had been as lucky as Blanche. Some of them had gone to Prome to stay with Uncle Eric and Aunt Mary: there, Uncle Clifford's daughter died, Eunice's daughter died and Uncle Arnie and his daughter died, all of cholera or dysentery. They and many tens of thousands of soldiers and civilians had paid the ultimate price for the freedom of their country.

'Towards the end of 1946, I went to live with Irene in her big house. There, I taught dancing. Many people came, soldiers from all over, British, Chinese, Indians. I taught the waltz and the tango. I used to charge 30 rupees a lesson. Great fun, it was. Then my young cousin Juju, Irene's daughter (her real name was Camellia), she knew how to jive, and she used to teach it. More people came to that class. The Americans could jive, and they would come to our big house and dance for hours. We had an old gramophone with a big horn loudspeaker—His

238

Master's Voice, I think it was. It had the badge with the small dog sitting beside a gramophone with his head to one side. We used to play all the records, and the soldiers would bring their favourites. We had some Indian records, and they would tell us to put them on, and they would jive to them as well. Those were good times, happy times after so many years of sadness.'

The troops began to leave for home, and through 1946 and early 1947, life gradually returned to normal. Manu's business, the General Electric Company, began to prosper. 'We had our own shop selling radios and spares. In those days, there were no televisions or fridges. There were no transistors or any fancy things. Then, the radios had glass valves and resistors and condensers, and we had lots of stock. Repairing a radio took a lot of skill and concentration. I remember I wasn't allowed to touch the glass valves because it affected them somehow. Our shop was in Fraser Street, at the other end from Irene's house. It was just next to the big bookshop, Smart & Mookerdum. Things were very quiet compared to what we had been through.'

Money was still tight in Burma, and Manu continued to work in the evenings broadcasting news for Burma Radio. He would come home sometimes after midnight and had to get up early the next morning to open the shop.

Austin joined the Burmese navy as an

engineer officer and they saw less of him from then on. He would later marry a Burmese woman, Ma Kyi. Eunice met and married a British officer, Richard Clift, who had served with distinction in Force 136, a branch of Special Operations working in Burma. Because of his knowledge of the country, he had been dropped behind enemy lines and tasked with setting up resistance groups to harass the Japanese, and, with his Karen fighters, he had been highly successful.

In January 1947, Aung San went to London to negotiate with Clement Attlee for Burmese independence and succeeded. Within a year, Burma was to be free of colonial rule. On the morning of 19 July 1947, Aung San was chairing a meeting of the Executive Council in the Secretariat Building when armed men burst in and assassinated him and several of his colleagues. The finger was pointed at U Saw, who had been prime minister under the British before the war. He was tried and sentenced to death, although there was some controversy and talk of conspiracy. A national monument, the Martyrs' Mausoleum, was built by the Shwedagon Pagoda and 19 July was designated Martyrs' Day. 'On the day of the shooting, we didn't know what was going on. I was living nearby . . . there was shooting going on, shouting and people running madly. What a confusion, my goodness. We asked, "What's happening, what's happening?" and we were told, "They shot all the VIPs." The bodies were taken away quietly, but we went to the place where they were buried and saw their graves. It was never discussed, who really killed them. It was all hushed up.'

After the assassination, life became quiet once more in the streets of Rangoon and the other major cities. In the outlying states, however, things were not at all peaceful as increasing dissatisfaction among ethnic groups such as the Karen manifested itself in violent insurgency.

Rangoon, although a city of some size, was also a place where news travelled fast. One day, Blanche discovered, through an announcement in the local paper, that her stepmother Daisy Boyce had survived the war and had returned to Rangoon, having remarried. Blanche and her family had more pressing developments to contend with, however. During the monsoon of 1948, Blanche contracted malaria and had to be admitted to the Seventh-Day Adventist Hospital, where she spent many weeks fighting for her life. Two doctors, one German, one Jewish, looked after her, and Blanche owed her life to their constant supervision and dedication.

In January 1949, the Karen National Union took up arms to demand an independent Karen state, and throughout the 1950s much of the countryside was under the control of insurgents. In 1952, Chinese Kuomintang troops entered Shan State, some 300 miles to the north-east of

Rangoon. This caused a massive military recruitment drive and a large-scale restructuring of the Burmese army. Blanche was living in Brooking Street, near the Secretariat Building, and she and the children would often hear shouting and screaming as impassioned debates carried on into the night.

By the early 1950s, the people of Burma began to suffer shortages of once plentiful basic commodities, and then came rationing of clothes, materials and food. It became difficult to buy anything freely, and travel was also restricted. The family took the decision to sell the shop on Fraser Street, as the business, like so many others, was starting to struggle. Manu went to work for Gestetner Duplicators, a multinational company that made copy machines.

For the children, life went on as normal. They would wake up early and help cook the food, wash the clothes and clean the house. After school, they would come home, do their homework and eat dinner. They rarely went out, although they had friends to stay and they would return these visits. When they did go out, it was to celebrate festivals such as Diwali, with all the sweets and lights and candles. At the time of the water festival in March, trucks were brightly decorated and girls rode on the backs, performing elaborate dances and looking like angels, as the floats drove through the streets. At Christmas time, the family attended the annual party organised by the boss of Gestetner in Burma. Then they would all dress up in their finest clothes and the children had to be on their very best behaviour. Often, Manu's friends visited, and the house would reverberate to the sound of laughter.

However, the political situation was gradually worsening, until, in 1958, the army had its first taste of control when, amid serious unrest, a caretaker government led by military leader General Ne Win was appointed. The writing was on the wall: Burma was changing forever.

CHAPTER TEN

1958–70

SYBIL

HUNTLY, SCOTLAND

The journey to the Flory family's new home passed largely in silence, the Buick's occupants thinking their own thoughts and keeping their natural anxieties to themselves. The younger children eventually dropped off to sleep.

Huntly was a thriving market town with a population of about 4,000. It was located some 35 miles north-west of Aberdeen on the main road to Inverness, through the Glens of Foudland, known to locals simply as 'the Glens', a winding, treacherous stretch of road, often impassable in bad winter weather. A few miles further on, the road improved, and they soon arrived at the town of Huntly, set in a dip in the landscape. In the words of a local rhyme:

The Ba' Hill, the Battle Hill,
The Clashmach and the Bin,
They a' form a circle,
And Huntly lies within.

The road north took the family past the busy Huntly Mart, the market, where livestock auctions were held, down the hill and under the railway bridge. On the other side of the bridge was the entrance to Huntly station, a small but important halt on the Inverness rail link. Carrying straight on, they came to Duke Street and proceeded to climb towards the town centre. Just as they approached the main shopping area, Reid turned sharply left and stopped outside their new home. Unlocking the door, they went in to explore. The house needed a good lick of paint, but it was fine for their needs. When Reid's friends arrived with the van, they moved their possessions in and the family sat amidst piles of cardboard boxes. It would be several weeks before everything had found a place and the house became more like home.

The building occupied a long corner plot on a hill. Reid proudly took his family down the steep wooden steps to his new dispensary and shop below. The dispensary was a room of around 15 ft square, the walls shelved and covered with large pill containers. Glass-fronted storage units housed the less frequently used medicines, and a locked cabinet near Reid's bureau contained bottles of liquid medicines. Right at the top were rows of dark-green bottles clearly marked POISON. There were two enormous storage areas. One was built into the hill, a large, very cold room, perfect for storing chemicals and products that needed a lower temperature to remain stable. From the dispensary, another steep stair went up to the even larger store above the shop, on the same level as the living area. Although bulk tubs of tablets and stone flagons and glass demijohns of liquids lined the entire side of one wall, most of this store was given over to products normally sold in the front shop: soaps, perfumes, make-up, gift sets and more mundane items such as rubber gloves and toothpaste, deodorants and nappies. Next to this store was a small galley-shaped darkroom, and, although Reid did move in some photographic equipment, he rarely did his own developing and printing. Once bitten, twice shy.

The front shop was essentially a larger version of the shop in Aberdeen. Two bay windows flanked a frosted-glass main door, and the walls were lined with mahogany storage drawers, with glass-fronted cabinets rising from chest height up to the ceiling. Public access to these cabinets was prevented by a wide counter on which sat a large till. This layout meant that customers could access very few items for themselves, having to ask for help when a purchase was to be made. Reid saw this as a distinct disadvantage, but there was little he could do about it at the time. There was one member of staff, Bill Gauld, a tall, smart and friendly dispensing assistant, who continued to work in the shop. Bill had been a military policeman during his national service, and had at one point been part of the guard at Buckingham Palace. It was obvious from his appearance that he still maintained the same high standards of dress and behaviour that would have been expected of him in the army.

The smell was the same as that of the shop in Aberdeen, and Reid and Sybil felt very comfortable in their new surroundings. Sybil's thoughts returned to Prome and her uncle Eric's pharmacy. Surrounded by dark mahogany and tall china jars, she felt that Uncle Eric would have been very much at home here. Her memory took her back to the life she had left behind, her parents, uncles, aunts and her brother and sisters, and she once more felt a great weight descend on her. She was shaken out of her melancholy by the children running around excitedly exploring their new home.

On their second day, Sybil and the children explored the town, walking up Duke Street past the baker, newsagent, butcher, haberdasher and ironmonger, as well as the other main pharmacy in the town, which belonged to a larger-than-life local character called Norman G. Connell. They arrived at the square, with its fountain and statue of the Duke of Gordon. At the four corners were the Brander Library, the Huntly Hotel, the Gordon Arms Hotel and Boyd's drapers and haberdashers. There was also an assortment of banks and offices, solicitors' firms and other shops. On the corner of the square and Duke Street was a smart menswear shop, and

Sybil went in to buy socks for the children. The owner was a small, dapper man with impeccable manners. He smiled and introduced himself to Sybil. He was Jack Brander, a relative of the library benefactor, and it turned out he lived next door to Reid and Sybil in Church Street. They would become lifelong friends as well as good neighbours.

They made their way back down Duke Street, having made a few purchases, and then called in at the newsagent's to place a regular order for the local newspaper (the *Huntly Express*), the Aberdeen *Press and Journal* and Sybil's favourite magazine, the *People's Friend*. Over the next weeks and months they met their new neighbours, including Vince Webster, a soft-spoken and charming man who ran the jeweller's across the street and called in to Reid's almost every day for a chat and a cup of coffee.

The daily routine varied little. Sybil would get up early to clean out and light the fires in the dining room and living room. She would then make Reid's breakfast, a plate of porridge, a soft-boiled egg and toast, followed by a cup of tea. At eight, he would open the shop, and between customers he would complete his paperwork and read the trade journals. His work consisted of serving in the shop, ordering stock, ensuring the shelves were neat, tidy and well stocked and, of course, filling prescriptions. At around eleven each day Reid would drive to the doctor's surgery to pick up prescriptions. To begin with, there were only a small number, as the business had been running down. On the first day they opened, they filled only five, but over time this grew to a peak of around sixty to seventy prescriptions a day, sometimes as many as one hundred. The front-of-shop turnover had also been poor, and Reid made a great effort to attract customers, bringing in new lines of well-known brands of cosmetics and more exclusive perfumes and toiletries. Aware of the potential business to be had from supplying veterinary products, Reid studied hard and soon began to attract a strong farming clientele. He enjoyed his work. Each day presented different challenges and new opportunities. As time went on, the back shop became a social hub for many of the town's businessmen and farmers.

Sybil also played a role, helping in the selection of make-up and perfumes, ensuring that the best was stocked. She attended courses run by Max Factor and Lancôme cosmetics, learning more about the favourite pastime of her youth, the subtle application of make-up. She became highly skilled in using cosmetics to emphasise the positive features of her clients. If only, Sybil thought, she had been as skilled when she had first applied make-up to her dear sister Blanche!

Lunch became something of a ritual for the family, with set meals on set days. Monday was always stovies, made from the remains of

Sunday's roast beef. Tuesday and Saturday were mince, tatties and mealie pudding, a white pudding made of oatmeal. The mince was never the ordinary stuff, as Reid liked lean meat, so Sybil would buy lean sirloin steak and the butcher would mince it for her, an extravagance that would have surprised and horrified most of the townspeople, and which Sybil insists on to this day. Wednesday was the only day when there could be a variation, although the fare was usually stew. On Thursdays, they had braised steak with delicious gravy, and on Friday Sybil served fish bought from the van or the local fishmonger's.

That was not the only ritual, however, as every week Sybil would drink one spoonful of Epsom salts dissolved in a cup of water. No one knew exactly why she did this, but of course it was a habit she had first picked up at St Philomena's convent school in Rangoon. Sybil talked so little about her past that to some extent she was a mystery even to her own family.

On Sundays, Sybil and the children would go to Mass at the local church of St Margaret's, and on one Sunday in the month the family would drive down to Ellon to visit Reid's mother. They always spent Easter Sunday at Brackenridge, where Flora would have prepared a hard-boiled egg for each of them. Everyone would paint their eggs before standing at the top of the steep hill in the grounds and rolling them down. Sometimes chocolate eggs were hidden

250

around the garden, and the children would set off to find as many as they could.

During the war, Reid had started to smoke cigarettes as a means of coping with the carnage and death that surrounded him and his friends. He continued to smoke and would even do so in the pharmacy, something that would not be allowed now. When he had been working in Aberdeen, Sybil hadn't known how much he smoked and wasn't really affected by it, but with the move to Huntly, where the house was attached to the shop, it was impossible to escape from the smell, which pervaded the whole building. It became apparent that Reid was smoking more than 60 cigarettes a day. In the evening, Reid would light a cigarette and Sybil, who disliked the fumes, would place her clean and perfumed handkerchief over her nose and mouth, a habit that the children found highly amusing.

In 1959, Sybil and Reid acquired their first television set. Sybil loved music and dancing, and *The White Heather Club* with Andy Stewart was a firm favourite. She would sing along with 'Stop your Ticklin', Jock', which would have her in stitches. Holidays took the family to the west coast of Scotland, and there were frequent visits to Garve in the Highlands and to Inverewe Garden, in Wester Ross, where the Gulf Stream allowed both traditional plants and more exotic ones such as palm trees to grow. For Sybil, it brought back memories of the beautiful

251

botanical garden at Maymyo.

While Sybil continued to look after the house and concentrated on bringing up the children, as well as occasionally helping out in the shop, in 1960 Reid was persuaded to stand as a local councillor. He and his wife were popular in the town, and he was elected with a handsome vote. At the end of his term of office, Reid was re-elected to the council by an even bigger vote and appointed junior baillie, which was a more responsible post in the council and carried with it the role of lay magistrate in the local court. By the end of the decade, he would be the town's senior baillie.

In the mid-'60s, Reid and Sybil decided to modernise the shop. Everything but the prescription medicines and high-value products was to be within reach of the customer, to encourage impulse buying and allow the customer to see more clearly the range of goods on offer. By this time, the prescription turnover was at a consistently high level and the sales of veterinary and agricultural medicines were also reaching a peak.

In 1965, the film *The Sound of Music* came to Aberdeen. Reid and Sybil had been frequent cinema-goers over the years, but of all the films she'd seen, this one made the greatest impression on Sybil, and she went to see it five times during its run. Perhaps the film brought back memories—the nuns at her school and the musical performances she'd taken part in as a girl—and there was also an obvious parallel in the Von Trapp family's escape to Switzerland from a militaristic occupying power with her less happy experiences. In any case, although she usually kept her emotions hidden, she was often tearful during and after the film, so it obviously had a profound effect on her.

Two years later, Sybil discovered a secret that Reid had kept from her for 24 years. The revelation came about because of changes to the organisation and funding of NHS hospitals. There was a major drive by the Government to treat as many patients as possible outside of institutions. The principal reason behind this was, as so often, a need to save money, and little thought seemed to have been given to the question of how those who had been institutionalised for long periods would survive in the outside world. This new policy forced Reid and his close family to reveal a secret that they had kept for many years. One Thursday afternoon, Reid explained to his wife and children that they were going to Aberdeen to meet his father. Now, this was something of a surprise, because as far as Sybil and the children knew, his father was dead. All the official documents, including Reid's army papers and enlistment details, stated that his father was deceased. It was therefore in a state of some uncertainty and confusion that they travelled to the Royal Cornhill Hospital and were let in to a locked ward where they were introduced to Reid's father, Walter Flory. It was a shock to be confronted with a man whom they didn't know existed but an even greater shock to see that he and his son Reid were as alike as two peas in a pod. Later, they were to hear more about Walter and his hospitalisation and discover that during Reid's monthly visits to Aberdeen to see his accountant, he would pop in to the hospital to visit his father. The story slowly began to unfold.

Walter Flory had been an electrical engineer at the outbreak of war in 1914 and had joined the army. The Royal Field Artillery had a distinguished history, and the regiment was to add to its battle honours during the Great War. In 1914, it fought at Mons, Aisne and the Marne; in 1915, it took part in the Battle of Ypres. Walter was lucky to survive. One of his bravest actions during the war took place away from the field of battle, however. On 23 February 1915, while on a short leave in Stowmarket, he spotted a man in difficulty in the River Gipping. Walter plunged into the fast-flowing, swollen river to save the life of the drowning man. For that brave act, he was awarded an honorary testimonial from the Royal Humane Society.

On his return to France, he continued to be involved in the action. During a mortar attack, the forward command bunker in which he was working sustained a direct hit. Many of the men with whom he had been working a few minutes earlier were killed instantly, and others were badly wounded. The entrance to the bunker collapsed and they were trapped inside. In ankle-deep mud, in pitch darkness and with the moans and cries of the injured all around him, Walter felt a fear he could barely control. He felt rats crawling around him and brushed them off. He knew that they would eat the flesh of his dead and wounded comrades, and the thought made him sick. It was some hours before the survivors were released from their tomb. Walter began to have nightmares and was terrified to go to sleep. He had difficulty working in confined spaces and preferred to be out in the open, despite the higher risk.

The Royal Naval Air Service was looking for qualified and experienced engineers, and in 1916 Walter made the decision to transfer, hoping that it might help him to forget what he had experienced. Once more, he served in France, where his RNAS unit supported the Royal Flying Corps. He suffered from claustrophobia, manageable at first but worsening over time. He served through some of the heaviest fighting of the conflict, including the month of April 1917, 'Bloody April', when the Allies lost 150 aircraft and some 316 crew. Walter was physically uninjured but mentally scarred, and in September 1917 he was transferred to the RNAS base at Longside air station, Aberdeenshire.

While there, he met and fell in love with a

255

local girl, Flora Reid, and so smitten was he that he proposed to her. They wasted no time, and on 3 December 1918, at the Church of Scotland in Ellon, they became husband and wife. The young couple settled into their new home, Craiglea, on Station Road in Ellon. Although Walter adjusted to civilian life as best he could and had married a strong and supportive woman, he still had nightmares and found it hard to sleep, often waking up exhausted and drenched in sweat. In 1920, Flora gave birth to their son Reid, and three years later a daughter, Janet, was born. It seemed that at last Walter was finding peace, and he and Flora were content.

It was a cruel twist of fate that tore their world apart. Walter was carrying out some electrical work on a large house in the country, and he was finishing off some wiring in the attic when his workmates decided to play a trick on him. It was a childish prank that they thought would be amusing. Knowing that Walter felt ill at ease in small spaces, they switched off the light in the attic and locked the trapdoor shut. The confined space was plunged into darkness. Walter was back in the turmoil of battle in France, surrounded by the smell of rotting corpses and tortured by the screams of the dying. Terrified by the rats he imagined swarming over him and the incessant sound of shelling in his head, he snapped and began screaming hysterically. Even when the trapdoor was opened, he continued to scream and didn't stop until the local doctor had been summoned and had administered a sedative. Walter had suffered a severe mental breakdown and was admitted to the Royal Cornhill Hospital in Aberdeen. The stigma attached to having a family member in a mental asylum was at that time so strong that the family decided to keep Walter's condition a secret.

In 1967, the change in policy had resulted in a visit to Brackenridge from two well-meaning civil servants, who assured Flora and Janet that Walter, who had spent four decades in hospital, was ready to come back out into the community. Thus was the secret uncovered. However, in the course of his first few trips out of the hospital, it became apparent that Walter was not able to cope outside that environment. For 40 years, he had contributed to the life of the hospital. He was well educated, funny, well liked and respected by both patients and staff, and the Cornhill was by this time the extent of his world, a world in which he still achieved things and was of use and in which he felt very comfortable. He was institutionalised and simply unable to return to life outside.

Reid and Sybil continued to visit him as often as work would allow, and the children went from time to time, too. Sybil grew very fond of Walter. She saw in him many of the people she had met during her own troubled times fleeing the Japanese. He was a warm, sensitive and gentle man who had been placed in conditions

257

that he simply did not have the mental or physical strength to cope with.

What disturbed and saddened Sybil was that Reid had felt it necessary to hide his father's existence from her, had felt that somehow she would not understand or that it would have changed their relationship. How wrong could he have been? She, more than any other member of the family, understood the physical and mental destruction that war could bring, having witnessed it at first hand. She hoped there would be no more revelations.

Throughout the decade, the pharmacy continued to thrive, with Sybil and Reid complementing each other's strengths. Sybil loved the over-the-counter side of the business and chatting to the women who came into the shop, many of whom became firm friends. In 1968 Reid bought his first small yacht and named it *Aref's Lady*, a play on his initials. The boat would prove to be a great source of relaxation and escape for him. Like Reid's, Sybil's role in the community was growing. In 1970, she was appointed president of the local Roman Catholic Church Guild, a position she held for a number of years. For relaxation she joined the bowling club and was an active member, enjoying her new sport and taking part in competitions throughout Scotland.

The children were now off their hands, pursuing their various careers. Ian studied at Duncan of Jordanstone College of Art in Dundee and went on to become an art teacher, as well as an accomplished jeweller and silversmith. Flora studied English and geography at Aberdeen University, and on graduation she married her fiancé, becoming a full-time wife and mother. Evelyn completed a degree in primary-school teaching in Edinburgh, a vocation she took to like a duck to water. Evelyn found teaching very rewarding and enjoyed the fact that many of the children she taught went on to have their own children, whom she also taught. Meanwhile, I pursued a successful career in the pharmaceutical industry.

BLANCHE

CALCUTTA AND MADRAS, INDIA

'In 1958, my husband asked if I would like to move to India, and I told him I didn't mind. I thought, "Let's try some other place." Things were looking bad in Burma. Manu's parents were Indian, living in Bombay, and he wanted to go back to see them.'

Gestetner offered Manu a transfer to India, and the way was clear for them to leave Burma. All the arrangements were made, and on 9 July the family—now made up of Blanche, Manu, Leslie and Raymond, now grown up, and younger daughters Anita and Yvonne—left the port of Rangoon on the SS *Santhia*, a 9,000-ton ship owned by Mackinnon & Mackenzie. It was a beautiful ship, and on the bulkhead was a brass plate that said it had been made by Barclay, Curle & Co., Glasgow, in 1950. On 12 July, they landed in Calcutta, the city that was to become their home.

The family spent a month in a hotel near the centre of Calcutta before buying a house and putting the girls in school. Their arrival in India was not without its hiccups, as Yvonne recalls: 'Not long after we came here, we went to the New Market and we got lost. We didn't know where we were or how to get back to our house. So comical, it was. Eventually, the police escorted us home.'

260

Leslie secured a job in the manufacturing division of Gestetner, Raymond trained to be a motor mechanic and Anita and Yvonne went to school at the Queen of the Missions convent. It wasn't easy for the girls, as the curriculum was very different from that taught in Burma. On top of this, all the children, like Blanche, had to learn Hindi and Bengali, their first language in Burma having been English and their second Burmese.

In late 1958, Blanche went to see the much-publicised film *The Bridge on the River Kwai*. 'It was a very good film. So many prisoners were sent to the bridge to build the railway, so many of them died. Many Burmese were sent, too. If they did anything wrong, they were sent; even if they didn't, they were still sent. They died in their tens of thousands. You didn't see that in the film. One life was lost for every sleeper: 120,000 sleepers were laid in the building of the railway, and 120,000 people died. What wickedness.'

Blanche and her family enjoyed the hustle and bustle of their new surroundings. Despite the language barrier, people were friendly and helpful, and their neighbours made them very welcome and were particularly good to the children. 'Coming to India was nice. We enjoyed ourselves. I suppose we had to like it because we were never going back. At first, my husband went back every year to see our family and friends and keep up his contacts. Then, just before the military coup of 1962, he suggested giving up our Burmese passports and becoming Indian nationals, as all our friends had left or were leaving. We had no intention of going back when the military was in power. Manu said, "Let's stay here. The children are settled and doing well, and we don't know what Burma will be like." So we stayed and were very happy when we became Indian nationals. It was a proud day for us all.'

In Burma, all businesses and industries were nationalised. Army trucks and tanks rolled into the capital and took up strategic positions. Soldiers thronged the streets. Shop owners turned up for work on 2 March 1962 to find officers of the army had taken over their businesses, reducing the owner's role to little more than manager. Burma was changing once again, and the consequences would be lasting.

In 1964, Irene, Eunice, their families and their friends the Lintons left for Hong Kong, realising that things would never be the same again. Irene eventually settled in Bangkok, and the Linton family finally made their way to Perth, Australia. Eunice, Richard and their sons John and Patrick emigrated to Australia in 1973. Their children Kathleen, Warren and Adeline had married and were settled in and around Rangoon, and they had stayed behind in Burma. Austin and Ma Kyi also remained in Rangoon. Things were becoming more and more unsettled, and the likelihood of Blanche and her family returning even for a short visit seemed even more remote.

One Sunday in Calcutta, while Blanche was walking to church, a woman calling out 'Sybil! Sybil!' stopped her in her tracks. Blanche turned and was confronted by a complete stranger. The woman apologised, saying she had mistaken her for a friend called Sybil. Blanche was shocked and replied that she was Sybil's sister. They chatted for a while, and the woman, who introduced herself as Mrs Orchard, told Blanche that she had been a friend of Sybil's during the war and that she had attended her wedding to a Mr Flory. She told Blanche as much as she could and arranged to meet later in the week to talk further.

At that meeting, she gave Blanche a photo of Sybil in her army uniform. 'Mrs Orchard gave me the photograph and the negative of Sybil, and so we began to search again. We went to everyone—the papers, the Salvation Army. We would say, "We are looking for a Mr Flory," and they would say, "Mr Flory—what is his Christian name?" and, of course, we didn't know. Mrs Orchard hadn't been able to remember. They found so many Florys all over India, so which Flory was it? We didn't know. I gave the photograph of Sybil to the Salvation Army, but I didn't get it back. Lucky I kept the negative.'

In 1968, Blanche and Manu moved to Madras. The children were by this time settled in Calcutta and remained behind. He had been offered a promotion within Gestetner's to area accountant, in charge of all southern India. He was very popular and was invited to all the parties and celebrations on occasions such as the firm's golden jubilee. When Manu had completed 15 years' service with the company, he was presented with a fine leather-bound book. For his 30th year of service, he would be presented with a gold watch, but for now he was very proud of his book. 'We would meet the bosses Mr Jessop, Mr Bowman and Mr Gestetner, not old Mr Gestetner but his son. They were very nice; the whole company was nice. They often gave us lovely buffet meals.'

On 8 December 1970, Manu returned from work feeling unwell. 'He had a massive heart attack. We rushed him to the hospital, but they couldn't save him. He was a good husband and a good father. A nice, kind, gentle man. I missed him very much.'

They had lived through good times and bad, and they had faced an often uncertain future together, each growing stronger because of the other. Now Blanche had to tackle life's challenges on her own.

CHAPTER ELEVEN

1971–2007

SYBIL

HUNTLY

In the early '70s, after working with Reid and Sybil for 14 years, Bill Gauld decided he would try pastures new and left the business. Sybil now joined Reid as his full-time assistant and learned the ropes quickly, getting involved in ordering all products, especially her beloved cosmetics and perfumes. She would turn her hand to anything, and they made a formidable team. In 1973, Reid was elected to the position of provost of Huntly—the equivalent of a mayor in England. He was the last provost of the town, as in 1975 local-government reforms saw the old-style town councils disappear. In June 1973, Reid and Sybil travelled down to Holyrood Palace in Edinburgh to attend the Queen's garden party, to which all the provosts of Scotland were invited. They set off in Reid's recently acquired second-hand Mercedes 220 SE, after carefully and none too discreetly displaying the Holyrood Palace car pass in the front window. They had an unforgettable time at the party, and although the Queen didn't actually speak to them, she did pass by very near, and that was excitement enough for Sybil, a staunch monarchist.

At this time, Sybil was actively involved in fund-raising as area president of Action for the Crippled Child and as a committee member of the local branch of the Arthritis Research Campaign, so she was attending official events in her own capacity, as well as in her role as provost's wife. Fund-raising, charity events and the sedate sport of crown-green bowling reflected the more refined and genteel side of Sybil's character, but all that changed on a Saturday afternoon at four o'clock, when she sat down to watch the wrestling on television. Suddenly, this 4-ft-11-in. lady became almost unrecognisable as she watched Les Kellet, the masked wrestler Kendo Nagasaki and the massive Giant Haystacks and Big Daddy performing half nelsons, armlocks and Boston crabs with a dexterity that belied their size. She shouted at the villains, Jackie 'Mr TV' Pallo and Mick McManus, telling them what she would do if she could get at them. Bert Royal and George Kidd were the heroes of the hour, although they often took a pounding from their arch-rivals.

It was quite entertaining to watch, but Sybil took it all very seriously and wouldn't miss her wrestling for anything. While Kent Walton provided relatively calm and unflustered commentary, Sybil's shouts of encouragement to the goodies and disparaging and often brutal remarks towards the villains could often be heard in the back shop, much to Reid's amusement. Sybil was not alone in loving the spectacle; rumour had it that two other distinguished ladies also watched the wrestling on a Saturday afternoon: the Queen Mother and Margaret Thatcher, herself as formidable an opponent as any wrestler.

This wasn't the only unusual practice in the household, however. On their frequent visits home, the Flory children were always amazed at the amount of food that Sybil had stockpiled. The freezer was always packed full, and the fridge was the same, but even these stores were put in the shade by the number of tins of fruit, corned beef, beans, tomato soup and other foods that were hidden away in every available cupboard in the kitchen. One thing was for certain: Sybil and Reid would never starve. In the mid-'70s, there was a threat of a sugar shortage, and Sybil, by carefully shopping around in the area, managed to amass a stock of granulated sugar that would have lasted several years had she kept the bags to herself. Instead, she gave them away to family and close friends who were beginning to suffer the occasional blip in their sugar supply. This need to hoard food was thought of as simply part of Sybil's character, as was her reluctance to throw away any books or magazines she had bought. She kept every one, telling people that she never knew when she might need them. The magazine piles grew into something of a paper mountain over the years.

Reid continued to enjoy his yachting and also commissioned the construction of a small clinker-built fishing boat. It was called the *Sybil M*, a fitting tribute to a woman who had sailed some turbulent seas with him and had been the rock he had clung to when times were tough.

On 26 May 1977, Walter Flory was finally released from the anguish that had haunted him during his lifetime. He was buried the following week in the small cemetery in Ellon. Sybil attended the funeral with the rest of the family and grieved deeply for a man whom she had become very fond of, regretting only that she had not known him sooner.

In the same year, Sybil was elected to the position of president of the Townswomen's Guild, and she served for four years. During that time, she took an active role in the TWG's amateur dramatic productions. She played the part of a Gypsy, was a nun in a short play called *The Twelve Apostles* and sang in a musical revue called *Wartime Favourites*. For this, she borrowed the uniform of a local lieutenant colonel, who happened to be of diminutive stature. On the opening night, she appeared on stage with the uniform looking immaculate, the Sam Browne belt polished until it shone, the brass buttons sparkling in the light and her shoes shined until you could see your reflection in them. It was the first time she had worn a uniform since late 1943, but she looked every inch a soldier. Sybil didn't tell her fellow entertainers, some of whom were too young to remember the war, that she had sung most of the songs while the Japanese had been waging their brutal war against the Allies. The musical brought back memories of Vera Lynn and of India, and it caused Sybil to reflect more on the fate of her family in Burma. Her memories were dimmed by the passing years, and the images of her family she had sworn to keep sharp in her mind had faded like old sepia photographs, gradually becoming less distinct. The only reminder of her mother and sisters came when she looked at her reflection in the mirror each morning. Then the image looking back at her was like her mother, and she could still picture her sister Blanche, who had always looked so similar to her.

In January 1979, at the age of 55, Reid's sister Janet passed away after a long illness. In 1980, on 3 September, Auntie Tan died at Brackenridge.

In 1981 Reid and Sybil had their first holiday abroad, flying to Malta. They thoroughly enjoyed it, visiting all the historic monuments and relaxing on the stony beaches. Shortly after the holiday, on 24 August 1981, the day after her 87th birthday, Reid's mother died. She had been admitted to hospital, where she died of heart failure.

In 1988, after 30 years as a pharmacist in the

community, with Sybil having spent 16 years working beside him, Reid decided to retire. In 1990, they resolved to undertake a trip to New Zealand to meet two of Reid's cousins whom they had never seen but often written to. They made it a memorable trip, calling at Los Angeles on the way out to meet up with Florence, Uncle Arthur's daughter. After a few days sightseeing, they flew on to New Zealand, where they discovered they had not just two cousins but in fact a large family of over thirty relatives. A grand party was organised so they could meet everyone, and they spent a very happy month there before moving on to Honolulu. There they visited the USS *Arizona* memorial at Pearl Harbor, where another Flory had died in the Japanese conflict. Max Edward Flory, Seaman 2nd Class United States Navy, was serving aboard the *Arizona* when the Japanese bombed the naval base. He was one of many hundreds who died on that terrible day. From Honolulu, Reid and Sybil travelled back to Scotland full of tales of their adventures and with pictures of all their new-found relatives.

In early June 1994, after an illness lasting several months, their eldest son, Ian, passed away. He had felt unwell for some time and had been admitted to hospital, where tests had shown he had a form of leukaemia. Despite a brave struggle, he finally had no strength left and his fight was over. It was a devastating loss to his family. He was artistic, witty and clever, and he was always a gentleman. Sybil took strength from what she had already been through in a life full of challenges and from her strong faith.

On 4 January 2003, Reid went about his day as normal. His daughter Flora was visiting, and they had a quiet but pleasant day. Reid complained of indigestion and discomfort but was otherwise his usual cheerful self. Flora left just after lunch, and Reid went for his customary afternoon nap. He didn't appear for his evening meal, so Sybil went upstairs with a cup of tea for him to find that he had died peacefully in his chair. He was buried a week later in a quiet spot at the cemetery in Huntly, after a Requiem Mass was said for him. Although Reid was not Catholic, the bishop led what must have been a rather unique service, such was the esteem in which Sybil was held in the local Catholic community. It was a moving ceremony, with the chapel packed to overflowing with mourners, made up of Reid's family, friends and former colleagues. The service was a very sad occasion, difficult and heartbreaking to endure. Reid had led a colourful life, achieving more in his 82 years than most people do, and he had served his community with distinction.

Tragedy was again to strike with the death in December 2005 of Sybil's grandson Keith, the youngest son of Flora and Sonny, handsome, intelligent, funny and a talented film maker. He was interred with his grandfather Reid.

Over time, Sybil settled back into a routine. Although now in her mid-80s, she was as sharp as ever and still an amazing cook. A fall at the end of 2006 made her a little more wary, but she soon bounced back and was as mobile as ever, attending church every day and going out with her closest friend, Beldie, for coffee. The year 2007 looked like being much the same as any other, with the same rituals and the same visits. That was, until the events of 11 June.

BLANCHE

MADRAS AND CALCUTTA

Following the death of Manu, Blanche remained in Madras. Christmas 1970 was a very sad time, for she had lost a friend, a wonderful husband and a kind, gentle and loving father to their children. She had to remain strong.

'I didn't know what I should do with the body, but I said, "Let Manu be cremated." When his family came from Bombay they asked what had been done with his body. They were very pleased when I said it had been cremated. They took the big urn containing his ashes and they scattered them on a sacred river.

'Manu used to say that the food at the wake should not be given to the priest and the family. He'd say, "Why should they have it? They are

272

well fed." Some of the family we never saw. They only turned up at funerals. What is the point of turning up only when someone is dead? Manu said it was better to give the food to the needy and poor, so that's what we did. In his name, we continue to feed the poor, the homeless, the aged and the lepers. Every Christmas, we make lots of extra food and give that and anything else we can to those less fortunate than ourselves.'

While Blanche stayed in Madras for the remainder of 1971, trying to come to terms with her husband's death, in the north of the country, things were taking a turn for the worse.

During that year, political conflict between West and East Pakistan erupted into warfare. Pakistan was created with the Partition of India in 1947, the new country consisting of two predominantly Muslim areas to the north-west and north-east of India. By 1971, the Bengalis of East Pakistan were demanding independence from the traditionally dominant West Pakistan. When in 1970 the East Pakistani Awami League won a majority in the lower house of the Pakistani parliament and were denied the right to form a government, the military, made up mainly of West Pakistanis, was called in. Civil war broke out and East Pakistan declared its independence under the name Bangladesh.

The knock-on effects of this conflict in India were many. In March, India, under the leadership of Indira Gandhi, declared its full support for Bangladesh. Refugee camps were established along the border as millions fled the conflict in Bangladesh to India, and this caused instability and economic difficulties in border states such as West Bengal. In Calcutta, the shortages began to bite, and all resources were stretched to the limit. There was an increase in taxes, and food and commodity prices also went up.

In December, Pakistan and India officially went to war as a result of Pakistani air strikes against north-west Indian airbases, including Agra some three hundred miles from the border. Too few planes were used to have any real impact, and the Indian armed forces responded immediately. In Calcutta, this war brought new dangers. Movement was restricted and a curfew imposed. This was done at such short notice that it left many people stranded and unable to return home.

As Blanche's son-in-law Iqbal, Yvonne's husband, recalls, 'Calcutta was the headquarters of the Indian Army operation. It was the focal point—everything took place there. We saw a lot of troops. It affected the economy of West Bengal. A lot of refugees came, and many stayed with their relatives. Our own cousins stayed for more than two months with us.'

In Madras, all was peaceful, but in many parts of India there was much strife. Blanche heard about the situation from her family, and the short war brought home the horrors of the past. Blanche's daughter Anita had over the years befriended a small, dark-haired elderly lady, who used to visit her at work. They would sit talking and drinking tea whenever they could, and they became great friends. When the conflict with Pakistan escalated in December, India was put on a national war footing, and there were frequent blackouts. During one of these, while Anita was taking tea with her friend, she confessed to the older woman that she was frightened by the events that were taking place. The elderly lady held her hand and said that there was no need to be frightened because she was there to look after her. Then, quietly, she explained that she had been a prisoner of war in Germany during the Second World War. She showed Anita the prison number tattooed on her arm, and again she reassured Anita that they would be all right. The war lasted only two weeks, until the Pakistani forces surrendered on 16 December. The elderly lady continued to visit Anita often, but she never again mentioned her time in captivity during the war.

In 1972, Blanche returned to Calcutta at the request of her family. They all sorely missed her, and, more grandchildren having arrived, they all agreed that it was best if she came back to live with her relatives.

Blanche had brought many precious items to India from Burma, but one of the more unusual was a film reel of original archive footage of

Mahatma Gandhi, obtained through one of Manu's many contacts in the Rangoon media. She had carried it through customs and had paid duty on it, and had the film stamped and given an official seal. It featured Gandhi in his early days with the Congress Party and had footage of some of his speeches. It showed the period when he renounced all clothing save for a homespun loincloth and shawl. It covered his first pronouncements on independence and his ongoing battle with the British Raj, which more often than not resulted in a term of imprisonment. There was newsreel coverage of Gandhi's 1931 visit to London and his meeting with King George V at Buckingham Palace. All the major political events were represented, up to the day of his assassination, and even the radio announcement of his death was included.

'I brought that film all the way from Burma and showed it in a cinema owned by my son-in-law Iqbal's family in Asansol. Richard Attenborough wanted it and one of his assistants tried to persuade me to sell it, but I didn't want to. He went on to make his wonderful film, and I think he used original newsreel for some of it. I wish I had sold it, as I ended up getting nothing for it. In 1975, my sons persuaded me to get rid of it. They went on at me about the old celluloid being a fire risk until I became frightened. How I wish Manu could have been there to guide me. In the end, I just got rid of it. It would have been worth a lot of money now.'

In 1984, Blanche made the journey to Bangkok to visit cousin Irene. She had a wonderful time and enjoyed the Thai food, as it reminded her of Burmese cooking. Blanche planned to visit the beautifully maintained war cemetery at Kanchanaburi (the last resting place of many of the workers who died constructing the Burma–Siam railway) and the Buddhist-run museum nearby in tribute to the many Allied soldiers and Burmese civilians forced to give their lives in the construction of the deadly railroad. She hoped to stay for a night, visiting the Kwai Bridge and the memorial there the next day. She had made all the plans, but at the last minute she was overcome with such a feeling of despondency and sadness that she felt she didn't have the strength to undertake the arduous and emotional trip. It was a decision she would later regret.

In November 1987, Blanche made her next trip, this time to Australia to stay with Eunice. Arriving in late November, Blanche spent Christmas with her Australian relations, and she rather admired their free-and-easy lifestyle, their generosity and the delicious barbecues. She also visited her old friend Marjorie Linton and her daughter Hilda, who had married and become Mrs Hilda Soord. Marjorie and Blanche had been best friends in Rangoon after the war, and as a consequence Hilda had been close to Anita and Yvonne, and the girls had spent many

277

happy hours together in each other's homes.

While she was there, Blanche discovered from Eunice that Daisy Boyce and her family lived nearby. After much soul-searching, Blanche called her up and arranged to visit the following week. She went with the express wish of asking Daisy for a photograph of her father, William, as all her early family photographs had been lost during the war. On the afternoon of the visit, Daisy was most welcoming, and they sat and talked about old times in Burma, about the war and their lives since then. They got on well and chatted happily for hours. Blanche couldn't find it in herself to bring up the subject of her father and the photograph. Daisy had been the perfect hostess and very kind to Blanche, and she felt it was time to let old wounds heal, to forget the past and move on. Eunice phoned Blanche in India regularly, and some years after the visit she mentioned that there had been an announcement in the newspaper: Daisy Boyce had died. Another chapter of their old life in Burma had closed.

In June 1988, not four weeks after Blanche returned from Australia to Calcutta, her son Raymond died of cancer. He was only 46 years of age. Raymond was an extrovert who was often the life and soul of the party, and Blanche was shocked and saddened by the death of her son at such a young age.

In the years that followed, she suffered sad loss after sad loss. Austin was killed by

278

tuberculosis in 1991, and Eunice died in 1995. Austin had been musical and artistic, extremely gregarious and fun-loving, and he had lived life to the full until his illness. When he had begun to feel tired and feverish and had little appetite, it was put down to influenza, and by the time the correct diagnosis had been made the illness was at an advanced stage and nothing could be done to save him. Eunice had spent the late 1980s nursing her husband after he had suffered a stroke. When he died in 1991, Eunice was distraught, and she never really recovered from the loss. She died peacefully in hospital of liver failure. Eunice was a tough character who had never had a day's illness. As Blanche had found on her visit to Australia, she was never happier than when cooking for old friends or attending Christmas or birthday parties, when she could relax and tell stories and jokes. She was deeply religious, but she enjoyed her bingo nights, and she was a lucky player who had frequent wins. With the deaths of her siblings, Blanche couldn't help but wonder if she was the sole survivor among the Le Fleur children, but she never gave up hope that Sybil was alive, and indeed she became even more determined that she would one day find her missing sister and that they would be reunited.

In June 2000, Blanche's remaining son, Leslie—a hard-working dedicated family man who took great pride in his children—passed away. He too lost his life to cancer. For

Blanche, these were terrible blows, but she coped with dignity. Her faith and the love of her family helped her through. Her grandchildren were a constant source of joy to her and she delighted in their company. Blanche would sit for long periods of time watching her beloved Indian cricket team, and she would despair when they failed to reach the highs expected of them. Her knowledge and understanding of the game made her a match for any pundit, and she would often become embroiled in debates over team selection, strategy and tactics.

Life had taken on an established pattern for Blanche, but in early 2006 she and her family had something special to look forward to. Their family friend Hilda was planning to visit in March, the first time Anita and Yvonne would have seen her since they had all been together in Rangoon in 1958. It was an eagerly awaited reunion.

CHAPTER TWELVE

11–13 June 2007

DEREK

MILNATHORT, SCOTLAND

The morning of 11 June 2007 dawned bright and warm. It was just another Monday, even if our routine had changed slightly, as my wife, Caroline, was to attend a short training course on genealogy in Perth. Caroline works as a library assistant in our local branch, a job she has been doing for more than ten years and which she enjoys immensely. That night, we sat down for our evening meal while Caroline told me enthusiastically all about the course and how she had been able to trace my grandmother Flora's family through the 1901 Scottish census. She presented me with a list of details, including my grandmother's birth in 1894, along with information on every member of the household at the date of the census. Caroline's enthusiasm was infectious, and I was fascinated by the information and the level of detail.

After we'd finished our meal, I said I was going to phone Mum and tell her what Caroline had been doing, as well as make sure that she was all right. At 86 years of age, she was physically fit and as sharp as a tack mentally, but that didn't stop us worrying about her. I asked Mum how she was doing and she said she was fine, just the usual shopping and visits to church. As always, I asked if anything exciting had happened. The reply was always the same: no excitement really, just the same old things. Occasionally, someone I should know or whom I vaguely recollected had died, but on 11 June, nothing untoward had happened.

I launched enthusiastically into telling Mum about Caroline's course and what she had been able to find out. The names of Flora's parents and siblings, their ages, their occupations and their address at the time of the census were all there in front of me. Mum responded by filling in the details about some of them: William Reid, the Ellon butcher, and Mary Ann, the matron who had worked in London and nursed a member of the royal family, one of the princes. She had been invited to a tea party at Buckingham Palace as a result. It was exciting to hear about these people, my mother's link with the past and her husband's family.

'Do you think Caroline could have a look for my family?' she asked, and with those words, a whole new strand of our family story began.

We ended our conversation, and I went through to the lounge to finish my cup of tea with Caroline. 'Mum was all excited about you finding out about Dad's family. I read out all the information you unearthed, and she was very impressed. She's even asked if you could try to find her family.'

To our knowledge, this was the first time Mum had mentioned the possibility of tracing her long-lost relatives. Though other family members had asked her before if they could search, Mum's reply had always been negative—she had been afraid of disappointment, of finding nothing, and also feared discovering bad news—so little had been attempted. I had, from time to time, tried to find the family using Google, but with no success, and in 2005 I had finally given up on even the occasional search. My work had begun to take up more of my time, and because of rapid developments within the company, meetings and consultations seemed to dominate my life. This time it was different. I was now semi-retired, and whether it was the enthusiasm that Caroline had shown about the genealogy course or simply fate, I'll never know, but I jumped to my feet and said, 'I'm going to start looking right now.'

I went straight to the computer in the study and switched it on, not really knowing what to do next. 'Google is as good a place to start as any,' I thought. I typed in various family names, but nothing relevant came up. On the third try, instead of giving the name as it should be spelled, Le Fleur, I incorrectly typed 'lefleur rangoon'. The search page appeared on the screen and the first result was for an unfamiliar website, headed 'Planet Burma—from the

Britain-Burma Society'. The extract read: 'Siblings: Austin, died in Rangoon, Burma. Eunice Clift, née Lefleur, died in Perth, Australia. Blanche Desai, née Lefleur, now living in Calcutta . . .'

I stared at the words, clicked on the link and found myself on a page titled 'Lost Relatives Who Once Lived in Burma'. Scrolling down, I found an entry for '1940s—Lefleur'. Again, I clicked on the link and read the words that appeared in front of me. I felt a shiver run down my spine as I read and read again the contents of that page.

Sybil Maud Lefleur
Born 8 April 1920 in Syriam, Burma.
She was a sergeant in the Royal Medical Corps.
Married a Mr Flory in Mussoorie? India.
Siblings: Austin, died in Rangoon, Burma.
Eunice Clift, née Lefleur, died in Perth, Australia.
Blanche Desai. née Lefleur, now living in Calcutta, India, and is desperately seeking her sister and would appreciate hearing from anyone who knows or knew her.
Please reply to Hilda Soord by clicking here.

I couldn't believe what I was reading. I called out for Caroline but didn't get a reply. I read the words again and shouted once more. I went through to the lounge and discovered she was in the garden reading the newspaper. 'Caroline, come quickly and see this,' I said, so urgently that it was as if I were afraid I had dreamt it all up and the words would disappear from the screen. Caroline could hear the anxiety in my voice and immediately followed me back to the study. She sat behind me reading the words that I had read so many times in so few minutes. Caroline was as incredulous as I was, and we sat and stared at the screen for a while before I asked her what she thought I should do. My heart was pounding and my mouth was dry. What if it were some cruel hoax or even a scam designed to get private information out of people?

Caroline, always the calm one, suggested I simply reply using the link at the foot of the entry, and we would wait to see what happened. 'What do I write?' I said, completely losing the ability to think logically. Between us, we came up with the following, which we typed in and sent off who knew where:

Sybil Maud Le Fleur is my mum, and although she is 87, she is in great health. Eldest brother was Austin, sister was Eunice Olga and younger sister was Blanche Miranda. She married Reid Flory and had four children, of whom I am the youngest, Derek Reid Flory. I told Mum that my wife had just completed a course at work in tracing ancestors, and she was keen that I try to find any of her relatives, more in hope than expectation, but it looks like there may be a happy ending. Please get back to me as soon as possible, as no one is getting any younger. You can reply to my email address above.

Caroline and I were so excited we chatted until late that night, wondering if the situation was genuinely as promising as it looked and what the outcome would be. We thought of all sorts of scenarios. The entry had been posted on 25 April 2006. What if no one was checking for replies after such a long time? What if Blanche had passed away? The 'what ifs' continued, accompanied by a growing worry as to whether what we were doing was right. We hardly slept at all, we were so excited at what we had found and so worried about what we might yet discover. At seven the next morning, I went back down to the computer and switched it on, going straight to my emails. My heart was pounding as I saw a new message in my in-box. It was from Hilda Soord.

Dear Derek,
I have goosebumps all over me and can hardly wait to ring your Aunt Blanche in Calcutta. Actually, I will speak to her elder daughter Anita first and ask her to break the good news, as Blanche is recovering from a fall that she had about four months ago.

I am unable to write a longer letter right now but will do so some time this evening, after I have spoken to them.

I am so very happy to hear from you.
Please write again.
Regards,
Hilda

I rushed upstairs to tell Caroline the good news. When we had calmed down and gathered our thoughts, I sent a reply.

Dear Hilda,
After I read your posting yesterday, I went into shock . . . I cannot believe that after all these years, there is a whole other side to the family that I never knew about. Many years ago, my sister Flora tried to trace Aunt Blanche and the rest of the family, but it was before the World Wide Web and improved communications, and trying to get information out of Burma was impossible. Mum has probably been torn between desperately needing to know what happened to her family and fearing the worst, and as we kept drawing a blank, we just let it lie. I kept trying to find her dad, William Le Fleur, on Burmah Oil websites, but although I found out some general information, there was nothing specific to the family . . . And lo and behold, here we are now talking about my aunt and my

cousin Anita, who I never knew existed.

Aunt Blanche has a large family in Scotland and England: two nieces, a nephew—sadly my elder brother Ian died of leukaemia in his early 50s—several grand-nieces and -nephews and four great-grand-nieces and -nephews, with another two on the way in November and December.

I can give you more details when you email me back, and I would like to send a digital photograph of my mum holding me as a baby, along with some others. I'll also send a picture of my daughters, as I think Nicola may well have a strong family resemblance. I haven't told my mum yet, as she is on her own at present and I worry that the shock may be too much for her, so if you get back to me as soon as possible, I will travel north to see her on Thursday morning to break the news to her in person.

I cannot tell you how much I look forward to your reply. I just hope my heart can take the stress!

Best wishes,
Derek

On that Tuesday, we received a stream of emails. Hilda sent a message to let us know that she had spoken to Blanche and Anita:

Dear Derek,

I have just got off the phone to your aunt Blanche. I didn't tell her about your mum but left it to her daughter to do so, in case she got a shock. Anita was as happy as I am. I also sent your email address to Anita's granddaughter to pass on to her. Here is her email address . . . She is 15 and her name is Chicku. She lives with her parents in the flat above Blanche and Nita.

I am sure your mum would want to talk to her long-lost sister as soon as possible.

Please feel free to keep in touch if I can be of any help.

All the best,

Hilda

I immediately sent an email to Chicku explaining the situation and how exciting it was to discover that I had a new family.

Hi Chicku,

I am Derek Flory, and, believe it or not, I am Blanche's sister Sybil's son, so Blanche is my aunt. I have tried to work out what relation I am to you, but I am so excited and emotional that my brain seems to have given up. I have forwarded the message I sent a few minutes ago to Hilda Soord, and now I have your email address, I can contact you direct.

It is all very strange having discovered a

whole new family in India, and I am finding it hard to take in. I can attach some photos of Mum and my brother and sisters and also my daughters Nicola and Rebecca to the next email . . . Please reply as soon as possible. I am almost shaking with all the emotion and find it difficult to be patient. I said to Hilda that I would travel north to tell Mum on Thursday, but Caroline and I may head up there on Wednesday afternoon, as I don't think I can wait much longer.

Give my love to everyone, and if we can manage to persuade Mum, then I think a visit to Calcutta may be on the cards soon . . .

I'll send the photos in a few minutes.
Love,
Derek

I rushed around the house taking digital photos of all our framed pictures and emailed the results to Chicku and Hilda.

Hilda replied explaining her part in the whole jigsaw. When Hilda had visited Blanche and her family in Calcutta for the first time in March 2006, spending a month there, Blanche had talked a great deal about her family, and many nights she and Hilda had stayed up late reminiscing. Blanche had talked about Austin and Eunice and of course about Sybil, whom she hadn't seen since 23 December 1941.

Blanche told Hilda that she had always believed she would find Sybil and spoke fondly of the times they'd spent together.

Just before Hilda left to return to Australia, Blanche had asked her if she would do one enormous favour for her: would Hilda try to find Sybil, using the Internet or any other means she could come up with? She gave Hilda all the information she had about her lost sister. It was a long shot, but Blanche refused to give up hope, to abandon her belief that she would see Sybil again one day. When Hilda returned to Australia, she looked into how she might go about the task that Blanche had set her. She came across the Britain-Burma Society 'Lost Relatives' web page and created the entry, little believing that anything would come of it. She told Blanche and Anita what she had posted on the Internet. Each time Hilda phoned Calcutta, Blanche would ask if there had been any replies, and each time Hilda had to tell her there hadn't been any. Over a year passed, and Blanche kept asking and praying and saying that she knew she and her sister would meet. Finally, after 14 months, and completely out of the blue, the reply she had been waiting for arrived.

Hilda went on to give me Blanche's address and told me that my aunt loves receiving letters, keeping them and rereading them at leisure. This struck a chord, as Mum also likes doing that. Hilda gave a brief history of the family. I

291

discovered that Blanche, like Mum, had had four children, two girls and two boys, and that her great-grandchildren included Sunny, Chicku and Teddy. She finished with: 'I shall await the news of how your mother takes it and will ring Auntie Boo Boo again for her reaction.'

More emails arrived, and it seemed I would spend all day replying to them and printing out photographs of our new family to take up north for Mum. The family likeness was strong, and the similarity between Blanche and Mum was particularly striking. On reflection, that should hardly have been surprising, although, at the time, having just found Blanche, everything seemed astounding.

Chicku emailed in reply to my message.

Hi Uncle Derek,

Thank you so much for your mail, which I just received. It's so exciting to get in touch with you all. My great-grandmother is thrilled, and she has so much to say. She's already looking forward to seeing her sister after so many years. Blanche lives with us, and even though she is 85, she's full of life.

Please keep in touch with us, and so will I with you. I will send you photographs of the family in my next mail. Hope to hear from you soon.

Love,
Chicku

With the excitement building, I decided we couldn't wait even until Wednesday afternoon to speak to Mum. We changed our plans, deciding to travel early in the morning. I phoned my sister Evelyn to ask her and her husband, Angus, to be at Mum's the next morning and to get her to invite my other sister, Flora, to be there as well. I couldn't tell Evelyn the reason for this over the phone but asked her to be patient. The rest of the day was a blur, and again that night Caroline and I couldn't sleep. The concern now was how we should tell Mum. In the early hours of the morning, we began to feel unsure about what we were doing. Were we right to unsettle Mum with the news? How would she take it? As the minutes and hours dragged on, we became less and less convinced that we knew what we were doing.

I had sent an email to Calcutta late on the Tuesday evening saying that I would phone at around 11.30 their time on Wednesday morning, just before we set off for Huntly, to check that I had the correct number and that they would be ready to take a call from Mum. At 7 a.m. our time, I told Caroline that I was going to phone India and asked what she thought I should say. 'Don't worry,' she said, 'you'll think of something.'

Nervously, I picked up the phone and dialled the number. No reply. I tried again, and again there was no answer. I left it a few minutes and checked I was calling the number I had been given. 'Third time lucky,' I thought as I dialled once more. If the call didn't go through, we would have to leave, otherwise we would be late getting to Huntly. This time, the phone was answered, and I found myself talking to my cousin Anita. We chatted about how marvellous it was to find each other and how we would have to meet up soon. It felt like we had known each other for years. Anita handed the phone to Blanche, and I was shocked to hear her voice. It was just like Mum's—again, on reflection, hardly surprising, because they had been educated at the same convent by the same British nuns. She chatted and laughed, and it felt so comfortable. She was very easy to talk to, just like Mum. Caroline kept telling me that we needed to leave or we would be late, but I found it hard to end the conversation. Finally, I said that we would ask Mum to phone them around mid-afternoon their time and said goodbye.

Within minutes, we were on our way. The debate about what we were doing and whether it was right or wrong continued, and we grew increasingly concerned. That journey felt the longest we had ever made and I thought we would never arrive. Suddenly, however, the turn-off was upon us, and we headed along the road we had travelled on that first journey to Huntly in 1958, past the now closed Mart, under the railway bridge and past the station. We arrived at Church Street not long after half past ten. Mum answered the door, and she was surprised to see us. We rarely visit during the week because of Caroline's work and hadn't told her in advance for fear of worrying her. We went in to find Evelyn and Angus already there, but Flora had been unable to make it, as she was on holiday in the Lake District.

Evelyn made us all a cup of tea and we sat down in the dining room. I began to tell Mum the news. 'Remember on Monday night you asked if Caroline would look for members of your family?' Mum nodded. 'Well, we have managed to find out some information for you. We've discovered that your brother Austin survived the war but died in Rangoon in 1991 and that your sister Eunice moved to Western Australia, and she died in 1995. We've found out much more about Blanche and her family, though, and I've got some photographs to show you. When you've looked at the photos, I can tell you a bit more about them, or you could just pick up the phone and call Blanche and ask her yourself.'

Mum was sitting in the corner, clasping her hands together tightly. Evelyn was next to her, with tears in her eyes. Mum seemed very shocked, and she was speechless until Caroline passed the pictures to her. She knew Blanche right away and began asking about the other people and commenting on likenesses to our side of the family. I was choked up by the whole event, so Caroline took over explaining who each person was and how they fitted in. We raised the idea of making the journey to Calcutta, but Mum was adamant that it was too far, so we didn't press the point. I asked her if she was ready to give Blanche a call, but she was reluctant. It was all very sudden and she seemed frightened or unsure. After a gap of almost 66 years, it is a huge step to talk to someone you love so dearly.

I offered to make the call for Mum, and she agreed. I went straight to the phone and dialled the number. Mum followed me. The call connected, and Blanche answered. After a brief chat, I said that I would pass her to Mum and handed the phone over. We could hear Auntie Blanche saying, 'Is that really you, Sybil? What happened to you, Sybil? Why didn't you come home from your Christmas shopping?' And then they talked as if they had to make up for 66 lost years in that first conversation. Mum laughed out loud and spoke about never forgotten friends and relatives. We listened for a few minutes and then left them to it, but we did hear Mum say, 'I'll be coming to Calcutta to see you very soon.'

They talked for an hour before Mum said goodbye to her sister. She was so happy. She explained that she had laughed out loud because Blanche had told her that Daisy Boyce had died. Mum seemed like a changed person. She looked taller and more upright, as if a load had been taken from her shoulders. She was so obviously happy that we knew we had done the right thing. The rest of the day went by quickly as Mum talked more openly about her past than she had ever done before. In one of her emails, Hilda had asked me about Mum's pet name, and I hadn't known what she meant. I questioned Mum about it and she told us that to the family Austin was Buddha, Eunice was Buddie, Blanche was Boo Boo and she was Baby. When she went upstairs, we could hear her singing, and she had a spring in her step. It felt like we had won the lottery, except this was an even bigger prize, as no value can be placed on finding a lost relative or making your mum so happy.

Later that afternoon, Mum phoned Calcutta again. She was coming to terms with what she had discovered and desperately wanted to chat to her sister. This time she spoke to Blanche, Anita and her son Peter, and again there was much laughter. At one point, Blanche said, 'If you think I'm funny on the phone, then wait till you meet me!' She was full of life and fun. She asked when Mum would come to see her, and although she told her it would be soon, Blanche stressed, 'If you don't come to see me soon, I will fall over again, and you'll be to blame.' She then burst out laughing again, and so did Mum.

The sisters had been reminiscing about the meals they used to have, and Anita asked Mum if she ever cooked Burmese food. She replied that she had never learned to cook Burmese meals, and when Anita asked how she'd survived in Rangoon before the war, Mum replied, 'Blanche cooked, I ate,' and we all laughed.

It was late before we dragged ourselves away. Mum had been on the phone for two hours and was clearly over the moon. When we left, Mum hugged Caroline tightly and thanked her for inspiring her to find her sister. The journey home was a joyful one. We could not believe how well everything had gone and how Mum had taken the news. Her happiness had been infectious. When we spoke later to Evelyn, who had stayed at Church Street that night, it turned out that Mum had been up until late talking about her past and making plans for the future. This was extremely unusual, as Mum always went to bed around seven, reading her magazines and listening to her radio for some time before falling asleep. She had done this every night for many years.

CHAPTER THIRTEEN

June–October 2007

MILNATHORT, SCOTLAND

The emails and photographs continued to come thick and fast. It was almost a full-time job answering them, but it was also incredibly exciting. All the messages were printed out along with the photographs and posted to Mum. The day after the sisters' first phone call, we received an email from Anita telling us how happy Blanche was at finally finding the sister she had longed to see for so many years:

Dear Derek,
This is Anita, Auntie Blanche's daughter (your cousin) writing to you. Mummy is so excited and overjoyed after reading your email and can hardly wait to get in touch with your mom, her long-lost sister whom she used to keep telling us about many a time.

It's thanks to my good friend Hilda's efforts in tracing Auntie Sybil that we are now able to communicate with you.

We are so excited and can't wait to meet you all in person. Thanks for all the photos you sent us. Your wife and daughters Nicola and Rebecca are really pretty. We shall be sending you some of our photos as well.

More from us later.

With all our love,

Anita, mummy and family.

We sent off more photographs, including a recent photo of Mum, receiving this response:

Hi Uncle Derek,

We loved the photos, and I was just going to show them to my nana and tell her how alike the both of them look . . . the first time I saw the photo, I thought it was my nana and was surprised to see the resemblance . . . Nana Sybil is as beautiful and sweet as my nana even now, I hope you tell her that.

Love,

Chicku

On 15 June, we had another surprise: Eunice's son Patrick emailed us from Australia, saying he was delighted to hear news of his mother's sister. He had attached a photograph taken at a wedding. In the picture, at the back, stood a man in a dark suit who looked exactly like my brother Ian. When I enlarged the photograph, the resemblance was even more obvious. It turned out that this was Eunice's son Warren. I emailed to thank Patrick for the photo and tell him that we were all very excited at the prospect of travelling to Calcutta to meet our new family.

He replied informing us that he had managed to speak to his sister Kathleen in Burma to tell her the good news. We now had another branch of the family, this one still living in Rangoon. Patrick had attached a wonderful picture of Austin, whom I had never seen before and knew very little about. It was very moving to see him in his navy uniform, and I knew Mum would cherish the picture, as she had so little to remind her of her past.

Chicku told me that the nuns at her school were so touched by the story of her nana finally discovering that her sister was still alive on the other side of the world that they had asked her to write an article for the school magazine, an extract from which follows:

'Ask and you shall receive, seek and you shall find.' These words of Jesus Christ in the Holy Bible proved so true in the remarkable story I am about to share with you—the story of Blanche and Sybil, two sisters who got separated in Burma during World War Two. They are now about to be reunited after 66 years. Yes, 66 years— almost a lifetime for many a person. How do I know this story? Well, one of these sisters, Blanche, happens to be my dear great-grandmother.

301

It was the year 1941 and Japanese troops were invading Burma. Every now and then the wailing of sirens would warn the people of Rangoon of an impending bombing raid by Japanese planes, which would send everyone scrambling for cover to the nearest trenches and bomb shelters.

During one such night, in the midst of the family dinner, the dreaded sirens sounded again, sending my great-grandmother, her four children and her sister scurrying to the safety of the trenches in the graveyard across the street. On discovering that her sister had not reached the trench, Blanche began to call out to her, trying to make her voice heard above the din of exploding bombs in the pitch darkness, anxiously expecting a reply—which she never got!!!

The years rolled by, Blanche travelled to India with my great-grandfather, who was a radio broadcaster, and their four children, finally settling down in Calcutta in 1958. Her children grew up, had inter-caste marriages and got occupied in their respective careers. But all along, right through the years that followed the separation, Blanche held on to the hope of finding her sister some day. Anyone who had the remotest connection with Burma would be beseeched by Blanche to find some news regarding her missing sister. But all attempts proved futile, until technology decided to lend a helping hand . . .

. . . As I went to wish my great-grandmother goodnight, her phone rang. She picked up the receiver, remaining speechless for a few seconds. It was her sister Sybil on the line. The first words that she finally spoke were: 'Do you know, the night I called out to you over and over again, waiting for a reply, I never realised it would take me 66 years to get it.' I tiptoed silently from the room, unable to control the tears that fell from my eyes. This Christmas could well see one of the most eagerly awaited and tearful reunions ever.

Chicku had used a little artistic licence, but it was a beautiful and moving report. She told us that when she'd read it out to her class, her teacher had cried at the story. Mum loved the article and read it over and over.

All was going well when we had an email to say that first Peter, Blanche's grandson, and then Chicku had fallen ill with chicken pox. Then came the news that Blanche was also not well, and suddenly we began to panic. After all these years, it was very worrying to hear that Blanche was unwell. Apparently, the monsoon had caused flooding, which had brought disease. We were desperate to hear further news and relieved when we finally received an email from Chicku telling us that everyone was well again.

In late June, we got an email adding another piece to our family jigsaw, this time from Eunice's daughter Bernice. That wasn't the end of the journey of discovery, as in early July we received a message from Mum's great-niece Bridget, also living in Australia. I sent her the photograph of Mum that I had taken the day we visited Huntly to tell her the news about Blanche. Mum continued to phone her sister every Sunday, and the calls lasted three hours or longer as they talked about their lives and recalled their times together.

I began to realise how little we had known about Mum and her life before she moved to Scotland. I had been told a superficial amount about her father and the Burmah Oil Company, and also about her siblings. I knew she had attended a convent school and that she had had to flee the Japanese when they invaded, that she had ended up in India and joined the British Army, that there she had met and married my father. Even her early years in Ellon were largely a mystery to her children, and, on reflection, I could only marvel at the way she fitted so well into an alien environment, totally removed from her country of birth and her upbringing.

After she spoke to Blanche on 13 June, it was as if an invisible barrier had been broken down, and slowly but surely, like a rock gathering momentum, her true story started to come out. Mum would tell me snippets about her life before Scotland, and I would scribble the stories down furiously, wishing I had learned shorthand at school. Stories led to questions as I realised what great gaps there were in my family knowledge, simple questions about her journeys, what she did, what she heard, what had happened to her and her companions. Mum remembered events that had been unspoken of for many years. It clearly still caused her pain to relate some of the more difficult things she had been through, but her contact with Blanche seemed to give her the strength to unload the terrible burden she had been storing up all those years.

At times, I was amazed at how much she did remember given that the events had taken place some 60-odd years before. It is difficult to imagine recalling sometimes very small details after such a period of time, but the intensity of feeling as her happy and orderly life was transformed into one of great uncertainty must have made such an impact on her that memories were etched on her mind forever.

I wondered how she had travelled from Agra to Ellon 6,000 miles away, so one evening I asked her. She told me her friends had helped her pack her few possessions and she had travelled with Ian and Flora by train to Bombay, where she boarded a ship to Britain. I asked her if she happened to remember the name of the ship, and she told me it was the MS *Batory*. A quick search on the Internet revealed the very ship, and Mum was excited when I said I had found a picture of it.

One night in July, I phoned Mum to see how she was. She started to tell me about her latest Sunday conversation with her sister. Blanche had been telling Mum about a night when she had been robbed by dacoits. It was some time after the war, when she was living in Rangoon with Eunice, and the bandits had broken in and threatened Blanche with death if she opened her mouth or made any sound. Blanche sat very quietly with her mouth clamped tightly shut while they ransacked the house, taking some of her belongings and much of her precious jewellery. The dacoits ran off, and at that moment Eunice came home and found Blanche sitting with her mouth still clamped shut. She saw the damage, guessed what had happened and started to console her sister over the loss.

Blanche opened her mouth and took out several gems, rings and bracelets, telling Eunice that when she heard the thieves breaking in she had quickly managed to hide her most precious jewels. It was providence that had made the thieves insist that she keep her mouth shut and not say a word. Unfortunately, it was then that the bandits, who had been hiding, came back in and took the jewels that Blanche had successfully hidden and would have kept had it not been for the return of Eunice.

Well, Mum started chuckling almost as soon as she started telling the tale and had difficulty finishing it as she laughed more and more. On Sunday, when Blanche had told her the story, they had been in stitches at the image of Blanche producing the jewels from her mouth and the thought of the untimely arrival of Eunice. I had never heard Mum laugh so much, and she started me off too, as so often happens. What other revelations and tales would we hear from Blanche?

In August, I posted letters enclosing several photographs of the family to Calcutta. Some of the photographs of my mother had been taken in the late '40s and early '50s, so the Sybil in those pictures would have been quite familiar to Blanche, looking almost the same as when they were parted. One of the photographs was of Mum and Dad, taken in the front shop before they retired. Blanche had examined this closely and noticed a Strepsils display. When she spoke to Mum, she mentioned this and asked her to bring her some Strepsils when she came to Calcutta. We now planned to make the trip in October.

I had mentioned in my letter the season of television programmes to commemorate the 60th anniversary of Indian independence. When I next spoke to Blanche on the phone, I told her about one of the programmes I'd seen, the Calcutta episode of *India with Sanjeev Bhaskar*. I was about to tell Blanche who Sanjeev

Bhaskar was when she told me that she watched him all the time, as *The Kumars at No. 42* was her favourite programme. She especially liked Meera Syal's character, who she said was a typical Indian grandmother in that she was very generous and kind and gentle but always inquisitive and asking hundreds of questions. She asked me if I liked *Mr Bean*, as it was another thing she enjoyed on TV. I promised myself I would watch both programmes if I got the chance, as it seemed strange that my aunt knew all the episodes of these British comedies while I had watched so few.

As the summer drew to a close, Mum began to show signs of anxiety and tension over the forthcoming trip. She realised that she wasn't getting any younger, and it was only on rare occasions, such as for her grandson Matthew's wedding in Belfast, that she actually left Huntly. Even before that short journey, she had displayed an initial reluctance to go, although she'd managed better than most when the time came to fly. On 13 September, the required visas were obtained from the Indian Consulate in Edinburgh. Our flights were booked for 25 October (we were to stay for three and a half weeks), inoculations administered and travel insurance obtained.

Meanwhile, news was breaking of demonstrations in Burma against the all-powerful military junta. Thousands of Buddhist monks in their traditional scarlet or orange robes had taken to the streets of Rangoon, Mandalay and Sittwe to protest against the government. Smaller demonstrations had been sparked by a 100 per cent increase in the price of fuel imposed by the government in August. By late September, after the government had used troops to break up peaceful marches, monks had joined students, pro-democracy campaigners and other citizens in their thousands on the streets. These people had been deprived of their rights for decades, and now, armed with stones and bricks, they faced the Burmese army. News reports showed violence on the wide tree-lined streets of Rangoon. The octagonal Sule Pagoda, more than 2,000 years old, its gold dome rising above the city centre, was one of the focal points of the protests, and pictures of it filled the television screen. The wide street leading to it, Dalhousie Street in the days when Mum and Blanche had lived there, was packed with protestors.

There were shots of the Shwedagon Pagoda, too, another centre of unrest. We could see at the entrance the two enormous stone lions, called *chinthes*, which are the traditional guardians of Burmese temples. They were a formidable sight, but not formidable enough to deter soldiers from entering and arresting some monks. A number of religious leaders and civilians were taken to detention centres throughout Burma and reports, later discovered to be false, came through that Aung San Suu

Kyi, the daughter of Aung San and leader of the movement for democracy and human rights, had been taken to the notorious Insein Prison. In New York, the UN condemned the harsh treatment of the protestors and urged the Burmese government to show restraint.

On 27 September, the armed forces opened fire on demonstrators. Although the junta reported only nine killed in suppressing the revolt, most estimates had the number of dead at around 200. One of the people killed was a Japanese photographer, shot at point-blank range. We watched in horror as his death was played out repeatedly on television. We saw him fall to the ground. He raised his arms above his head, his cameras clearly visible. The soldier approached, wearing a dark-green combat uniform and a steel helmet. In his hands, he held a machine gun at waist level. The gun fired, and the photographer moved no more. The sight was made all the more incongruous by the fact that the soldier, who walked on without a second glance, had on his feet a pair of flip-flop sandals. I associated flip-flops with holidays in the sun, not blood and death, but television footage showing the scene of a protest had images of sandals lying in the street, lost as their owners fled beatings and gunfire.

The following day, crowds taunted soldiers and police as they erected barricades in an attempt to prevent further demonstrations in Rangoon, but generally the streets were quiet as people stayed in their homes, perhaps remembering the outcome of a similar uprising in 1988, which was brutally crushed, resulting in the deaths of more than 3,000 protestors. There was further outrage when the military appeared to have cut off public access to the Internet, isolating Burma more than ever from the rest of the world. Access to the Internet and to telephones was not widely available anyway, as I had found out when I had asked for my cousin Kathleen's email address. I was informed that she had no email and the only way to contact her was to call a phone box at the end of her street in the hope that someone would answer the call and arrange to fetch Kathleen at an agreed time when I would call back. This in a country that had once been the most advanced in Asia.

UN special envoy Ibrahim Gambari arrived in Burma for talks with the military leaders. Near the house of Aung San Suu Kyi, where she had been under house arrest for many years, four deep rows of barbed wire had been set up, flanked by machine-gun posts, in order to prevent any contact with her. Stories continued of small groups of protestors being beaten by large numbers of well-armed troops. Reports came in that an intelligence officer had defected after refusing to massacre Buddhist monks. The man, Hla Win, claimed that many thousands of civilian protestors were dead and that hundreds of monks had been executed and their bodies dumped in the jungle.

During this period, Mum had been telling me for the first time about her flight from Burma, and about the refugee camp at Myitkyina. She was remembering more of the events that occurred in the camp, and I was beginning to wonder if she had actually forgotten anything of that traumatic time. She mentioned the old sewing machine on which she worked for long hours altering traditional Burmese dresses. It was black and sat on top of a wooden table supported by two wrought-iron legs. It was an old Singer, the brand name inscribed in gold. The machine was powered by a treadle, and she talked of sitting for hours mending, cutting and stitching until her legs ached and she became exhausted with the effort, the heat and the lack of food. While she sewed, she wore the tattered and faded dress she had put on on 23 December. Although the people in the camp did their best to keep clean, it was nigh on impossible given the lack of facilities or privacy. There was even a shortage of carbolic soap, which people had learned to covet. Some months earlier they would all have turned their noses up at the thought of using such soap. There was no doubt they all smelled, but there were worse smells to be found around the camp. Few ventured into the jungle, which had its own scent, a sweet, sickly stench of rotting vegetation and other life forms.

At 21 years of age, Mum was little different

from young Western women of today, from my own two daughters, Nicola and Rebecca. Life was about having fun, going to the pictures and listening to the radio. It was about fashion and make-up and perfume, about reading books and even going out with boyfriends. It was about working to earn enough money to do the things she liked, and it was about adventure. At 22 years of age, her life was about being shot at and bombed by the Japanese, about watching as people died all around, from bullets, bombs or the diseases that claimed the lives of even more. It was about trying to preserve the one item of clothing she had left. It was about trying to remain sane in a world gone mad. It was about working each day to help others, making do with the limited food and resources available. Life was about nothing more than survival.

I wondered how I would have coped in that situation. I hated to imagine Nicola and Rebecca being faced with those terrors, with the older adults around them powerless to help in any way. Our daughters are intelligent, strong, determined and wilful, so they might well have adapted to such circumstances, but the thought of their being faced with that kind of challenge saddened me.

I wanted to find out more about the camp at Myitkyina—there might even be some old photographs—and I decided to look on the Internet. Typed into Google, the words 'Myitkyina refugee camp' brought a surprise. It seems that a large number of refugee camps still exist in Burma, home to the many people fleeing persecution by the oppressive military regime. These internally displaced persons (IDPs) have become virtual prisoners in their own country. If they escape into a neighbouring country, they become stateless people, often living in camps near the border, vulnerable and impoverished. Some estimates have the number of IDPs in Burma as high as two million, while millions more have taken refuge in countries such as Bangladesh, India, China and Thailand.

In Thailand, for example, there are some 140,000 Burmese refugees living in camps alone. In one border town, Mae Sot, there are twice as many Burmese residents as Thais. In the three main camps around the town— Umpiem Mai, Nu Po and Mae La—there are at least 70,000 refugees. Life in the camps is hard, but for many it is far preferable to deportation to their homeland, where some 75 per cent of the population are living on or below the poverty line and human rights abuses are commonplace. Even in the major cities, poverty and lack of education affect many thousands of Burmese.

How can all this happen and the Western world remain largely ignorant of it? If you asked the man in the street where Burma (or Myanmar) is located, I doubt that he would be able to tell you, let alone that he would know of the conditions within the country. In the aftermath of the protests, the military junta paid renewed lip service to the principle of moving towards democracy, but only time will tell whether representative government and respect for human rights will return to Burma.

With only days to go before our departure for Calcutta, we began the task of packing for the 18-day trip. Clothes were sorted, packed and unpacked several times, but even then we were unsure. My sister Evelyn phoned to tell me that she was having some difficulty with Mum's packing. Blanche had been telling Mum that the weather in Calcutta would start turning cold while we were there, so Mum decided she needed to pack her thermal underwear and her woollen cardigans. Although Evelyn tried to explain that the temperature would be dropping to the high 20s centigrade, Mum was not convinced. In the 66 years since she had left India, Mum had forgotten how hot and humid the weather could be. Evelyn decided it would be best to go along with Mum's wishes to avoid causing her any anxiety—more light clothes could always be bought in Calcutta if necessary—so into the suitcase went sets of thermals and several thick cardis. With our suitcases packed and ready to go, we realised it would not be long before we met our new family, and our excitement was beginning to mount.

CHAPTER FOURTEEN

25 October–18 November 2007

CALCUTTA

Caroline, our brothers-in-law Angus and Sonny and I travelled to Glasgow airport in our car, while Mum, Evelyn and Flora were picked up by a limousine sent by Emirates and transported in luxury to the airport. Nicola, her partner, Ewan, and Rebecca were to join us in the second week of the holiday. By midday, we were all checked in. Mum looked splendid in her bright-red woollen coat, and, as always, she was immaculately made up. She was adorned with her gold jewellery—earrings, rings and bracelets—as she always is when she goes out. The distinctive scent of Shalimar perfume followed in her wake as she was wheeled to the Emirates lounge. She had opted to use a wheelchair because, although she is fairly mobile and her pride initially prevented her from seeking help, we had managed to convince her that there would be too much walking to be done. We chatted excitedly about our thoughts and expectations for the trip, but Mum remained fairly quiet and calm, watching each of us and smiling in the same gentle way she has always had.

Our flight was called and we boarded the plane. Mum, Evelyn and Flora were travelling business class, as we felt the journey would be more bearable for Mum at her age if she wasn't cramped in economy with the rest of us. The business-class passengers were settled in their comfortable surroundings before we were even allowed to board the plane. When we eventually found our seats, however, we were pleasantly surprised by the amount of room we had. Right on time, the plane gathered speed down the main runway and suddenly the noise of the tyres rolling along the tarmac ceased, our ascent into the clear blue skies above Glasgow punctuated only by the noise of the engines straining to lift us ever higher.

The flight was a very comfortable one. At one point, we ventured forward to business class to see how Mum was doing. She was reclining in a large soft armchair with her feet up and looked very relaxed. In one hand she had a glass of orange juice and in the other a plate of hors d'oeuvres, the first of what turned out to be many courses served to her during the flight. She was really enjoying herself and praised the cabin crew for the way she was being treated. The purser started chatting to Mum and asked her where she was flying to, perhaps because it isn't that common to find someone of Mum's age making such a long journey. Mum told her that she was on her way to meet the sister she hadn't seen since December 1941 and gave her a potted version of the story. The purser started to weep and held Mum's hand tightly. When she recovered herself she told the rest of the crew, and they too struggled to keep their emotions in check. The purser then had her photograph taken with Mum. It wasn't long before the other business-class passengers had been told of the extraordinary story of the two sisters parted by war in 1941 who had only now found each other again. There was a round of applause for Mum from her fellow passengers, and she was very moved by the warmth shown to her by these complete strangers.

We arrived in Dubai on schedule, but there wasn't much time before our connecting flight to Calcutta. Even at midnight, the temperature was enough to take your breath away, and I wondered how Mum was coping. We economy passengers waited in a long queue to clear passport control and security before making our way to the departure gate. Occasionally, I caught a flash of Mum's bright-red coat as she was wheeled imperiously along like some head of state, with her daughters in tow like ladies-in-waiting. We caught up to them and walked with them to the departure area where they were again whisked off to the business-class lounge.

The flight to Calcutta took off just after 2 a.m. on Friday, 26 October, and we settled in for yet another round of eating and sleeping. Before we knew it, the captain was announcing our descent into Calcutta. We had our first experience of Indian tarmac as the plane bounced along the uneven surface before finally slowing enough to make the turn towards the terminal. We came to a stop, and virtually every passenger stood up, jostling for space. Waiting for a reasonable gap in the human traffic, we made our way to the exit and were immediately hit by the high temperature, accompanied by humidity of 98 per cent, which we—Mum excepted, of course—had never experienced before. The short walk to the terminal entrance left us drenched in sweat.

We took our turn in one of the many queues to clear customs. Some things in life never change, and our queue proved to be the slowest. At last, our entry forms were stamped and we were through. There was Mum, still in her red coat despite the heat, being wheeled along and pursued by Flora and Evelyn. We all collected our baggage and made our way out to meet the family we had first found and contacted only five months before. I thought of their photographs and hoped that we'd have no trouble recognising them.

Entering the arrivals hall and walking down the long corridor, we spotted a colourful banner held aloft by a large group of people. Its message was clear to all: 'Welcome Nana Sybil and Family'. It had been made that morning by a very excited Chicku, Teddy and Sunny, and it made us laugh and cry at the same time. They had also brought a traditional garland of bright, sweet-smelling marigolds for each of us. We walked swiftly towards them. Reaching the centre of the group, Mum stood up from her wheelchair and embraced her sister Blanche for the first time in a lifetime. Blanche placed a garland of flowers around her sister's neck and hugged her tightly. Mum's heart was pounding, and, as she fought to hold back the tears, all she could say was 'Hello, Blanche, it's so lovely to have found you.'

'Hello, Sybil' was all Blanche managed to say before dissolving into tears, and we watched as her tiny frame shook with her sobbing.

They wept tears of joy mixed with sadness and regret for the time they had spent separated from one another. They were overwhelmed with happiness but at the same time they couldn't help but feel anew the cruelty of the fate that had forced them apart without so much as a chance to say goodbye. The last time they had seen each other, they were carefree young women; now they were frail and elderly. We had to wipe our eyes as we took in the remarkable scene being played out before us. Here were Sybil and Blanche, hand in hand, sisters who looked every inch twins—the same hairstyle, the same laugh and smile. We warmly hugged our new family and were introduced to each member in turn, sobbing in each other's arms as if we had known each other all our lives. Blanche needed no introduction as she clung to Mum, smiling, laughing and crying. In contrast to her diminutive stature, she had a giant personality and a great sense of humour. Over the next weeks, we would get to know them all, but for now it was difficult just to separate the two sisters, who hugged each other and laughed and sobbed and laughed again.

Standing in the entrance hall of Calcutta airport, we must have been a strange sight, an obviously Western family, dressed in dull winter clothing, clinging tearfully to an equally emotional and obviously Eastern family in beautiful brightly coloured traditional dress. No one would know that the two families were one or that the link, which had been broken for 66 years, had finally been joined again.

Here in our arms were the people we had been talking to and emailing for the past five months: Blanche, Anita, Anita's son Peter, his wife, Shenaz, and their two beautiful children, Chicku and Teddy. They made up less than half the welcome party, however, as we were introduced to the family we had only heard about and seen in the occasional photograph. Blanche's daughter Yvonne and her husband, Iqbal, their sons Raja and Sonu and daughter Mumtaz, and finally Sunny, the other creator of the magnificent welcome banner and Mumtaz's youngest son.

Mum and Blanche held each other tightly, talking quietly for a long time, until we were the only people left in the arrivals hall. Eventually, we made our way to the exit. Cars, jeeps and taxis swallowed up what must have seemed an absurd amount of luggage for so few people, and once Peter was assured that were all accounted for and everyone was comfortable, we set off for our hotel. Mum and Blanche sat together in the back of Peter's car.

Peter had arranged breakfast for us all on our arrival at the hotel, and we sat together and talked excitedly. Our eyes more often than not returned to Mum and Blanche, sitting together, so small and neat, like porcelain dolls. They had the same mannerisms, the same way of resting the head on one hand, the same way of talking, the idiosyncratic phrases learned many decades ago in school and never forgotten. Even their facial expressions of joy, surprise and shock looked identical. It was quite uncanny. They chatted excitedly, and every now and then they both suddenly threw their heads back and laughed out loud.

After a brief interval allowing us to shower and freshen up, during which time Mum refused to be parted from her sister even for a minute, we were whisked off to have lunch at Peter's house. Mum and Blanche sat together all day in Blanche's room, holding hands and laughing as they had done when they were little girls. They would occasionally stop what they were doing and look at each other intently, studying a face that was so familiar but which had been unseen for so long. We all sat around them as they started to exchange gifts. As we watched, we realised how alike the sisters were in nature as well as in appearance and mannerisms. Both hoard more food than they could ever eat and Blanche had several secret stashes of chocolates, biscuits and snacks, just as Mum keeps selection boxes, biscuits and crisps. Blanche had every surface covered in trinkets, photographs and ornaments, just as Mum does. The cabinets full of bric-a-brac and items she had collected over the years would not have looked out of place in Sybil's home in Huntly.

We took Mum back to the hotel that evening exhausted but very happy. Caroline and I returned to the home of our cousins Yvonne and Iqbal, where we were staying, and spent a wonderful evening chatting and getting to know them better. We slept soundly that night. Meanwhile, Mum and the rest of the family settled in to their hotel. The Novelty was very reasonable, clean and well run by an English-speaking manager, and it served quite exceptional food.

The next day, Saturday, started off slowly, as we allowed ourselves to get more used to the craziness that is Calcutta. The noise of traffic, the constant sound of vehicle horns—the potholed roads being shared by cycle rickshaws, motorbikes, cars, yellow taxis, ancient buses, highly decorated lorries and the occasional cow or water buffalo—assailed our senses as we ate our breakfast. Later, the entire family were to join us at Yvonne's, and we were going to go on a shopping expedition for spices. For now, we relaxed with Yvonne and Iqbal. As we got to know them better, we realised that the similarities between Sybil and Blanche were mirrored by the parallels between their children. Both women had two boys and two girls. Yvonne is bubbly, talkative, excitable and considerate, always fussing to make sure everyone is well looked after, and she reminds us very much of Evelyn. Anita is very much like Flora: quiet, reserved and reflective. Leslie and Raymond seem to have been like their Scottish cousins. Leslie was the gentle, shy, sensitive and artistic son, just like Ian, while Raymond was a bit of a lad with an outgoing personality and a devil-may-care attitude, and I suppose some would say that I'm like that too.

When we went shopping, leaving Mum and Blanche at Yvonne's, they were sitting together talking, Mum in her Western clothes, a high-necked blouse and a skirt, and Blanche in her traditional Indian garments, a cool and comfortable salwar kameez. They had so many things in common. They wore the same jewellery, rings on the same fingers and gold bracelets on their wrists. Both suffered from arthritis, affecting the same fingers. When we returned, they were lying sleeping side by side on the bed, facing each other. Such was their small stature that they lay sideways on the bed rather than lengthways. They looked like bookends. When they awoke, Blanche told us that when they lay down together they had started talking, and it was only after several minutes of conversation that she noticed Sybil had fallen asleep. Blanche too drifted off, and for the first time in 66 years, she had slept secure in the knowledge that her sister was safe by her side. It was as if an enormous weight had been lifted from her, and she thanked God for her great fortune.

Sunday was Peter's day off, and he had organised trips to various city sights. First on the agenda was the magnificent Birla Mandir temple and we all stood outside while photographs were taken. The day was extremely hot, and, although we were wearing light clothing, the humidity was energy-sapping. Back in the Calcutta traffic, we made our way to the famous Victoria Memorial, one of the finest and most impressive reminders of the British Raj in all India. By now, the heat was even more intense. Iqbal purchased the 17 tickets we needed to enter, and while we strolled on through the gardens, Mum, Blanche and Anita sat quietly in the shade beneath a tree, the wide moat spread out in front of them. It was only when we approached the entrance to the memorial hall itself that one of the curators drew our attention to a small problem. He became quite agitated and spoke rapidly to Iqbal and Peter. They seemed to give as good as they got, but it looked like there was no way we were going to gain access to the inside of the memorial. It turned out that Iqbal had purchased 17 entry tickets at 10 rupees each, the fee for Indian nationals. The curator was pointing out that it looked suspiciously like 7 of the group were not Indian nationals and should have paid 150 rupees each. Iqbal and Peter were arguing that we were all the same family, which the man seemed to find difficult to believe. Eventually, however, the curator seemed to decide to give us the benefit of the doubt and allowed us to carry on.

By the time we came out, it was early afternoon and time for lunch. We made our way to the Millennium Park, where we found a quiet spot under a round gazebo and sat down to have our picnic. Mum and Blanche were inseparable as usual as they tucked in to a selection of delicious snacks brought from Anita's restaurant. Their conversations were lively and often punctuated by loud laughter, and when they were not eating or drinking they sat clasping each other's hands tightly. We were surprised by how well Mum was coping with the heat and humidity, as the rest of the Florys were feeling the effects, although, of course, she had forsaken her thermals by now and was in a cotton blouse and loose skirt. Our final stop of the day was Nalban Park, where we boarded a couple of *shikaras* (long, narrow boats with a canopy to provide shade and seating for six or so people) for a relaxing trip on the lake, a chance to catch our breath after the whirlwind tour of Calcutta.

Monday was a more restful day, and Mum and Blanche spent it together while Caroline and I sat and talked to Iqbal and Yvonne. All the food was prepared with fresh ingredients, and the chicken curry we had for lunch that day was one of the best I have ever eaten. Dinner that night was the meal that Mum had talked about for months, ever since discovering her sister was alive: ohn-no khaukswe. The basis of this dish is a mild chicken curry made with coconut milk, with a thin consistency like that of chicken soup. A serving of noodles is placed in each bowl, and spoonfuls of the curry are ladled on top. The final step is to add a garnish of finely chopped red onions, a sprinkling of fresh coriander and the freshly squeezed lime juice. The result is the most delicious mix of flavours. No wonder Mum loved it. I stopped after four helpings! Our new relatives introduced us to many delicious foods. Breakfast, for example, consisted not only of the familiar fried eggs and toast but also of *halwa puri*, a pancake stuffed with semolina, and *nahari*, which is bone marrow cooked overnight to produce a thick gravy into which you dip *dal puri*, discs of flatbread stuffed with lentils. The nahari was delicious and unlike anything we had ever eaten.

We spent Tuesday at Blanche's home, where we had lunch and sat and listened as Mum and

Blanche talked of their childhood. For four hours that afternoon, Blanche told us of her experiences on 23 December 1941, of the horrors of the war, of her life in post-war Burma and her move to India. This was to be the first of many such conversations as she relived her sometimes painful but often contented past. At the end of the day, as the light faded and they sat together side by side holding hands, Blanche and Mum began to sing the songs they used to perform as girls. We were treated to beautiful renditions of 'Moonlight on the River Colorado', 'Carolina Moon' and 'Among my Souvenirs'. The last song they sang was by Vera Lynn: 'We'll Meet Again'. Rarely can a song have been so movingly appropriate, and tears started to flow as they had done so many times in the past few days. As the song came to an end, Mum and Blanche got to their feet and danced slowly hand in hand before finally rubbing their noses together as they had done when they were children.

We left Mum with her sister. They were having a sleepover, as there was to be little movement in Calcutta the next day because of the *Bandh*, a strike causing a shutdown on all traffic. The term 'sleepover' might be more commonly used of children, but as Mum and Blanche always called each other 'girl' ('Come and sit with me, girl,' or 'What are you doing, girl?') it seemed appropriate.

On Thursday morning, the heat was intense

and it was very humid. The sky darkened, and suddenly there was a loud crack of thunder and, very close to us, a flash of forked lightning. The raindrops came slowly at first and we were told that a shower was on its way. We were totally unprepared for what happened next. The wind started blowing strongly, causing the palm trees to sway violently. I watched to see if any fruit would be dislodged but was to be disappointed. The rain began to fall more heavily until it was positively torrential, at least as heavy as anything I had ever seen in Scotland. To the family, it was little more than a shower, and they went about in the same light clothes, with a small umbrella to ward off the rain. If this was a light shower, what must the monsoon be like?

The days passed with visits to see Blanche and to look at the many family photo albums. The volume of photographs was so great and our extended family so large that in the end we began to get confused. We discovered that some of the superstitions and customs that we have at home are also part of life in our Indian family. For example, when perfume is given as a present, a penny must be handed to the giver. When Yvonne dropped a pan in the kitchen, she ran out exclaiming that they would soon get a visitor, just as Mum does. Everything was both strange and familiar.

On the Wednesday of the second week, we took Mum to visit Nicola, Rebecca and Ewan at the Oberoi Grand. Driving in through the front gates was like entering another world. The noise of Calcutta disappeared, and all was calm. Security guards checked the vehicle before allowing us to proceed, and when we drew up outside the front door we were immediately helped from the car by extremely courteous doormen. We strolled through the grand interior to the poolside, where Ewan was sitting reading the paper and drinking ice-cold beer. The pool was set in a courtyard at the centre of the hotel, and it was hard to believe as we sat there watching the clear blue water lapping against the tiles that we were at the heart of one of the biggest cities in the world. Mum thought it was wonderful, and we visited again later in our trip, vowing to stay there on our return to Calcutta, whenever that might be.

On 7 November, a big party was held for the sisters. Peter had invited lots of family friends and some of his business colleagues, and the games and dancing went on till late that night. The highlight was undoubtedly when Mum and Blanche sat together sharing a microphone to sing some of their favourite old songs. It was just one moving moment among many.

Two days later, we celebrated Diwali. Huge quantities of fireworks were purchased, and we went out onto the roof of Blanche's house to see the display. Mum and Blanche sat together holding sparklers as they had done at Diwali in Syriam all those years ago. It was a wonderful evening, but Mum couldn't believe how noisy

330

the festival was, with drums beating constantly and bands playing in the streets. The music continued all through the night. While Blanche loved the hustle and bustle, the noise and the proximity of people, Mum had grown to prefer peace and tranquillity. Another difference between the two women was that while Mum enjoys Indian and Chinese food occasionally at home, she has spent the past 60 years eating a comparatively plain Scottish diet, and it took her some time to get used to the delicious but spicy meals—meals that she had grown up eating.

In between our visits to Blanche, we managed to fit in a trip to the botanical gardens, the Sir Stuart Hogg market, more commonly known as the New Market, which has to be seen to be believed, and the splendid Marble Palace, which was simply outstanding, the highlight of our visit to Calcutta. The city was beautiful, but we continued to be amazed and horrified in equal measure by the traffic, the noise and the pollution. The final week passed in a blur of activity—shopping, visits to the family, excursions to the countryside—and all too soon the final day of our reunion arrived.

On Sunday, 18 November, after a leisurely start, the entire family got together at the hotel for a last meal together. The usual chatter arose, and there was constant toing and froing around the table as the food was eagerly devoured. When it was time to make the journey to the airport, the suitcases were loaded into minicabs and our convoy headed off, taking us on our last journey through the streets of Calcutta. It proved to be another traumatic experience, with one of our taxis narrowly escaping a collision. Hearts were in mouths as the horror of being involved in an accident almost became a reality. The traffic was like a huge carefully choreographed ballet, with cars, taxis, lorries, rickshaws and pedestrians intermingling and making seemingly impossible manoeuvres within inches of each other. Miraculously, we all made it to the airport safely.

In the departure lounge, Peter, normally confident, composed and erudite, began to make a short speech, but the enormity of the situation finally overcame him, and he was choked with tears. Everyone was hugging and kissing and crying openly, but naturally it was the sisters who felt it the most. They stood and hugged each other tightly, neither wanting to let the other go. Blanche was racked with sobs, tears flowing freely down her cheeks. Sybil was crying terribly too and holding on to her little sister as if her life depended on it. Blanche and Sybil realised that this might be the last time they would see each other, and that awareness was extremely hard on them.

When finally we had to leave, we walked with heavy hearts past the security guards, turned one last time and waved to our family. Everyone was weeping. Then we were through security and on our way to the departure gate, and there was no use looking back.

EPILOGUE

During the flight from Calcutta to Dubai, everyone was very subdued. Mum wouldn't eat or drink and fought to keep her tears back and her emotions hidden. She had made the trip to India to see the sister she had been so cruelly parted from 66 years before, and now she had had to leave her once again. The pain was almost unbearable and caused her tremendous heartache. The best efforts of the cabin crew and Sybil's daughters could not get her to eat. She simply had not the will.

The purser noticed this and became alarmed, encouraging Mum to at least drink some water. As the plane neared Dubai, the purser discussed the situation briefly with Evelyn and made the decision to ask for a special meal to be arranged for the flight from Dubai to Glasgow, as she knew that Mum could become dangerously weak if no food or liquids were taken. On the next leg of the journey, Mum was presented with a meal of specially prepared foods—light, bland dishes and fresh fruit. It was just what was required, and she managed to eat everything and drink some much-needed water. It was another example of the kindness of the Emirates crew. By the time we were nearing Scotland, Mum had recovered somewhat and was more like her old self.

Glasgow International Airport was a welcome sight as the plane made its way to the gate. Passport control and customs were swiftly negotiated, and we stepped out into the cold, clear air. We were immediately struck by the difference in temperature. When we had left Calcutta, the temperature had been 30°C; the thermometer in Glasgow was hovering around 3°C, and a cold wind was blowing. The journey up to Aberdeenshire only served to underline the differences in the two countries. The air was fresh and clear, with little hint of pollution, and the traffic seemed positively sparse after Calcutta. We were initially taken aback by the lack of use of car horns, so accustomed had we become to the constant blare. It was in eerie silence that we drove home, although I still flinched when cars and lorries approached from side roads. It took me some time to remember that they weren't going to pull out, causing me to brake hard, swerve and slam my right palm down on the horn before uttering a curse and carrying on at high speed.

It was good to be back in Scotland, to return to our house and sleep in our own bed. Our friends and family were all as anxious to hear about our trip and the reunion as we were to tell them of the instant when my mother met her beloved younger sister for the first time in 66 years. We talked enthusiastically about each member of our wonderful family, and we choked back tears when we described the many touching moments we had witnessed when Mum and her sister were together. We emailed everyone in India to tell them we were home safely and thank them for looking after us so well and for all the gifts they had given us. They really are an extraordinary family, and we felt very proud and privileged to have met them and to be part of their lives.

As the days turned to weeks and the weeks to months, we missed them more and more, their kindness and generosity, their affection and their willingness to share everything with a group of people who only a few months before had been completely unknown to them. We could not have wished to meet a nicer group of people or a finer family than that which we now have in Calcutta. There is little doubt that we will remain close and that we will all eventually return. Not even 6,000 miles can dull the memories we have of our reunion in Calcutta.

Mum continues to telephone Blanche every Sunday afternoon, and as well as remembering the times they spent together as children, they now also talk fondly of their most recent memories together. None of us will forget the emotional first meeting between the sisters after 66 years or the wonderful times we had together. None of us, least of all Mum, will forget the incredible sadness we experienced when we had to return home. Whether Mum and Blanche will meet again, only God knows, and as neither is getting any younger, the chances of many more meetings are greatly diminished. But no one can take away the time they spent together in October and November 2007. It is a memory to cherish forever.

ACKNOWLEDGEMENTS

My biggest thanks go to the two wonderful ladies who made this book possible: my mum, Sybil, and my aunt Blanche, whose courage, determination and resourcefulness are an inspiration. I thank them for sharing details of their lives both joyful and terribly sad, details that in many cases had never been shared with anyone else. They faced and conquered challenges that could have defeated even the strongest, and they made new lives in countries very different from the land of their birth. I found their story inspiring. Everyone should have heroes to look up to and admire, and now I have two of the greatest in my own family.

To those dearly loved and greatly missed members of the family, from all continents, sadly no longer with us, you would have had so much joy from the events of 2007 and are always in our thoughts and prayers.

We are eternally grateful to Hilda Soord, who was presented with a formidable challenge by Blanche in April 2006. Hilda took up that challenge, little knowing where it would lead or the impact it would have on our lives. I doubt that even she could have imagined the outcome. Thank you.

Thanks to Google, never a bad place to start if you are looking for something.

My thanks to my sisters, Flora and Evelyn, and their husbands, Sonny and Angus, who kindly allowed me to use a selection of their photographs from the reunion in Calcutta; to Nicola's partner, Ewan, for his support on the trip, and Rebecca's partner, Peter, for his from a distance. I am also very grateful to my sister-in-law Madeline, who spent weeks searching through family photographs and supplied most of the black-and-white images of Scotland.

To my nephew Ian Flory at www.originallight.com, thank you for producing such excellent maps, particularly since you and Kate had your hands full with the birth of Etienne.

To Iqbal, Yvonne, Mumtaz, Raja, Sonu, Ronnie, Sunny, Anita, Peter, Shenaz, Chicku, Teddy, Patrick and Denise, and all our other family members in Calcutta and beyond, you are a wonderful, kind, generous and loving family, our family. When we met you, it was as if we had known you all our lives.

What can I say about Jenny Brown, my fantastic agent, and her colleague Lucy Juckes? I am greatly indebted to them for their immediate realisation that this was a story worth telling and especially to Jenny, who motivated, encouraged and directed me when at times I felt lost. I was very lucky to find you both.

Three people at Mainstream have been of enormous help: Fiona Brownlee, who persuaded us by her undoubted enthusiasm and commitment to the story that Mainstream was the publisher to choose, not an easy thing to do on a mobile phone from the Frankfurt Book Fair; and Graeme Blaikie, who helped turn my manuscript and random selection of photographs into the book you are now holding; but most of all I must thank Claire Rose, my editor, who has the patience of a saint and the wisdom of Solomon. Her thoroughness and professionalism saw us through to the end, and she was a joy to work with.

While most of the book is based on the recollections of Sybil and Blanche, I am indebted to a small number of invaluable sources for additional information regarding the bombing of Rangoon and military details of the four-year conflict. The website www.warbirdforum.com contains invaluable information on the December 1941 raids on Rangoon, based on Japanese histories. Two books provided essential background information: Louis Allen, *Burma: The Longest War 1941–1945* (J.M. Dent and Sons Ltd, 1984); and John Latimer, *Burma: The Forgotten War* (John Murray, 2005). Thank you to the University of Chicago Library for permission to reprint the photograph of Rangoon after the war in the picture section.

Finally, I would like to thank my wife and daughters. To Caroline, who has been my biggest supporter and my best friend for the past

34 years, words cannot describe the love I feel for you. Thanks to your editing and patience, the book ended up 20,000 words shorter and considerably better for it. Nicola and Rebecca, thank you for coming with us to Calcutta and being so helpful, encouraging and supportive. Thank you above all for being everything we could ever wish for.

I apologise if I have left anyone out.

Derek R. Flory
May 2008